The Politics of Technology in Latin America (Volume 2)

This volume focuses on the hyper-mediatization of Latin America from the citizen's perspective, considering the social impact and how people embrace information technologies to improve their living conditions, engage in political issues, and the role of digital journalism in promoting democratic values in Latin America.

The book is divided into three parts:

- "Digital Media and Daily Life in Latin America" explores cases related to the integration of digital media such as mobile devices, social platforms and, even, drones to diverse commercial, private, and social activities.
- "Information Technologies and Civic Engagement" gives special attention to the new political practices triggered by the irruption of smartphones and platforms, especially inside organizations and social movements in Latin America.
- "Journalism and Media Integrity in the Age of Post-truth" centers on the study of digital journalism and the new media landscape, and related issues like precarization of labor conditions and the crisis of reliability in media.

This second volume in a two volume set will be important reading for scholars and students of social use of digital media in Latin America, civic engagement, and the connections between politics, journalism, and technology.

David Ramírez Plascencia is a professor at the University of Guadalajara, specializing in the study of information law and digital policies.

Barbara Carvalho Gurgel has a bachelor's degree in Political Science from the University of Massachusetts Dartmouth (USA), and is working toward a master's degree in Journalism from the Harvard Extension School (USA).

Professor Avery Plaw specialized in political theory and international relations, with a particular focus on strategic studies.

Emerging Technologies, Ethics and International Affairs
Series Editors: Steven Barela, Jai C. Galliott, Avery Plaw, Katina Michael

This series examines the crucial ethical, legal and public policy questions arising from or exacerbated by the design, development and eventual adoption of new technologies across all related fields, from education and engineering to medicine and military affairs. The books revolve around two key themes:

- **Moral issues in research, engineering, and design**
- **Ethical, legal, and political/policy issues in the use and regulation of technology**

This series encourages submission of cutting-edge research monographs and edited collections with a particular focus on forward-looking ideas concerning innovative or as yet undeveloped technologies. While there is an expectation that authors will be well grounded in philosophy, law or political science, consideration will be given to future-orientated works that cross these disciplinary boundaries. The interdisciplinary nature of the series editorial team offers the best possible examination of works that address the "ethical, legal and social" implications of emerging technologies.

For more information about this series, please visit: https://www.routledge.com/Emerging-Technologies-Ethics-and-International-Affairs/book-series/ASHSER-1408

Contemporary Technologies and the Morality of Warfare
The War of the Machines
Jean-François Caron

American Security and the Global War on Terror
Edwin Daniel Jacob

The Politics of Technology in Latin America (Volume 1)
Data Protection, Homeland Security and the Labor Market
Avery Plaw, Barbara Carvalho Gurgel and David Ramírez Plascencia

The Politics of Technology in Latin America (Volume 2)
Digital Media, Daily Life and Public Engagement
Edited by David Ramírez Plascencia, Barbara Carvalho Gurgel and Avery Plaw

The Politics of Technology in Latin America (Volume 2)

Digital Media, Daily Life and Public Engagement

Edited by David Ramírez Plascencia, Barbara Carvalho Gurgel and Avery Plaw

Routledge
Taylor & Francis Group
LONDON AND NEW YORK

First published 2021
by Routledge
2 Park Square, Milton Park, Abingdon, Oxon OX14 4RN

and by Routledge
52 Vanderbilt Avenue, New York, NY 10017

Routledge is an imprint of the Taylor & Francis Group, an informa business

British Library Cataloguing-in-Publication Data
A catalogue record for this book is available from the British Library

Library of Congress Cataloging-in-Publication Data
A catalog record has been requested for this book

ISBN: 9780367360115 (hbk)
ISBN: 9780429343247 (ebk)

Typeset in Times
by KnowledgeWorks Global Ltd.

This editorial project is dedicated to the memory of Dr. Avery Plaw.

Contents

List of figures

List of tables

List of contributors

Editors

David Ramírez Plascencia is a professor at the University of Guadalajara, specializing in the study of information law and digital policies. His previous works include "Concerning at distance: Digital activism and social media empowerment between Latin-American migrants in Spain" in the journal ESSACHESS and "Education reform, teacher resistance and social media activism in Mexico, 2013–2016" in the journal *The Educational Forum*, Taylor & Francis. His research has focused on the study of the possibilities and dilemmas of information technologies in developing countries. He is interested in digital activism, information control, and social media use in Latin America.

Barbara Carvalho Gurgel has a bachelor's degree in Political Science from the University of Massachusetts Dartmouth (USA), and is working toward a master's degree in Journalism from the Harvard Extension School (USA). Her latest pieces involve such subjects as violence against journalists, online radicalization, and literary analysis of Childish Gambino's Grammy-winning record This Is America. Barbara has worked on various research projects and publications regarding extra-territorial uses of force, and the history and practice of drone strikes by the United States. Her published work *Super Soldiers: The Ethical, Legal and Social Implications,* with Avery Plaw, was part of Ashgate Publishing's *The Super Soldier as Scholar: Cultural Knowledge as Power.* She is currently working as lead editor at the Israeli Center for the Study of Targeted Killing (ICSTK), a project mapping targeted killing throughout the Middle East. Barbara has also published her prose and poetry.

Professor Avery Plaw specialized in political theory and international relations, with a particular focus on strategic studies. He is the author of *Targeting Terrorists: A License to Kill?* (Routledge, 2008), and the editor of *The Metamorphosis of War* (Brill, 2012) and *Frontiers of Diversity: Explorations in Contemporary Pluralism* (Brill, 2005). He is also co-author of the textbook *The Drone Debate: A Primer on the U.S. Use of Unmanned Aircraft Outside Conventional Battlefields* (Rowman & Littlefield, 2015).

Contributors

Jorge Andrés Cruz Silva is an associate professor and a researcher for the Research Group in Communication Sciences (GicCom) at Pontificia Universidad Católica del Ecuador. He is a PhD candidate in Communication and Contemporary Information at Universidade de Santiago de Compostela, Spain. He has a master's degree in research in Digital Media and Culture by The University of Edinburgh, United Kingdom. Holds a BA in Communication with emphasis in Journalism for Printed Media, Radio and Television by Pontificia Universidad Católica del Ecuador.

David Andrés Mayorga Naranjo is a lawyer by Pontificia Universidad Católica del Ecuador and holds a Postgraduate degree on State attorney management by Instituto de Altos Estudios Nacionales del Ecuador (IAEN). He holds a Higher Specialization in Procedural Law by Universidad Andina Simón Bolívar. Has been a collaborator in the Pan-Hispanic Dictionary of Legal Spanish of the Royal Spanish Academy of Language.

Dra. Virginia Villaplana Ruiz is Professor of Media Studies at Murcia University, Cultural Studies at Colef Social Sciences University Baja California Tijuana, and researcher of the Institute of Communication at Autonomous University of Barcelona. Villaplana is the author of the books *Softfiction. Políticas visuales de la emocionalidad y el deseo* (Consonni), *El instante de la memoria* (Ministry of Education and Culture) and co-editor of *Cárcel, de amor. Relatos culturales sobre la violencia de género* (Reina Sofía National Museum). She is a member of the Research Network Project *Unearthing Pre-HIV/AIDS Queer Sexual Cultures* at the European Science Foundation. Additionally, she has written a number of articles and book chapters about communication and digital memory communities in several contexts of social exclusion as working sex, prison and border. Her current research projects include feminist and queer politics in Europe and Latin America: transnational violence, social movements, resistance and social change in digital media. She is also co-editor of the academic Journal *Art and Politics of Identity*.

Dra. Alejandra León Olvera is Feminist researcher and activist. PhD in Cultural Studies from El Colegio de la Frontera Norte. Master in Gender Studies from El Colegio de México. Social Anthropologist from the Universidad Autónoma de Querétaro. Her lines of research are the conformation of gender identities, uses of social networks, analysis of cultural consumption by young population, emphasizing the critical analysis of hyperconsumption and power relations in the online space, as well as the representations and practices by youth cultures in the offline space. She is expert in qualitative methodology, specifically ethnography and netnography. Since 2014, she has focused on studies of Mexican narcoculture, hyperconsumption, and gender identities. In early 2020, she ventured into digital media with the YouTube educational content channel: Alejandra León: Educación Circular Social. In which the content focuses on the importance of the social sciences in everyday life and is aimed for all audience.

Sergio Yagüe Pasamón is a gender and linguistic discourse researcher. He was awarded a degree in English Studies from University of Zaragoza, which he further complemented with a degree in Primary Education at UCJC, a master degree in Specialized Translation at UCO, specializing in scientific and technical texts in EN-ES and FR-ES; and a master's degree in Translation and New Technologies: Translation of Software and Multimedia Products at IUMP and ISTRAD. Currently, he is elaborating on his pre-PhD project under the direction of Dr. Rivas Carmona at University of Córdoba (Spain). Throughout his professional career, Sergio taught linguistics in the bachelor's degree in Spanish at the Norwegian University of Science and Technology (NTNU, Trondheim-Norway) and translated videogame guides and monographs as *Safe Computing is like Sex: You Have to Practice it to Avoid Infections*. Currently, he works as linguistic advisor for the Spanish Ministry of Education and Sport (MECD) and British Council in Aragón, coordinating English bilingual programs for the promotion of linguistic competence, designing bilingual module-based pathways for BRIT-Aragón model; and teaching CLIL modules at Primary Schools in the Autonomous Community.

Stuart Davis is Assistant Professor in the Department of Communication Studies at the City University of New York, Baruch College. He has roughly 20 pieces published or forthcoming in journals including Communication Theory, Communication Monographs, International Journal of Communication, International Communication Gazette, Popular Communication, Digital Journalism, Journalism Practice, Development in Practice, and The Journal of Latin American and Caribbean Anthropology as well as edited collections including *Mapping Citizen and Participatory Journalism* (2020), *Protests in the Information Age* (2018), *The Pink Tide: Media and Political Power in Latin America* (2017), *The Routledge Companion to Global Internet Histories* (2017), and *Civic Media: Theory, Design, Practice* (2016). He is a co-editor of the forthcoming *Sanctions as War: Anti-Imperialist Perspectives on US Geoeconomic Power* (Monthly Review Press). He is also finishing a book manuscript examining the relationship between mass protests, digital media activism, and the rise of right-wing political movements in Brazil as well as starting a new project looking at public transportation struggle as a comparative framework for mapping class-based and racial conflict in Europe and the Americas.

Melissa Santillana is a PhD student in the Department of Radio-Television-Film at the University of Texas at Austin. She received her MA in Communication with a concentration in Latin America and Border Media Studies from Texas A&M International University. Her research focuses on international media flows, border studies, activist movements, feminist activism, digital media, and digital inequality.

Yunuen Ysela Mandujano-Salazar is a Professor at the Autonomous University of Ciudad Juarez (Mexico). She holds a Doctorate in Social Sciences with a specialization in Cultural Studies and a master's degree in Studies of Asia and Africa specialty Japan. Her research interests are media discourses, gender and national identity construction, and Japanese culture and society. She is a member of the Mexican National System of Researchers (SNI). Her most recent publications include *'Media idols and the regime of truth about national identity in post-3.11 Japan' in The Routledge Handbook of Japanese Media (2018),* the article *'Exploring the construction of adulthood and gender identity among single childfree people in Mexico and Japan' in SAGE Open (2019),* and *'Pop idols, mediatized places and identity-oriented performances of fans as domestic tourists in Japan' in The Routledge Companion to Media and Tourism (2020).*

Luis Antonio Becerra-Soria is a Professor at the National Autonomous University of Mexico (UNAM). He holds a master's *degree in Studies of Asia and Africa specialty Japan and is a Doctorate student of Literature.*

Milton Fernando Gonzalez-Rodriguez is a Postdoctoral Research Fellow at the Centre for Latin American Research and Documentation (University of Amsterdam). Previous affiliations include University of Iceland, Malmö University and University of Cambridge. His research has mainly focused on the representation of indigeneity in Latin American cinema, animated series, television, and material culture. He is mostly interested in visual framing, stereotypes in media, digital cultural artifacts and the nexus between visuality, imaginaries, and material culture.

Laura Pinzón Cardona is a PhD candidate of the School of Architecture, Planning and Landscape at Newcastle University, fully funded by the Research Excellence Academy (REA), specializing in citizen participation and digital media uses in urban planning. Her previous articles include "Beyond connectivity: the impacts of social media in urban development in Puerto Ayora, Ecuador" (2013). ISSN 1474-3280. DPU Working Paper No 160. UCL, London. She has done fieldwork in Galapagos Islands, Ecuador, and Manizales, Colombia, with social and government organizations at the neighborhood and city scale. Her research has focused on the uses of digital, and traditional, media on participatory processes around urban planning, and the impacts these have in shaping new dynamics of activism and city-making. She is particularly interested in the relationship between new technologies and local communication trends with more inclusive ways of developing Latin American cities.

Jean-Marie Chenou is an Associate Professor at the department of Political Science of the Universidad de los Andes, Bogotá, Colombia. He obtained his PhD in Political Science from the University of Lausanne, Switzerland, and a masters' degree in International Relations from the University Panthéon-Assas (Paris II). Prior to joining the Universidad de los Andes, he was a lecturer at the University of Lausanne and a visiting researcher at the Copenhagen Business School. His research interests include Internet governance, the global political economy of the digital era, and the regulation of digital markets in Latin America.

Daniel Cabarcas Velandia is bachelor's degree candidate in Economics with a minor in Law at the Universidad de los Andes, Bogotá, Colombia. He is a member of the research incubator in Global Studies at the Department of Political Science at the Universidad de los Andes.

Maria Nicoll Sepulveda Marin holds a bachelor's degree in Political Science with a minor in sociology from the Universidad de los Andes, Bogotá, Colombia. She is a member of the research incubator in Global Studies at the Department of Political Science at the Universidad de los Andes. She has diverse research interests that include international security, specifically disarmament and the non-proliferation of weapons, international institutions, and political polarization both at national and international levels.

Ramón Salaverría is Associate Professor of Journalism at the University of Navarra, where he serves as Associate Dean of Research at the School of Communication. His research focuses on digital journalism, a topic in which he is a highly referred researcher. He was a research scholar of the Digital Media Research Program at the University of Texas at Austin (USA) during the academic year 2014–2015. He has also served as visiting lecturer in several universities in USA, Chile, Colombia, Guatemala, Paraguay, Peru, Portugal, Puerto Rico, Ukraine, and Venezuela, among other countries. He counts over 200 publications, including books such as "Ciberperiodismo en Iberoamérica" (2016), "Periodismo integrado" (2008), "Cibermedios" (2005), "Redacción periodística en Internet" (2005) and "Manual de redacción ciberperiodística" (2003).

Silvia-María Corzo is a researcher at Digital Unav—Center for Internet Studies and Digital Life, bound to the School of Communication at the University of Navarra, where she is currently working toward a PhD degree. Her research focuses on digital media in Latin America. In the 2016–2017 academic year, she worked in the Digital Communication Service of the University, where she carried out the planning, management, and evaluation of content in digital platforms, audience analysis and segmentation and online strategies. In 2015, she earned a Master's in political and corporate communication at the same university. From 2011 to 2015, she worked in television and print media in Guatemala City. In 2019, she was a visiting researcher at Northwestern University's Department of Communication Studies.

Javier Serrano-Puche is Associate Professor of Journalism at the University of Navarra, where he serves as Associate Dean of Academic Affairs at the School of Communication. His research focuses on news consumption, media and emotions, and the digital public sphere. His publications on these topics have appeared in publishers such as Palgrave MacMillan, Springer, IGI Global, McGraw Hill and in journals such as Communications, International Journal of Communication, Journal of Iberian and Latin American Research or Comunicar. He has been a visiting scholar at the London School of Economics (LSE).

Carmen Beatriz Fernández is a PhD candidate and lecturer at University of Navarra (UNAV), doing research at the Centre for Internet Studies and Digital Life at School of Communication. She is a professor of Political Communication at IESA (Venezuela). She holds a master's in business administration (IESA, Venezuela) and Electoral Campaigning (University of Florida, USA). She is CEO at DataStrategia Consultores and leads the Ibero-American political portal e-lecciones.net. Her works in cyberpolitics made her worthy of the Aristotle Excellence Award 2010, being part of the "Global Dream Team" that recognizes the best political consultants in the world. She has also been awarded with Eikon Regional (2013) and Victory awards (2014, 2017).

Jordi Rodríguez Virgili is Associate Professor of Political Communication at the University of Navarra, where he serves as Associate Dean of Teaching Staff at the School of Communication. He is a researcher at the Centre for Internet Studies and Digital Life at the UNAV. He has been a visiting scholar at the Graduate School of Political Management at George Washington University. He has also served as visiting lecturer in several universities in Uruguay, México, Germany, Poland, and Peru, among other countries. In 2016, he was awarded the Victory Award Merit for Excellence in Teaching in Political Communication. He has been the director of the master's degree program in Political and Corporate Communication (MCPC) at UNAV.

Priscila Muniz de Medeiros (Brazil) is a professor at the Department of Communication at Universidade Federal de Alagoas (Brazil). She holds a PhD in communication from Universidade Federal de Pernambuco

(Brazil). She has experience in the fields of discourse analysis, cyberculture and environmental communication.

Natália Martins Flores (Brazil) is a postdoc researcher at the State University of Campinas (Brazil). She holds a PhD in communication from Universidade Federal de Pernambuco (Brazil) and conducted her postdoctoral research in Communication Strategies at Universidade Federal de Santa Maria (Brazil). She has experience in discourse analysis of media discourses.

Amaya Noain-Sánchez, PhD is a researcher. Her lines of research include: Digital Communication, Journalism, Social Networks, Privacy, Disinformation and Ethics. She has written extensively on aspects of Digital Media, Effects of SNSs, Privacy vs. Public Sphere, Data Protection, Surveillance and Media Ethics. Her Doctoral Essay, *The protection of privacy on the Internet: Information flows and contextual integrity on Social Network Sites 2004–2014,* obtained the 2015 National Research Award by the Spanish Agency of Data Protection (AEPD). Additionally, she obtained the "2017 Emerald Literati Awards for Excellence" for her research on privacy by default and informed consent on the Internet. Apart from her experience as a researcher, she works as a journalist for several mass media and is lecturer at the Communications and Sociology Department of the Rey Juan Carlos University of Madrid.

1 Introduction—digital media, daily life, and public engagement

David Ramírez Plascencia, Barbara Carvalho Gurgel and Avery Plaw

Introduction

As the world arrives to the second decade of the new millennium, more than 3.5 billion people spend a significant part of their lives using information technologies (The Economist, 2019a). Commerce, education, politics, and communication are now, in a greater or lesser extent, fused with digital media. E-commerce, one of the most popular activities online, has globally grown 300% in between 2014 and 2019 (Statista, 2020a). In Latin America there are about 453.7 million of users which represent more than two-thirds of the entire population (Clement, 2019). Latin Americans spend many hours per day online: reading online news, publishing content on social platforms, watching series, listening to music, and buying stuff online. The region, in spite of the lack of infrastructure and connectivity, shows a noteworthy increase of online shopping. The number of buyers grew from 126.8 million in 2016 to 155.5 million in 2019, about 30 million in a matter of some years (Statista, 2020b). Big international corporations have extended their presence in the region. Amazon, for example, is expanding operations in Mexico, Brazil, and Argentina (Thomson, 2018). Netflix, the media-services provider, has pondered Latin America along with Asia, as one of the most promising markets to undertake future expansions (AFP, 2019). Even fresh new technologies such as drones are arriving to the region. Drones, unmanned aerial vehicle (UAV), are taking particular relevance not just to surveil national borders or combat crime in urban contexts in Brazil or Mexico (as it was possible to observe in The Politics of Latin America, Volume 1), they have been incorporated into diverse economic and entertainment activities as well: to establish precision agriculture systems that employ drones for monitoring fields and obtaining relevant data in real-time (Sandvik & Martins, 2018). Media companies incorporated UAVs to improve broadcasting coverture (Knight, 2017). They have been a great ally when searching for lost people in the desert or evaluating damages after a natural disaster such as hurricanes or floods and fighting social health problems as pandemics.

But the Internet have allowed Latin Americans not only to consume content and acquire goods and services but to expand their social relations, stay in contact with their relatives, and share opinions and complains related with public services and community problems. Actually, social media has established as an important sphere for activism and the construction of alternative discourses to empower minorities and dissidents. Women approach social media to raise the voice against labor and social discrimination, and ethnic communities use the Internet to visibilize their culture and to complain against public mistreatment and the dispossession of their lands and natural resources. Recent protests in France (#yellowvest), Chile (#chileprotests), and the United States (#ICantBreathe) endorse the use of social platforms and mobile applications as key instruments for community and political activism. Candidates, political parties, and organizations invest important resources to create social media profiles, manage, and share information with their supporters.

Actually, the Latin American media landscape faces significant changes as well, greatly accelerated by the rise of the digital world and its continuous and instantaneous dissemination of information and the irruption of the digital journalism which has transformed the process of news production by improving news with multimedia elements (audio, videos, photos, animations), adding the possibility that readers could interact with the notes, and the prospect of reaching a worldwide public. This massification of the information, however, has caused the proliferation of untrusted sources that share doubtful and fake news to polarize and distort facts. Relevant events such as presidential campaigns, war conflicts, and public health problems, as the case of the COVID-19 pandemic, are flooded by a huge amount of news which contains trusted information along with fake and altered data (Spring, 2020).

The structure of the book

This second volume of The Politics of Technology in Latin America centers on the study of the social impact of digital media from a citizen perspective. How people embrace information technologies to improve their living conditions, in what way social media and mobile devices support the strengthening of alternative movements and the organization of public demonstrations against governmental actions, and finally what are the challenges of digital journalism in a context of political polarization and disinformation. **Part I. Digital Media and Daily Life in Latin America** embraces cases related with the integration of digital media such as mobile devices, social platforms and, even, drones to diverse commercial, private, and social activities. From the inclusion of drones for business purposes, the construction of feminist discourse among Mexican girls on social media platforms, and the use of technology to surpass the impact of COVID-19 pandemic in Latin American countries during the 2020. **Part II. Information Technologies**

and Civic Engagement gives special attention to the new political practices triggered by the irruption of smartphones and platforms, especially inside organizations and social movements in Latin America. Activists have found in these devices and applications novel options to express their discontent toward traditional problems in the region such as corruption, insecurity, poverty and social exclusion. And finally, **Part III. Journalism and Media Integrity in the Age of Post-truth** centers on the study of digital journalism and the new media landscape, how these novel sceneries stand, not only possibilities to set fresh models to provide contents and information to the public, but present hard and complex trials as well: the precarization of journalist labor conditions, the massive spread of fake news, and the crisis of reliability in media.

Digital media and daily life in Latin America

Along with social media and smartphones, Latin America has witnessed the irruption of inventive technologies as the case of drones. UAVs, commonly known as drones, have made the jump from the military to the domestic and commercial sector. Actually, the presence of drones in diverse areas as entertainment and media, logistics, construction, or agriculture has constantly grown (Business Insider Intelligence, 2020). Latin America has not been absent from this trend. Drones, besides the lack of technological infrastructure in the region, have been adopted in diverse security and civilian activities. As it is possible to observe in The Politics of Internet in Latin America Vol 1, drones have been incorporated to combat organized crime in countries like Mexico. But UAVs have gained presence in the agriculture and media sectors as well. This proliferation has triggered the enactment of novel regulations and the amends of traditional ones (The Economist, 2020a). Drones in Latin America not only stand promising effects, but legal dilemmas and controversies regarding privacy and security issues (Jones, 2017). More about the debate on how to properly regulate drones for civilian use could be consulted in the chapter **Drone Ethics and Legal Regulation, Comparative Drone Law in Latin American Countries** by Jorge Cruz and David Mayorga.

In our present hypermediated context, social activities are becoming more dependent on smart phones, electronic tablets, mobile applications, and platforms: companies and governments have digitalized their procedures, not only to save resources, but also to reduce the time to process citizen applications and deliver products to consumers. Actually, people can buy goods, pay taxes and, in some cases, become an entrepreneur using smartphone applications. There are even applications such as Tinder or Badoo which allow people to expand their romantic relations. The impact of digital media, however, not only stands in helping people to acquire goods or socialize but in supporting the construction of discourses that empowers sectors that have been traditionally discriminated as women, genre and ethnic minorities and migrants. Those groups have found on social media an alternative public sphere to raise their voice and generate public actions toward racism, xenophobia, women harassment, and discrimination. In Villaplana and León's work **Net-narcoculture. Discursive Trends on Femicide Violence and Youth Culture in the Consumption of the Narcorap Aesthetics versus Feminist Rap Resistances,** the authors describe how YouTube serves to visibly feminist rap, a visual discourse to encourage feminist resistance toward the dissemination of songs, lyrics, and videos that promote genre violence, as the case of the narcorap, a kind of music that is gaining popularity among youth whose lyrics idealize narco leaders, illicit activities and make explicit references to violence toward women as well.

However, besides public policies and massive protests, violence toward women remains as a persistent problem in developing and industrialized countries alike. This hostility emerges as the form of visual discourses, as described in the Villaplana and León chapter, but in labor discrimination, street harassment, and, in some extreme cases, homicide. The irruption of the COVID-19 has exacerbated domestic violence, among others social and economic problems: the loss of jobs, the rise of poverty, and mental health problems caused by the lockdown and the ceasing of physical contact and socialization (Kar et al., 2020). This last issue is analyzed by Sergio Yagüe-Pasamón in his chapter **COVID-19 Confinement-related Mental Disorders: Morbidity and the Remedial Use of ICT in Hispanic Societies**, the author makes an insightful comparative analysis of the potential negative effects triggered by the quarantine policies implemented in Spain and Latin America, and how information technologies become a partial solution to balance the absence of social communication and contact.

As the pandemic spreads across the globe, governments must face very challenging undertakings. One of them is to reduce the number of infected and casualties to prevent the overload of the hospitals and other health facilities. This assignment is especially complex in megalopolises with millions of inhabitants as the case of Mexico City or Sao Paulo. Latin America is extremely urbanized and highly unequal (Bilal, 2020), and authorities were ill-equipped and untrained to correctly respond to the epidemic (O'Boyle et al., 2020), these facts limit the impact of common strategies that have been implemented to combat the advance of the disease: quarantines and social distancing measures. It happened in Ecuador (Guayaquil), where the dead bodies of the victims lay for days on the street because of the overload of hospitals, funeral services, and morgues. In the last chapter of this section **Speaking for Communities and against Oppression: Digital Media Responses to COVID-19 within Marginalized Communities of Brazil and Mexico,** Stuart H. Davis and Melissa Santillana focus on how, due to a deficient public response to the COVID-19, many organizations in countries like Mexico and Brazil are using social media to facilitate mutual aid through the sharing of medical advices and the distribution of food and medicines to deprived communities.

Information technologies and civic engagement

Modern-day activism and civic engagement are strongly attained to digital media. Technology has become an inherent compound for the traditional strategies used by social movements to spread their agenda and organize public gatherings to complain toward unpopular governmental actions (George & Leidner, 2019; Milošević-Đorđević & Žeželj, 2017). Recent protests in Hong Kong and Chile cannot be understood without the presence of smartphones and social media. Thanks to mobile devices people were able to live stream the marches or to record police abuses during the incidents avoiding censorship or future retaliations from the authorities (Caballero & Gravante, 2018; The Economist, 2020c). Digital media, furthermore, provides a cheap, flexible, and less-censored channel to the expression of dissent voices. There are even hidden spaces as the Deep Web in where people promote issues that could be controversial in some countries such as the liberalization of drugs such as Marijuana, or the application of euthanasia for people with terminal diseases (Maddox et al., 2016). Digital technologies, however, could be a "double-edged sword," that bring advantages but also threats. Technology provides government with apps to surveil and control citizens' activities online and offline. This surveillance is not only based for the scrutiny of opinions and information shared on social media, but on the use of Artificial intelligence (AI) and high-definition cameras to capture protesters' faces, and to identify and arrest political protesters, as it happened during Hong Kong's massive protests in 2019 (Thorbecke, 2019). On the other hand, citizens use technology to protect their identity. They have incorporated computer programs to encrypt communications and data, obstructing government's scrutiny, and apps to update other members about their safety or their location, in case they have been seized by the police.

In Latin America, digital technologies have served as conducts to express discontent toward governments and to bring the spotlight upon traditional social and economic problems (Cavalcanti et al., 2019). Social media supported the organization of massive concentrations in Chile toward the rise of the Santiago Metro's Subway fare and the general increase of the living cost. Protesters used the Internet as an alternative media to broadcast the news about the protest, avoiding government censorship (NPR, 2019). In recent years, pro-women rights collectives have approached to platforms as Twitter or YouTube to broadcast diverse genre vindications (Binder, 2019). Digital technologies play a key role, not only to denounce street harassment (Fileborn, 2017), but to empower and globally spread women's social demands and complaints as it happened with the *#MeToo* movement. In December 2019 the Chilean collective "Las Tesis" video recorded and transmitted a flash mob chant called "Un violador en tu camino" (A rapist in your path), a protest toward street harassment and rape, which rapidly became a trending topic on social media, and was adopted across Latin America and Europe. In March 2020, diverse Mexican pro-women rights groups organized a series of public demonstrations to demand actions against the dramatic growth of women murder rates in the country (The Economist, 2020b). And for the first time in history, in March 09, 2020, there was a one day-strike in where women did not present at work or go to school. All those actions were planned and organized using mostly social media platforms. To know more about importance of the role of digital media in the irruption of the Latin American feminist new wave, readers may consult Mandujano and Becerra's chapter **Social Media as an Instrument of Activism for Feminist University Students in Mexico: The Cases of MOFFyL and Uni Unida.** Thanks to spaces as Facebook or YouTube, local movements have reached a global public as the case of indigenous resistances toward the privatization of tribal lands and the construction of oil pipelines in Canada or the illegal mineral extraction and the devastation of the rainforest in the Amazon (Budka, 2018). The Indigenous have incorporated digital media for the construction and spreading of an alternative discourse (Clark & Hinzo, 2019). Milton Gonzalez's chapter **Latin American Indigenous Media Productions: Digital Artefacts of Contestation** focuses on how indigenous groups have incorporated technologies to create and share visual discourses to contest official discourse about their culture.

In urban contexts, Latin Americans have to deal with diverse metropolitan problems like air pollution, mobility, water and food supply, and criminality. To face these problems, local administrations are gambling their resources on the consolidation of smart cities, looking to promote the development of integral solutions based on connectivity, the use of video surveillance, drones, and similar devices. Laura Pinzon studies in **Digital Media in Citizen Participation and Collective Action for Spatial Justice**, how the incorporation of social media like Facebook and other digital tools could support a more inclusive and open process of the decision-making in urban management cities. The last chapter of this section, **Social Media and Political Polarization in Latin America: Analyzing Online Discussions During the 2018 Presidential Campaign in Colombia** by Chenou, Cabarcas, and Sepulveda, analyzes the use of social media, more precisely, WhatsApp groups, that not only promote engagement and mobilization among youth during electoral campaigns, but political polarization through the creation of echo chambers and that of filter bubbles that centralize, constrain, and polarize the political debate.

Journalism and media integrity in the age of post-truth

In plain 2020, information technologies have consolidated as vital elements not only for everyday activities but for political contest and activism as well. Though, along with these possibilities, there are also controversies and glitches. One of them is related with how few technological firms control most social platforms, applications and devices: Facebook, Alphabet (Google), Apple, and Amazon (The Economist, 2019b). Outside them, there are few options to reach a global audience, perhaps only Twitter. Facebook, for example, has acquired popular applications such as WhatsApp or Instagram, and Google has followed a similar path by acquiring YouTube. This concentration not only stands a great risk for the incorporation of new players in the global media landscape, avoiding competition and innovation, but it could be a serious threat to democratic institutions as it happened with The Cambridge Analytica scandal. In 2018, this company was accused of using Facebook to harvest user's personal data and to deliver selective political advertising. This information served to produce specific electoral preferences which paved the Donald Trump's electoral win in 2016 (Lewis & Hilder, 2018). In addition to this problem, there is a growing concern about the irruption of disinformation campaigns to subvert political and economic instability and trigger social polarization about key social issues such as migration, free market, and democracy.

Besides these glitches, digital media has brought deep changes to traditional media (Salaverría et al., 2019). The incorporation of technology allowed the reduction of production's costs and enabled the growth of potential consumers. Many newspapers have ended delivering their content in paper and transformed into a just-digital format, under the scheme of subscriptions or displaying ads when the users access the information. But many local newspapers have been forced to close because they could not stand this digital transition (Takenaga, 2019). Digital media has not only radically affected traditional media, but it has prompted the irruption of fresh competitors that base their entire operations on Internet, and which have taken advantage of content platforms such as YouTube or Facebook to equal traditional big corporations (Darbo & Skjerdal, 2019). In this context of incertitude and political polarization, journalism still plays a key role, not only by giving a voice to alternative discourses and social vindications, but to forge an informed public opinion. In Salaverría and Corzo's chapter **Digital Native Media in Central America: Reshaping the Online News Sphere,** it is possible to understand the process of digitalization of traditional media in Central America, a region that besides high levels of insecurity, public corruption, and the lack of infrastructure, has incorporated digital journalism as a vital element to inform citizens and promote free speech. However, its consolidation is facing complex problems: precarization of labor conditions, harassment toward journalists, and the irruption of fake news and disinformation.

Because of the omnipresence of social media across the globe, people can access a myriad of information, however, not all the sources and news are reputable. Practically every event not only at a global level but also locally is susceptible of being affected by the flow of false and untrusted data. Two chapters in this volume aim to understand how fake news are used to diverge citizens. **Disinformation and News Consumption in a Polarized Society: An Analysis of the Case of Venezuela** by Serrano-Puche, Beatriz Fernández, and Rodríguez Virgili, emphasizes how people consume information, from trusted sources or not, according to their political preferences, pro-government and pro-opposition, and how this information causes social divergence in Venezuela. Muniz de Medeiros and Martins Flore, in **Social Media in a Post-truth Age: Discursive Roles of Fake News About Marielle Franco,** describe the use of disinformation campaigns to attack political dissents and activists as it happened with the murder of the Marielle Franco, a councilwoman of Rio de Janeiro. After the homicide, there has been a fake narrative to denigrate the public image of the politician, as a form to attack her political ideas and justify her killing.

Due to the increased usage of fake news to attack political opposition and create social instability, several collectives conformed by volunteers, journalists, and informatics have settled online platforms that review, confirm, or discredit online news, particularly during elections (CNN, 2018; Deutsche Welle, 2018) or global events and incidents as the case of the COVID-19 pandemic during 2020 (Verificado, 2020). To know more about the potential harms of fake news in Latin America and how some collectives are combating the flow of untrusted information the readers could refer to Amaya Noain's chapter **Collaborative Journalism versus Disinformation: An Approach to Fact-Checking Projects in Mexico, Argentina, Colombia, Brazil, and Spain.**

Final remarks

In 2020, the world has suffered the worst global pandemic since the Spanish Flu of 1918, almost 100 years ago. The Coronavirus disease (COVID-19) as it is widely known in media, has caused thousands of casualties and the shutdown of non-essential economic activities around the world (World Health Organization, 2020). However, the final number of casualties is far to be known as the pandemic spreads to other countries. In the meantime, people have been forced to seclude at home and stop their activities. But, despite the difficult context, social life did not really end. On the contrary, people's socialization, education, and labor mostly migrated to the Internet. People organized online video game matches, ordered food and groceries using smartphones, communicated with their relatives and friends with Skype or WhatsApp; even musicians broadcasted live concerts at home using YouTube or Facebook. Thanks to social media, the world witnessed the brave determination of hundreds of public services: medics, nurses, police offices, and functionaries to combat the spread of the disease. It was through social platforms that people got valuable information to protect their lives and the lives of their relatives (Chitkara, 2020). Government built robust public platforms and mobile apps to deliver online services and reliable information about the pandemic.

Though this "massive exodus" to the virtuality has amplified traditional problems in Latin America. It has deepened social inequality by showing that only a small segment of the population could stay at home and follow public ordinances related with seclusion and social distancing. To continue with daily activities at home became a class privilege, not a democratic solution. During the pandemic, many people have been compelled to labor in spite of the potential risk, many children were not able to follow classes due to the lack of proper Internet connectivity and a computer. As a matter of fact, the pandemic did not create inequality in Latin America, but it is definitely intensifying social exclusion and poverty. As this editorial project is conducted, the pandemic curve is reaching the peak in many Latin American countries as Mexico and Brazil. By now, there is not a certitude about the exact damage that this disease will bring to the region. However, the after-match will be severe. A massive loss of jobs, the reduction or cut of social services, and economic crises as many governments could not deal with their public debts. What is undeniable is that until there will be a universally accessible vaccine, social distancing, and virtualization of work and public activities will continue for, probably years. This hyper-technologization of social life will bring important undertakings to the region such as to grant a more equal access to Internet in a context where the connectivity has become an imperative to continue with essential economic and labor activities, and to promote the involvement of social organizations in the process of public decision-making about the economic recovery and the return to the "new normality," and finally, to strengthen transparency, accountably, and the open access to public information to guarantee the respect of human rights. This point is particularly important, since many governments, under the excuse of the pandemic, have limited constitutional guarantees, particularly in the case of migrants and genre minorities. In this context of political politization, misinformation campaigns, and incertitude about the future, the role of free press and social organizations will be crucial to denounce governmental abuses and to offer alternative spaces to channel people's opinions and complains.

References

AFP. (2019, December 17). *Netflix seeing strong subscriber growth in Asia, Latin America—France 24.* Retrieved from https://www.france24.com/en/20191217-netflix-seeing-strong-subscriber-growth-in-asia-latin-america

Bilal, U. (2020). *COVID-19 and Latin American cities.* LAC-Urban Health. Retrieved from https://drexel.edu/lac/media/blog/2020/March/COVID and LatAm/

Binder, I. (2019). Identidad y agencia colectiva del movimiento ciberfeminista en América Latina. El caso de [ciberfeministaslatam]. *Revista Digitos, 0*(5), 210–233. https://doi.org/10.7203/rd.v0i5.128

Budka, P. (2018, May 24). *Indigenous articulations in the digital age: Reflections on historical developments, activist engagements and mundane practices.* Paper at International Communication Association 2018 Pre-Conference "Articulating Voice. The Expressivity and Performativity of Media Practice," Prague, Czech Republic: Hilton, 24 May.

Business Insider Intelligence. (2020, March 3). Drone market outlook: Industry growth trends, market stats and forecast. *Business Insider*. Retrieved from https://www.businessinsider.com/drone-industry-analysis-market-trends-growth-forecasts

Caballero, F. S., & Gravante, T. (2018). Digital Media Practices and Social Movements. A Theoretical Framework from Latin America. In F. S. Caballero & T. Gravante (Eds.), *Networks, Movements and Technopolitics in Latin America: Critical Analysis and Current Challenges* (pp. 17–41). Springer International Publishing, Cham, Switzerland. Retrieved from https://doi.org/10.1007/978-3-319-65560-4_2

Cavalcanti, D. B., Bringel, E. P. B., da Costa, F. R. J., de Oliveira, T. M., & Zuccolotto, V. R. (2019). Digital activism and indignation nets in Brazil: The pressure groups. *Journal of Politics in Latin America*, *11*(1), 109–130. Retrieved from https://doi.org/10.1177/1866802X19840455

Chitkara, H. (2020, March 17). The surge in connectivity due to the coronavirus will likely spur operational changes. *Business Insider*. Retrieved from https://www.businessinsider.com/coronavirus-led-internet-traffic-surge-to-test-network-operations-2020-3

Clark, L. S., & Hinzo, A. (2019). Digital survivance: Mediatization and the sacred in the tribal digital activism of the #NoDAPL movement. *Journal of Religion, Media and Digital Culture*, *8*(1), 76–104. Retrieved from https://doi.org/10.1163/21659214-00801005

Clement, J. (2019). *Worldwide internet users by region 2009–2019*. Statista. Retrieved from https://www.statista.com/statistics/265147/number-of-worldwide-internet-users-by-region/

CNN. (2018, June 30). ¿Qué sigue para #Verificado2018 tras la votación del 1 de julio? *CNN*. Retrieved from https://cnnespanol.cnn.com/video/termina-verificado-2018-noticias-falsas-elecciones-tania-montalvo-intvw-digital-mexico-voto-2018/

Darbo, K. N., & Skjerdal, T. (2019). Blurred boundaries: Citizens journalists versus conventional journalists in Hong Kong. *Global Media and China*, *4*(1), 111–124. Retrieved from https://doi.org/10.1177/2059436419834633

Deutsche Welle. (2018, March 11). Lanzan iniciativa para verificar noticias electorales. *DW.COM*. Retrieved from https://www.dw.com/es/m%C3%A9xico-lanzan-iniciativa-para-verificar-noticias-electorales/a-42929135-0

Fileborn, B. (2017). Justice 2.0: Street harassment victims' use of social media and online activism as sites of informal justice. *The British Journal of Criminology*, *57*(6), 1482–1501. Retrieved from https://doi.org/10.1093/bjc/azw093

George, J. J., & Leidner, D. E. (2019). From clicktivism to hacktivism: Understanding digital activism. *Information and Organization*, *29*(3), 100249. Retrieved from https://doi.org/10.1016/j.infoandorg.2019.04.001

Jones, T. (2017). *International Commercial Drone Regulation and Drone Delivery Services:* [Product Page]. RAND. Retrieved from https://www.rand.org/pubs/research_reports/RR1718z3.html

Kar, S. K., Yasir Arafat, S. M., Kabir, R., Sharma, P., & Saxena, S. K. (2020). Coping with mental health challenges during COVID-19. In S. K. Saxena (Ed.), *Coronavirus Disease 2019 (COVID-19): Epidemiology, Pathogenesis, Diagnosis, and Therapeutics* (pp. 199–213). Springer, Singapore. Retrieved from https://doi.org/10.1007/978-981-15-4814-7_16

Knight, W. (2017, September 12). Drones y robots inteligentes amenazan con destruir los trabajos de inspección industrial. *MIT Technology Review*. Retrieved from https://www.technologyreview.es/s/9471/drones-y-robots-inteligentes-amenazan-con-destruir-los-trabajos-de-inspeccion-industrial

Lewis, P., & Hilder, P. (2018, March 23). Leaked: Cambridge Analytica's blueprint for Trump victory. *The Guardian*. Retrieved from https://www.theguardian.com/uk-news/2018/mar/23/leaked-cambridge-analyticas-blueprint-for-trump-victory

Maddox, A., Barratt, M. J., Allen, M., & Lenton, S. (2016). Constructive activism in the dark web: Cryptomarkets and illicit drugs in the digital "demimonde." *Information, Communication & Society*, *19*(1), 111–126. Retrieved from https://doi.org/10.1080/1369118X.2015.1093531

Milošević-Đorđević, J. S., & Žeželj, I. L. (2017). Civic activism online: Making young people dormant or more active in real life? *Computers in Human Behavior*, *70*, 113–118. Retrieved from https://doi.org/10.1016/j.chb.2016.12.070

NPR. (2019, November 8). How the price of the metro sparked mass protests in Chile. *NPR.Org*. Retrieved from https://www.npr.org/2019/11/07/777391505/how-the-price-of-the-metro-sparked-mass-protests-in-chile

O'Boyle, M., Adghirni, S., & Gillespie, P. (2020, March 20). Coronavirus news: Latin America isn't ready for coming onslaught—*Bloomberg*. Retrieved from https://www.bloomberg.com/news/articles/2020-03-20/latin-america-isn-t-ready-for-the-virus-onslaught-headed-its-way

Salaverría, R., Sádaba, C., Breiner, J. G., & Warner, J. C. (2019). A brave new digital journalism in Latin America. In M. Túñez-López, V.-A. Martínez-Fernández, X. López-García, X. Rúas-Araújo, & F. Campos-Freire (Eds.), *Communication: Innovation & Quality* (pp. 229–247). Springer International Publishing, Cham, Switzerland. Retrieved from https://doi.org/10.1007/978-3-319-91860-0_14

Sandvik, K. B., & Martins, B. O. (2018). Revisitando el espacio aéreo latinoamericano: Una exploración de los drones como sujetos de regulación. *Latin American Law Review*. Retrieved from https://doi.org/10.29263/lar01.2018.03

Spring, M. (2020, May 27). The human cost of virus misinformation. *BBC News*. Retrieved from https://www.bbc.com/news/stories-52731624

Statista. (2020a). *Global retail e-commerce market size 2014–2023*. Statista. Retrieved from https://www.statista.com/statistics/379046/worldwide-retail-e-commerce-sales/

Statista. (2020b). *Topic: E-commerce in Latin America*. Statista. Retrieved from https://www.statista.com/topics/2453/e-commerce-in-latin-america/

Takenaga, L. (2019, December 21). More than 1 in 5 U.S. papers has closed. This is the result. *The New York Times*. Retrieved from https://www.nytimes.com/2019/12/21/reader-center/local-news-deserts.html

The Economist. (2019a, June 8). The second half of humanity is joining the internet. *The Economist*. Retrieved from https://www.economist.com/leaders/2019/06/08/the-second-half-of-humanity-is-joining-the-internet

The Economist. (2019b, October). Dismembering big tech. *The Economist*. Retrieved from https://www.economist.com/business/2019/10/24/dismembering-big-tech

The Economist. (2020a, February). As delivery drones multiply, they may need to protect themselves. *The Economist*. Retrieved from https://www.economist.com/science-and-technology/2020/02/27/as-delivery-drones-multiply-they-may-need-to-protect-themselves

The Economist. (2020b, March). Mexico's new feminist wave. *The Economist*. Retrieved from https://www.economist.com/the-americas/2020/03/05/mexicos-new-feminist-wave

The Economist. (2020c, March). Young Africans want more democracy. *The Economist*. Retrieved from https://www.economist.com/middle-east-and-africa/2020/03/05/young-africans-want-more-democracy

Thomson, E. (2018, January 2). Customer service sucks in Latin America. Amazon may change that. *Bloomberg.Com*. Retrieved from https://www.bloomberg.com/news/articles/2018-01-02/customer-service-sucks-in-latin-america-amazon-may-change-that

Thorbecke, C. (2019, October 12). How tech has fueled a "leaderless protest" in Hong Kong. *ABC News*. Retrieved from https://abcnews.go.com/Technology/tech-fueled-leaderless-protest-hong-kong/story?id=66158665

Verificado. (2020, March 23). Cobertura especial: Noticias verificadas sobre el Coronavirus. *Verificado*. Retrieved from https://verificado.com.mx/coronavirus/

World Health Organization. (2020). *Coronavirus disease 2019 (COVID-19)* (No. 62; Situation Report). World Health Organization.

Part I

Digital media and daily life in Latin America

2 Drone ethics and legal regulation, comparative drone law in Latin American countries

Jorge Andrés Cruz Silva and David Andrés Mayorga Naranjo

Introduction

Since technology enabled people to operate devices and ships remotely, the use of unmanned vehicles aroused questions on a myriad of implications. From technicalities to ethical and legal constraints, the use of drones can be studied from different approaches. During the first two decades of the 21st century, these aircraft have become gadgets of great popularity and importance in industries as journalism, agriculture, civil control, etc. Drones have become a handful of curious eyes from the sky, aircraft that—in an Orwellian perspective—may control and monitor people or could enhance the pilot's vision and scopes to observe and modify realities. This dichotomy offers an ethical and legal discussion regarding the role of these craft to create or recreate narratives and their relationship.

Drones, equipped with high-definition lenses, may be considered a moving camera and their usages are closely related to dilemmas within the image capturing process: constraints on filming and photographing unaware people and the subsequent narrative construction for eager audiences. Drones may be seen as a cyborgist attempt to enhance human capabilities, but also as novelty devices within a complex social and cultural understanding of their role while they create a synthetic situation. This chapter aims to be an analysis to understand the research question: How legal bodies were shaped in Latin America for drone flights?

Although research on drone legislation and ethical constraints have been carried out in American and South American spheres, a Latin American perspective is mandatory to reinforce the understanding of this technological and social phenomenon. This region of the world, a so-called "Third World land," may find clever uses for drones that promote changes in people's realities. This chapter seeks to be a comprehensive guide to the legal state on drones into expectations of future understanding for pilots and stakeholders in this market. To achieve this, a Comparative Law method will be used, since the legislation on drones around the world has similar roots, but different geographical and historical contexts. All 26 Latin American legislations will be displayed around legal body aspects, operational limitations, a remote pilot-in-command certification and responsibilities and aircraft requirements; aspects that are derived from US legislation.

The understanding of the possibilities and constraints to deploy drones in Latin America is an important step to recognize the current state of the usage of one of the most disruptive devices of the information society. The legal control of these devices has to do with limitations but also offers a frame of reference for future work, theoretical, but especially, practical.

Drones: History, aerial viewing, and revenue

A modern definition for drones can be traced to the first years of the 21st century, nevertheless, the importance of devices that could be deployed to register aerial views is more ancient. One of the first projects to capture aerial sights is linked to Danish artist Melchior Lorck (Warner in Dorrian and Pousin, 2013). He produced panoramic landscapes of the Mecca and Constantinople from the hills close to those cities. This type of recordings created room for a different technique of mapping; examples of this can be traced in the work of Antonio Tempesta and his drawings of 16th-century Rome (Bury in Dorrian and Pousin, 2013); it also can be seen in the efforts of Gaspar Felix Tournachon or "Nadar," three centuries after Tempesta. This French balloonist is considered the first aerial photographer who used cameras and balloons to capture the first aerial views of Paris and the Seine River (Professional Aerial Photographers Association, N.D. 2013). This first period can be considered the ancient era of aerial footage.

The modern era developed through the 20th century, after the invention of modern aircraft. In 1917 the US navy modified a biplane to install a gyroscopic stabilizer to control the ship by radio; also, in 1935 the United Kingdom's Royal Air Force manufactured a prime reusable radio-controlled airplane (Brooks, 2012). A semantic perspective is helpful to understand the emergence of unmanned vehicles. The word *Drone*—a more simple, concise, and spread term—is linked to a flying machine from 1946, where a Popular Science magazine article addressed "radio-controlled crafts" used for military missions with that new name (Grumman Hatches a Mallard, 1946); within the publication, a ship was presented with the name Queen Bee, a nod to the previous usage for the term, referred to the male bee.

While the questions of "what is a drone?" and "where they came from?" were answered, the pyramid for a contextual understanding can be completed by addressing the potential applications of these aircraft. For this, Clarke (2014b) underlined possible usages for drones: Journalism, Voyeurnalism, Law Enforcement, Community Policing, Voyeurism, Passenger Transport, Hostile Load-Delivery, Hobby, and Entertainment Uses. However, to understand the use of drones, a key difference has to be acknowledged: the usage of drones for carrying purposes and for aerial viewing and control. While the first deals with technicalities and technology regarding capabilities to deliver or collect packages, the second usage is more complex as it deals with aesthetic and ethical standpoints.

The revenue and growth of the industry demonstrate the drone industry is still boiling. According to the FAA (2019), by the first day of 2019, more than 900,000 drone pilots were registered and by 2020 the industry will reach 2.4 million units in the United States. The industry revenue by 2025 is projected to have an annual income of 82.1 billion dollars (AUSVI, 2013). The commercial uses for drones, according to the FAA's Unmanned Aircraft System Report (Philly by Air, 2019), divide mainly in five key sectors where these devices present high impact and use: Real Estate/Photography (47%), Industrial/Inspections (28%), Agricultural (17%), Insurance (4%), and State/Local Governments (3%).

Regarding the aesthetic and ontological perspective, drones can be seen as devices that enhance and boost human capabilities. Aerial viewing, in particular, reveals formal chaos of the objects that are under aerial scrutiny (Dorrian and Pousin, 2013). With drones, activities related to recognition and search are enhanced as a cognitive process (Clark and Chalmers, 2010) as the drone footage is neutral and fair (Gynnild, 2014). Secondly, regarding ethical constraints, Culver (2014)—a researcher of drones and drone journalism—defines four ethical dimensions: safety, accuracy and context, privacy, and conflict of interest. These aspects can be also traced in legal bodies since laws determine some aspects related to the well-being as philosophic and ethical approaches.

Aviation law

From the beginning of the commercial activities with drones, states have been interested to create specific legal bodies to control the use of these unmanned vehicles. Regarding drones, Clarke (2014a) addressed six types of control: Natural, Soft regulatory forms for both organizational and industrial regulations, Pre-existing generic laws, Aviation laws, Privacy laws, and Surveillance laws. Countries like the United States or the UK have set the example, issuing new legislation, with some precincts from current aviation laws.

At first, to create new legislation it will be normal to face a relationship of forces, whereas to achieve political and social agreement, this connection can become contradictory, chaotic, or obscure (Galiana Saura, 2002). In this sense, not many lawmakers may change their standpoint, but the whole society should approach the topic ruled differently—a new form of social contract in the words of Rousseau.

Arnaud underlines a concept about legal regulation, useful to open this discussion, where this social regulation can be considered "a set of positive rules that the State establishes and controls" (2000, p. 166.). The legislator must direct his work to legislate, foreseeing possible problems that may occur, as long as the solution may come from a legislative regulation, considering the principle of legal certainty (Segovia Salcedo, 2013). For instance, in Venezuela an attack to president Maduro activated the discussion for drone regulations (How the Drone Attack on Maduro Unfolded in Venezuela | NYT—Visual Investigations, 2019)

On the other hand, lawmakers must carry out a detailed analysis that determines if it is necessary to create legislation not to fall into normative hypertrophy, excessive legal regulation (Cortés Sánchez, 2007). States must function as a guarantee, explains Ferrajoli (2010), to avoid idealistic and normativism fallacies; that is to say, it is not possible to be confused with law and reality. Lawmakers must be capable enough to analyze reality and translate it into the norm, thus giving a true fulfillment of the rule. The quality of a norm does not only depend on the fact that the legislative procedure is followed, but also that it is complied with and the ability to achieve the objective for which it was created.

Finally, it is key to identify which social actor should lead the legal processes; normally the only body or entity that can create, modify, or extinguish laws is the Legislative Function, which takes different names. National Assembly in Ecuador, National Congress in Chile, Congress of the Union in Mexico, and thus, respectively, in each of the countries. These institutions will share the role with some specific aviation regulatory institutions that will create the regulations.

In this sense, with the appearance of commercial flights, the need to legislate both nationally and internationally the use of airspace emerged, to regulate permits, operation, crew, and other activities carried out by both natural and legal persons. This, to avoid chaos in the airspace and to provide safe and accident-free spaces (ICAO, 2019).

In addition to country aerial legislation, it must be taken into account that there is the International Civil Aviation Organization (ICAO), an institution of the United Nations Organization which aims to "develop the principles and techniques of international air navigation and promote the organization and development of international air transport" (ICAO, 2007). This organization, founded in 1944, and with the subscription of 189 "contracting states," is responsible for ensuring compliance with agreements and international standards set for airspace (Convenio sobre Aviación Internacional, 1944). The macro agreement, signed in Chicago, determined respect for the exclusive sovereignty in the airspace over territories, a principle of utmost. Subsequently, there have been other international standards and conventions, which are part of the international aviation legislation, such as the Tokyo Convention of 1969 which mentions the infringements committed by aircraft (ICAO, 1969) which mentions the infringements committed by aircraft; Hague Convention of 1970 which regulates sanctions and crimes that can be committed by natural persons within an aircraft, for instance (United Nations (1970) which regulates sanctions and crimes that can be committed by natural persons within an aircraft, for instance.

Comparative law

In order to pursue the main objective of this chapter, a comparative law methodology will be used. This research method will take place in the analysis of 21 Latin American countries and their regulations related to unmanned aircrafts. These countries' drone laws will be scrutinized in two main aspects:

(1) date of issue, which explores how early each country acknowledged the need for this kind of regulations; and (2) particular specifications, following Operational Limitations, Remote Pilot in Command Certification and Responsibilities, Aircraft Requirements, and Model Aircraft (Waite, 2016).

Tardif defines Comparative Law as "an autonomous legal discipline or a simple method of analyzing the legal norms of various systems," (2011, p. 24). Cabanellas de Torres refers to this type of legal analysis as the branch that aims "to systematize the positive law in force in the various countries, already in general or in some of its institutions, to establish analogies and differences" (2017, p. 55). Additionally, Ajani et al. (2009) underlined the importance of Comparative Law as a promotor of the acquisition of a better understanding of the data belonging to a specific area of knowledge. While the importance of Comparative Law is clear, its application must be carried out with care, because to determine a universal Comparative Law "would be a monstrous and encyclopedic task, difficult and nearly impossible to read" (Alcalá Zamora In Barrera Martínez, 2011).

One key aspect of Comparative Law is related to nomothetic—legislative policy—in which, with the comparison and study of different legal institutions in the world, lawmakers innovate and update national regulations, as long as it implies consistency within the same. Bastide explains that "legislators around the world have observed that many times, there cannot be dictated good laws without resorting to Comparative Law, either through general studies or through specific reports on the subject in question" (2017, p. 587).

Latin American drone legislation

Argentina

The National Civil Aviation Administration, issued on May 27, 2019, the more updated document of the research: New Regulations unmanned airborne vehicles (UAVs) and Systems unmanned airborne vehicles (SVANT) (Proyecto de Nuevo Reglamento de Vehículos Aéreos No Tripulados (Vant) y de Sistemas de Vehículos Aéreos No Tripulados (Svant), 2019). A particular aspect of the legal body is that it divides drones in three different aspects: according to the character, as public or private; depending on the nature of its use: Recreational, Commercial and Scientific, or Experimental; and according to weight: Class A, up to 500 grams, Class B, between 501 grams and up to 5 kilograms, Class C, more than 5 kilograms and up to 150 kilograms, and, Class D, more than 150 kilograms.

The Resolution 527/2015, states, some specifications:

- Maximum height for the flight, 400 feet and 140 feet below controlled airspace
- 5 kilometers away from runways, 1 kilometer away from VFR/helicopter corridors

- Operation Manual and Safety Management System must be documented
- The operation over-populated areas (unless in segregated areas) is forbidden
- Daylight operation is mandatory
- Registration and Identification is required
- Medical fitness, theory, and practice certificates are required
- No simultaneous flights will be allowed

Bolivia

The General Directorate of Civil Aviation in Bolivia, issued on 30, April 2019, the Rules for flight and operations of Remote Piloted Aircraft (Boletín Reglamentario N° AAP-0149, 2019). The document underlines a difference regarding operations: recreational, from 250 grams of maximum takeoff weight, exclusively for recreational purposes; and Aerial work operations, with the same minimum weight. The regulation also indicates that the owner or pilot of a drone heavier than 250 grams must obtain a registration number from the AAC by filling out the Online Registration Form. Additionally, for drones with a weight equal to greater than 6 kilograms and up to 10 kilograms, the owner or remote pilot must make the payment of 50.00 Bolivians pesos (7.6 dollars) for registration.

Besides normal limitations regarding negligence or reckless operation of Remotely Piloted Aircraft (RPA), such as responsibility for the operation, psychophysiological aptitude of the operator, and limited use near airfield and heliports, it is important to mention that any drone can be operated in public events, concerts, festivals, sporting events, manifestations, or protests.

Brazil

The National Civil Aviation Agency issued May 2, 2017, the General Requirements for Civil Use Un-Crewed Aircraft (Requisitos Gerais para Aeronaves não Tripuladas de Uso Civil, 2017). The regulation states the remote pilot and observer requirements: All remote pilots and RPA observers must be 18 years of age or older; All RPA Class 1 or 2 remote pilots must have a valid 1st, 2nd, or 5th Class Aeronautical Medical Certificate (CMA); and, all remote pilots engaged in operations above 400 feet above ground level (AGL) or engaged in Class 1 or 2 Remote Piloted Aircraft System (RPAS) operations shall have a license and qualification issued or validated by the National Civil Aviation Agency of Brazil (ANAC).

Another specification worthy to mention is the requirements for the operation:

- Registration Certificate, Registration Certificate, or Experimental Trademark Certificate, as applicable, all valid;
- Valid certificate of airworthiness, if applicable;

- Flight manual;
- Insurance policy or insurance certificate with proof of payment, if valid, if applicable;
- Document containing the risk assessment referred to in paragraphs E94.103 (f) (2) and E94.103 (g) (2) of these Special Regulations; and
- Valid CMA license.

Chile

General Directorate of Civil Aviation issued the DAN 15: Operations of Remotely Piloted Aircraft (RPA) in Public Interest Matters, which are performed on populated areas on February 10, 2017. The legal body addresses some key aspects and rules:

- Maximum takeoff weight of 9 kilograms (without the parachute weight)
- Only RPAS-manufactured are allowed, with technical instructions and operating instructions (no homemade RPAS)
- RPAS must have a serial number from the DGAC
- Drones must have a parachute during operation
- Drones must be controllable at any time manually (not be fully automatic).
- Authorization is required by DGAC to fly (registration card, pilot credentials, insurance). The pilot certificate valid 12 months (18 years old, theoretical training, practice exam on a specific model, written exam)
- The operation must be carried out 2 kilometers away from airports
- Only one drone must be operative at a time with a maximum of 500 meters range horizontally
- Drones are not allowed to drop any object
- No operation is permitted in firefighting areas
- If autonomy is less than 60 minutes, the discharge cannot be more than 80% of the battery capacity
- The operation of the ship will be no closer than 20 meters over and 30 meters from non-participating people

Colombia

Civil Aeronautics of the Ministry of Transport issued the General Requirements for Airworthiness and Operations of RPAs, on July 27, 2015 (Requisitos Generales de aeronavegabilidad y Operaciones para RPAS, 2015). The document determines some key aspects for regulations: UAVs are not permitted to fly over people, or in high winds, or within 5 kilometers of an airport. Regarding this, an aspect particular to Colombia is that drones are not allowed to fly within 1.8 kilometer radius of the President,

Vice President, and other national and foreign authorities. Drones are forbidden above border lines.

Some other aspects are referred in the legal body:

- Maximum weight of 25 kilograms
- Maximum altitude of 500 feet
- Drones must remain within 750 meters from the operator, and within visual line of sight
- No special permission is required for photography

Costa Rica

The General Directorate of Civil Aviation issued, the Operational Directive regulating the operations of Drones or RPAS on February 13, 2018 (Directiva Operacional que regula las operaciones de Drones o Sistema de Aeronaves Pilotadas a Distancia (RPAS), 2019). The regulation states that the operation of drones does not require a DGAC approval, but it is mandatory to follow the safety guide. Only day flights are allowed, in visual weather conditions and areas outside agglomerations. All drones with a weight less than 25 kilograms must have an identification plate.

Within the document, the rules are expressed as limitations:

- Drones cannot fly near manned aircraft or out of the operator's visual range
- Drones cannot fly for paid or commercial activities
- Drones cannot fly more than 400 feet (120 meters) high or in a radius of 8 kilometers around Aerodromes, Corrections Centers, Presidential House, among others
- Drones cannot fly where they affect people's privacy

Dominican Republic

The Dominican Institute of Civil Aviation issued Resolution No. 008-2015 that regulates the use and operation of RPAS or drones in the national territory, which has a scope for all persons who carry out air operations with drones, regardless of weight or type of activity (No.008-2015, 2015).

The regulations establish that if the ship weighs of less than 4.4 pounds (2 kilograms) the pilot is not obligated to have authorization from the IDAC department; any drone that exceeds the limit weight, must obtain a license duly registered. (Resolución No. 008-2015)

Within the general rules, the operation should be done only when there is sufficient natural lighting. The flight is forbidden if the activity violates the rights of others in terms of privacy and/or intimacy. (No.008-2015, 2015) Finally, a speed limit of 87 knots (160 km/h) and a height of 400 feet above the ground are established, taking into account international regulations on drones. (No.008-2015, 2015).

Ecuador

The General Directorate of Civil Aviation (DGAC) issued in February 2018-Part 91, legal guidance for flight and general operating rules. Within the document, Appendix M deals with unmanned pilot aircraft, the appendix presents three considerations to add to the 2015 document, "Requirements for Operation System of remotely piloted aircraft known as drones or Unmanned Aircraft Systems" (issued on September 17, 2015). The three considerations are: general rules of use, granting of certificates and licenses, and request for authorization. The aspect regarding Certification and Responsibilities excels, it is the first time that Ecuadorian Drone Law considers the possibility of issuing certificates for aircraft or pilots and even creates a regulatory process for granting licenses; notwithstanding, the document clarifies that "norms related to certification and licensing have not yet been developed" (Aviación Civil, 2018).

A specific aspect within Ecuadorian legislation deals with the responsibility of the owner and the insurance involved: Pilots or owners must contract a civil liability insurance policy, of 3000 dollars minimum for a drone between 2 and 25 kilograms; and of 5000 dollars minimum for drones that exceed 25 kilograms.

El Salvador

The Civil Aviation Authority has not issued a specific legal body regarding drones, although in its website (¿Qué puedo hacer con mi DRON?, 2017), a press release discusses some aspects of the operation. Drones operated for recreational purposes weighing less than 2 kilograms do not require registration, ships that do require permission must go to the competent authority. On the other hand, there are some precautions:

- Flights within the operator's visual range and up to 120 meters
- The operation at night is prohibited, as well as if it is less than 6 kilometers from airports
- The drone cannot exceed 70 km/h
- The drone cannot fly over government institutions, penal centers, embassies, judicial centers, hospitals, among others

Guatemala

The General Directorate of Civil Aviation issued the Civil Aviation Regulations Manual: RAC—101: Regulation on Unmanned Aircraft, Modeling Aircraft and Fireworks, on July 22, 2013 (Manual de Regulaciones de Aviacion Civil: RAC—101, 2017), meaning this legal body is one of the first to be issued, but also one that has not suffered any update. The regulation states that the documents required for the operation are: (1) Name, address, and telephone number of the person who will operate the aircraft or if several persons are involved, the name, address, and telephone number of the person who will coordinate the operation; (2) the date and time of the operation and/or release and how long it will last; and, the specific area of operation.

Finally, a key aspect is in the Dangerous Operations Prohibited Section:

- A person must not operate an unmanned aircraft in a manner that produces a danger to another aircraft, another person, or property.
- The operation of a rocket includes a firework rocket, regardless of whether it can be raised more than 400 feet above ground level or not.

Honduras

On August 17, 2017, the National Congress of Honduras approved several reforms to the Civil Aviation Law, which was an initiative of the Executive Power, who observed that an update and reference was needed on the systems of RPAs. Article 56-A, added in this reform, stipulates that the "Aeronautical Authority must regulate the conditions of initiation, learning, flight practices and Operation of Remote Piloted Aircraft Systems (RPAS) through the Civil Aeronautics Regulation (RAC) respective" (Decreto No.65-2017, 2017).

The document also establishes that studies should be carried by the authority, which also should establish restrictions or prohibitions—related specifically to national security issues—on the use of drones in specific areas. The Honduran Civil Aeronautics Agency as a competent body and by following the aforementioned amended law, issued the regulations to regulate everything related to RPAS.

Mexico

On July 25, 2017, the General Directorate of Civil Aviation of Mexico issued the Mandatory Circular AV-23/10 R4 corresponding to the requirements to operate RPAS. The institution refers, in part, to the international regulations carried out by the International Civil Aviation Organization and defines RPAS as "The Remote Piloted Aircraft System (RPAS) is composed of a Remote Piloted Aircraft (RPA) and everything associated with the support team for its operation, such as, control station, link data, telemetry (…)" (Circular Obligatoria No. AV-23/10 R4, 2017, p. 4)

Among the regulations and limitations that apply to the three categories are the following:

- Micro RPAS, Small RPAS with private recreational use, and large RPAS with private recreational use only have to be registered in the database of the competent entity, while small and large RPAS for non-commercial and commercial private use must necessarily have authorization of operation by the Aeronautical Authority.

- Prohibition of operating the drone in restricted or dangerous areas, determined by the Competent Authority in Mexico or within enclosed spaces with more than 12 people.
- The RPA pilot is responsible for any damage, accident or incident, and information obtained during the operation of the aircraft.
- The maximum height of the flight is regulated by each type of category.

Nicaragua

The Nicaraguan Institute of Civil Aviation issued on November 28, 2014, the Resolution No. 34-2014, which prohibits the entry into the national territory of unmanned equipment and also restricts the use of this equipment to more than 100 feet high with 30 horizontal meters (RN34-2014, 2014).

According to the aforementioned resolution and the press release made by the government, this decision is justified since the use of this equipment would affect the airspace and could cause accidents since the Nicaraguan airspace is often occupied by civil and military Helicopters and ships from the National and International Aviation Authorities (INAC, 2014).

Panama

The Civil Aeronautical Authority of Panama approved on February 16, 2016, Resolution No. 120/DSA/DJ/DG/AAC corresponding to the requirements for the operation of RPAS. Drones are classified by their weight and by their type of operations. Due to its weight, there are four categories: (1) Micro from 0 to 250 grams of maximum takeoff certified weight, (2) Small, for more than 250 grams up to 25 kilograms, (3) Lightweight, for more than 25 kilograms up to 150 kilograms, and (4) Heavy, more than 150 kilograms. By its type of operations, they are classified in civil or state aircraft operations.

Within the general rules, it should be noted that Panama establishes that photography or filming non-consensual for third parties, observation, interference, or any similar activity, are not considered as sports or recreational use. (Resolución No. 120/DSAD/DJ/DG/AAC, 2016)

Paraguay

The National Directorate of Civil Aeronautics of Paraguay approved on November 21, 2017, through Resolution No. 2170/2017 to Resolution No. 1103 the regulation of RPA and RPAS. The application of the regulation focuses on the activities or operations carried out by drones, only if it is "used in the unsecured airspace from a height of one hundred and fifty (150) meters as well as in the vicinity of the aerodromes, their approach and takeoff paths" (Resolution No. 2170/2017, p. 10).

The Aeronautical Authority has considered making a distinction of RPAS by its size: (1) small, up to 10 kilograms; (2) medium, over 10 kilograms up to 150 kilograms; and, (3) large, above 150 kilograms (R1103, 2017). Within Chapter 3 of the aforementioned resolution, it regulates operations and limitations:

- Any recreational or sports operation will be limited "in a radius of not less than 30 meters horizontally and 10 meters vertically" (R1103, 2017, p. 15)
- The use of drones will be allowed when the usage is for recreational, entertainment, and similar purposes
- Limitation of operation of drones in populated areas as "cities, urbanizations, agglomeration of people, (...) prohibited, restricted and/or dangerous areas that have been established as such" (R1103, 2017, p. 16)
- Distant crew member requirement
- Insurance for damage liability must be contracted

Peru

The Congress of the Republic of Peru, approved on March 21, 2018, the Law No. 30740, corresponding to the regulation, use, and operations of distance piloted aircraft systems (RPAS). Despite being a concise law, it establishes several important regulations and limitations in the Peruvian territory (Ley No. 30740, 2018):

- Any person who wishes to manage or pilot an RPAS, without counting civil or practical use of aero sports, must have a license and authorization from the Ministry of Transportation and Communications through the General Directorate of Civil Aeronautics.
- RPAS owned by the State, used for military, police, or customs purposes are not required to obtain the aforementioned license.
- It establishes an important limitation, since it prohibits the use of drones when their usage intends to violate the privacy of any citizen.
- Establishes a geographical area for testing.

Puerto Rico

The Federal Aviation Agency of Puerto Rico regulated the use of Drones or RPAS in June 2016. Within the regulations, it is necessary to have a drone pilot certificate. Another aspect is the speed limit (100 miles per hour) of these devices and the flight (400 feet) and the operation is forbidden near any airport (Ortiz Musseden et al., 2017).

On January 24, 2017, the Government of Puerto Rico, through the Legislative Assembly, decided to approve the law on the Protection of the Airspace and Use of Unmanned Aircraft on security Facilities of the Commonwealth of Puerto Rico, in which the regulations issued by the

Federal Aviation Agency of Puerto Rico mentioned above reach the status of a law. Additionally, it establishes the penalties and fines that any person may be susceptible when using drones and violates the law and established regulations. (Ley. 667, 2017, p. 23).

Uruguay

The regulation in this country begins very early, with Decree No. 314/994 of July 5, 1994, which regulates the obtaining of permits for the operation of any type of airborne sensor. However, it is on August 29, 2014, that the National Directorate of Civil Aviation in Aeronautical Infrastructure, issues Resolution No. 291-2014 in which they regulate the activities carried out by drones.

The Aeronautical Authority makes a classification according to the weight of the RPAS in the following manner: (1) small, up to 25 kilograms; (2) mediums, with more than 25 kilograms; (3) big, more than 260 kilograms. Any RPAS can perform operations in prohibited and restricted areas and airports (Resolución No. 291-2014).

Small RPAS that are dedicated to recreation or sports issues do not need registration or certification or a license issued by the Aeronautical Authority. While minor RPAS for commercial use, no matter their purpose, must necessarily require the registration to have the airworthiness license and certification. (R.291-2014, 2014).

Venezuela

The Administrative Providence N° PRE-CJU-GDA-183-19 of April 8, 2019, which covers several topics corresponding to aeronautics, is currently in force, including the regulation of the operations of RPAS. It classifies them into four types: (1) mini, with less than 3 kilograms; (2) lightweight, with a weight between 3 kilograms and 25 kilograms; (3) middleweight, with a weight greater than 25 kilograms up to 150 kilograms; and (4) Heavy, with a weight greater than 150 kilograms (Providencia Administrativa N° PRE-CJU-GDA-183-19, 2019).

In Appendix B it states that all RPAS, without exception, must have authorization from the Aeronautical Authority, establishes many limitations of the places of operation of these aerial devices, including the high seas, restricted areas, dangerous areas, nearby airports, military bases, airfields, and any place that the authority deems necessary. (Providencia Administrativa N° PRE-CJU-GDA-183-19, 2019). The flights may not exceed the height of 122 meters and when it is flying over people it may not fall below 46 meters and within the regulations establishes a strong responsibility on the part of the pilot who manages the drone, regarding the damages and injuries that it could cause (Providencia Administrativa N° PRE-CJU-GDA-183-19, 2019).

Cuba and Haiti

The research carried out did not show any regulations related to drones and RPAS. In the case of Cuba, the use of importation of drones is not banned per se, but the regulation is constantly under the revision and final decisión made by the General Customs of the Republic (García, 2017).

Final considerations

This chapter seeks to show the current state of the regulations on drones in the region; it is clear that the particularities exist, but especially convergences appear allowing to speak in a common language. It has been exposed that since 2013, Latin American countries have assessed what pilots and ships should be able to do. Comparative Law, in this case, serves to describe aspects of legal bodies, but this is only the beginning of an investigative possibility. The drone industry grows, changes, and becomes a possibility for more people, for more ways of using it, to which lawmaking must adapt. It is clear that discussions such as the use of drones for the delivery of packages or commercial applications, as in the United States, are still away from the studied spheres. The comparison, description, and deepening of the procedures for obtaining permits and licenses for the operation of drones will be left for future investigations. Drone pilots, in addition to the technical and physiological characteristics will find high narrative, labor, and commercial possibilities in the upcoming days.

It is interesting to find that the use of drones in situations such as demonstrations or strikes may be compromised in several countries. It will be necessary to investigate in each one of the contexts to understand how a useful tool to understand the magnitude of social agglomerations is being prohibited. It is clear that the dichotomies between private and public or between public and state should be reviewed, as governments may want to control a tide of eyes in the sky. And this, because regulations should be designed to serve the common good, but above all in the possibility of putting them in the hands of the majority the disruptive technologies that can deliver better information for deeper and further decision-making. The use of drones should open new discussions, besides legal bodies; ethical dilemmas must be studied as future research as part of the importance of this usage in different countries. Another aspect should be training and how this process must be carried out, considering aesthetical, technical, and professional aspects.

References

¿Qué puedo hacer con mi DRON? (2017). Retrieved 4 November 2019, from https://www.aac.gob.sv/?p=3063

Ajani, G., Anderson M., Arroyo Amayuelas, E., and Pasa, B. (2009). *Sistemas jurídicos comparados.* Barcelona: UBE.

Arnaud, A.J. (2000). *Entre Modernidad y Globalización.* Bogotá: Universidad Externado de Colombia.

AUSVI (2013). *The Economic Impact of Unmanned Aircraft Systems Integration in the United States.* [Online] Available from: https://cms.qz.com/wp-content/uploads/2013/03/econ_report_full2.pdf [Accessed 03 September 2019].

Aviación Civil (2018). *Rdac Parte 91 Reglas De Vuelo Y Operación General.* [Online] Available from: http://www.aviacioncivil.gob.ec/wp-content/uploads/downloads/2018/03/RDAC-91-FINAL.pdf [Accessed 25 January 2019].

Barrera Martínez, C. (2011). *Introducción al Derecho Comparado.* Bogotá: Grupo Editorial Ibáñez.

Bastide, C. (2017). El derecho comparado en la jurisdicción constitucional brasileña. *Boletín Mexicano de Derecho Comparado*, 149, 581–612.

Boletín Reglamentario N° AAP-0149/2019, La Paz, Bolivia, April, 30 2019. [Online] Available from: https://www.dgac.gob.bo/trabajo-aereo-con-drones/ [Accessed 10 September 2019].

Brooks, M. (2012). The Drone Age. *New Scientist*, 216, 42–45.

Cabanellas de Torres, G. (2017). *Diccionario Jurídico Elemental.* Buenos Aires: Editorial Heliasta.

Circular Obligatoria No. AV-23/10 R4, Requerimientos para operar un sistema de aeronave pilotada a distancia (RPAS) en el espacio aéreo mexicano, Dirección General de Aeronáutica Civil, México—México, 25 de julio de 2017. [Online] Available from: http://www.sct.gob.mx/fileadmin/DireccionesGrales/DGAC-archivo/modulo3/co-av-23-10-r4.pdf [Accessed 10 September 2019].

Clark, A. and Chalmers, D.J. (2010) The Extended Mind. In: Menary, R. (ed.), *The Extended Mind*, Cambridge: The MIT Press, pp. 1–14.

Clarke, R. (2014a). The Regulation of Civilian Drones' Impacts on Behavioural Privacy. *Computer Law & Security Review*, 30(3), 286–305.

Clarke, R. (2014b). Understanding the Drone Epidemic. *Computer Law & Security Review*, 30(3), 230–246.

Convenio sobre Aviación Internacional, 7300/9 (April 4, 1944). ICAO. [Online] Available from: https://www.icao.int/publications/documents/7300_cons.pdf [Accessed October 22 2021].

Convenio sobre las Infracciones y ciertos otros actos cometidos a bordo de las aeronaves (December 4, 1969).

Cortés Sánchez, E.M. Vol. 1, N°. 2, (2007). Hacia una fundamentación filosófica de la educación en Derechos Humanos. *Magistro*, 343–354.

Culver, K.B. (2014). From Battlefield to Newsroom: Ethical Implications of Drone Technology in Journalism. *Journal of Mass Media Ethics*, 29(1), 52–64.

DAN 15: Operations of Distance Piloted Aircraft (RPA) in Public Interest Matters, Santiago de Chile, Chile, February 10, 2017. [Online] Available from: https://www.dgac.gob.cl/wp-content/uploads/2018/07/DAN_151.pdf [Accessed 15 September 2019].

Decreto No.65-2017, Ley de Aeronáutica Civil, Diario Oficial "La Gaceta," Tegucigalpa—Honduras, August 17, 2017. [Online] Available from: http://congresonacional.hn/wp-content/uploads/2019/03/decreto-58-2017.pdf [Accessed 10 September 2019].

Directiva Operacional que regula las operaciones de Drones o Sistema de Aeronaves Pilotadas a Distancia (RPAS), San José, Costa Rica, February 18, 2018. [Online] Available from: https://www.dgac.go.cr/wp-content/uploads/2018/02/COMUNICADO-DE-PRENSA-DRONES.-FEBRERO.pdf [Accessed 15 September 2019].

Dorrian, M. and Pousin, F. (2013). *Seeing from Above: The Aerial View in Visual Culture.* London: I. B. Tauris.

FAA (2019). *Unamanned Aircraft Systmes Report.* [Online] Available from: https://www.faa.gov/data_research/aviation/aerospace_forecasts/media/Unmanned_Aircraft_Systems.pdf [Accessed 03 September 2019].

Ferrajoli, L. (2010). Para una refundación epistemológica de la teoría del derecho. Anales de la Cátedra Francisco Suárez, 44, 417-434.

Galiana Saura, Á. (2002). La actividad legislativa en el Estado Social de Derecho. *En De Lucas & otros, El vínculo social: ciudadania y cosmopolitismo*, Valencia: Tirant lo Blanch, pp. 449–462.

García, L. (2017). La Aduana de Cuba emite nota sobre la importación de drones a la Isla. Retrieved 4 October 2019, from https://www.cibercuba.com/noticias/2017-05-11-u177600-e177600-aduana-cuba-emite-nota-importacion-drones-isla

Gynnild, A. (2014). The Robot Eyewitness. *Digital Journalism*, (June), 1–10.

How the Drone Attack on Maduro Unfolded in Venezuela | NYT—Visual Investigations. (2019). Retrieved 4 November 2019, from https://www.youtube.com/watch?v=EpFNCqCwVzo

ICAO. (2007). *Informe anual del Consejo—Documentación para el período de sesiones de la Asamblea de 2007.* Montereal: OACI.

ICAO. (31 de 10 de 2019). ICAO. Retrieved by https://www.icao.int/Pages/default.aspx

INAC, Restricción para uso de Drones en Nicaragua, Managua, November 28, 2014. [Online] Available from: http://www.inac.gob.ni/2014/11/restriccion-para-uso-de-drones/ [Accessed 10 September 2019].

International Civil Aviation Organization (ICAO). (1969). Convention on Offences and Certain Acts Commited on Board Aircraft available at: https://www.refworld.org/docid/3ddca03d4.html [accessed 23 October 2020]

Ley No. 667, Ley de Protection del Espacio Aéreo y Uso de Aeronaves No Tripuladas sobre Instalaciones de Seguridad del Estado Libre Asociado de Puerto Rico, Asamblea Legislativa, San Juan- Puerto Rico, 24 de enero de 2017. [Online] Available from: http://www.tucamarapr.org/dnncamara/Documents/Measures/a6ed5116-ac8e-461f-a5ce-343c217b89d5.pdf [Accessed 10 September 2019].

Ley No. 30740, Ley que regula el uso y las operaciones de los sistemas de aeronaves pilotadas a distancia, El Congreso de la República del Perú, Lima, Marzo 2019. [Online] Available from: https://leyes.congreso.gob.pe/Documentos/2016_2021/ADLP/Normas_Legales/30740-LEY.pdf [Accessed 22 October 2021].

Manual de Regulaciones de Aviacion Civil: RAC—101: Regulacion sobre Aeronaves No Tripuladas, Aeronaves de Modelismo y Fuegos Artificiales, Managua, Guatemala, July 22, 2013. [Online] Available from: http://www.dgac.gob.gt/drones/RAC101.pdf [Accessed 17 September 2019].

Ortiz Mussenden R., Santiago Gómez H., and Torres Báez J. (2017). *La Privacidad Y Los Aparatos Voladores A Control Remoto Recreacionales.* San Juan, Puerto Rico: Universidad Interamericana De Puerto Rico.

Phily by Air (2019). 33 Eye-Opening Stats About Drones for 2019. [Online] Available from: https://www.phillybyair.com/blog/drone-stats/ [Accessed 02 August 2019].

Professional Aerial Photographers Association (2013). History of Aerial Photography [Online] Available from: https://www.professionalaerialphotographers.com/content.aspx?page_id=22&club_id=808138&module_id=158950 [Accessed 17 August 2019].

Providencia Administrativa N°PRE-CJU-GDA-183-19, Gaceta Oficial de la República Bolivariana de Venezuela No. 6.462, Caracas-Venezuela, April, 8 2019. [Online] Available from: http://www.inac.gob.ve/wp-content/uploads/2018/proyecto_RAV/PROYECTO%20RAV%20%2014.pdf [Accessed 10 September 2019].

Proyecto de Nuevo Reglamento de Vehículos Aéreos No Tripulados (Vant) y de Sistemas de Vehículos Aéreos No Tripulados (Svant), Buenos Aires, Argentina, May 27 2019. [Online] Available from: https://www.anac.gob.ar/anac/web/uploads/upcg/resoluciones-dnaypi/seguridad-operacional/anexo-2019-368-vant.pdf [Accessed 15 September 2019].

Requisitos Generales de aeronavegabilidad y Operaciones para RPAS, Bogota, Colombia, July 27, 2015. [Online] Available from: http://www.aerocivil.gov.co/autoridad-de-la-aviacion-civil/certificacion-y-licenciamiento/Documents/PROYECTO%20BORRADOR%20CIRCULAR%20RPAS.pdf [Accessed 15 September 2019].

Requisitos Gerais para Aeronaves não Tripuladas de Uso Civil, National Civil Aviation Agency, Brasilia, Brazil, May, 2 2017. [Online] Available from: https://www.defesa.gov.br/arquivos/cartografia/dica/legislacao/rbac_e_94_anac_02_05_2017.pdf [Accessed 15 September 2019].

Resolución 34-2014, Instituto Nicaragüense de Aeronáutica Civil, Managua, 2014. [Online] Available from: http://www.inac.gob.ni/wp-content/uploads/2014/12/RESOLUCION_34-2014.pdf [Accessed 10 September 2019].

Resolución No. 008-2015, Resolución que regula el uso y operación de los sistemas de aeronaves pilotadas a distancia (RPAS) o drones en el territorio nacional, Instituto Dominicano de Aviación Civil, Santo Domingo de Guzmán- República Dominicana, 15 de julio 2015. [Online] Available from: http://idac.gob.do/descargas/4318/ [Accessed 10 September 2019].

Resolución No. 120/DSAD/DJ/DG/AAC, Requisitos para la operación de los sistemas de aeronaves pilotadas a distancia (RPAS), Autoridad Aeronáutica Civil de Panamá, Panamá-Panamá, 16 de febrero de 2016. [Online] Available from: http://www.aeronautica.gob.pa/images/seguridad_aerea/norma%202016/Requisito%20para%20las%20Operaciones%20de%20los%20Sistemas%20de%20Aeronaves%20Pilotadas%20a%20Distancia.pdf [Accessed 10 September 2019].

Resolución No. 291-2014, Dirección Nacional de Aviación Civil en Infraestructura Aeronáutica, Montevideo- Uruguay, 29 de Agosto de 2014. [Online] Available from: https://www.dinacia.gub.uy/operaciones/item/843-resolucion-n-291-2014-de-29-de-agosto-de-2014.html [Accessed 10 September 2019].

Resolución No.2170/2017, Reglamento de aeronaves piloteadas a distancia (RPA) y sistema de aeronaves piloteadas a distancia (RPAS), Dirección Nacional de Aeronáutica Civil Paraguay, Asunción- Paraguay, 2017. [Online] Available from: http://www.dinac.gov.py/Seguridad_Operacional/docs/DINAC_R1103_RPAS-2017.pdf [Accessed 10 September 2019].

Segovia Salcedo, A. (2013). *Nociones de Técnica Legislativa*. Bogotá: EDYTA.

Tardif, E. (2011). *Sistemas jurídicos contemporáneos. México: Limusa.*

Tremayne, M. and Clark, A. (2014). New Perspectives from the Sky. *Digital Journalism*, 2(2), 232–246.

United Nations. (1970). Convention for the Suppression of Unlawful Seizure of Aircraft. Available at: https://www.refworld.org/docid/3ddcaa774.html [accessed 23 October 2020].

Waite, M. (2016). The FAA's drone rules are here: What does it mean for journalists? [Online] Available from: http://www.dronejournalismlab.org/post/146262852202/the-faas-drone-rules-are- here-what-does-it-mean [Accessed 04 February 2020].

3 Net-narcoculture. Discursive trends on femicide violence and youth culture in the consumption of the narcorap aesthetics versus feminist rap resistances

Dra. Virginia Villaplana Ruiz and Dra. Alejandra León Olvera

Introduction to the net-narcoculture: Territory and web territory

Social research in netculture and gender studies, especially involving Web 2.0 social interaction, is becoming increasingly relevant to explain the narrative construction and assimilation of discourses that occur in the consumption of information media and network culture on the most popular social networks. It is necessary to emphasize that technological advances and the new ways that we relate to digital devices allow us to create new cultural and identity imagery (Villaplana-Ruiz & León-Olvera, 2019). These identities depend on online dissemination to have greater reach and consumption, and they feed upon events that occur daily in any given territory, as in the case of Mexican narcoculture. This culture generates violent discourses and representations in social networks based on the explicit violence that is depicted in the media. It is most evident in certain Mexican territories, but it also generates identities that reproduce sexist, consumerist, and individualist discourses at the transnational level.

Narcocorrido and narcorap, gender violence and resistances

We define Net-narcoculture as the distribution of the Mexican narcotraffic culture displayed on the Internet, through social media and audio-visual content platforms where this type of cultural consumption will have more impact on their favorite public: young people. The Internet is a worldwide platform, where people inserted in narcoculture will be able to access and create cultural consumptions that will influence the way in which identities are created and symbolized within this culture as well as outside of it. The forms of production of drug trafficking have been transformed also the forms of exhibition. Now the narcoculture has its greatest potential for distribution on the Internet, especially in the circulation of images and video clips. (León Olvera, 2019). On Instagram accounts, photographs are uploaded which are material for analyzes representations of power performances and on YouTube the video clips, of narcocorridos or narcorap, with explicit images are not banned. If we had to illustrate the net-narcoculture, we find it in these professional or amateur videos.

To speak of the explicit violence related to Mexican drug trafficking, represented in an aestheticized way and without metaphors in the products it creates, is to speak of the historical-political context of the Mexican Drug War. It was in 2006 when violent scenes from Mexican territories began to reach public awareness through the media. It was also when the name of Joaquín "El Chapo" Guzmán took relevance in the logics of cultural consumption of drug trafficking with greater force, and when products were created that would mediatize this culture even more. Within this context a website called "El blog del Narco"[1] appeared online, and became the first website to generate a compendium of the videos recorded by hitmen when executing or torturing.

The tradition of Mexican narcoculture has its origins in cultural products that narrate the reality of a lifestyle immersed in the culture of drug trafficking. The *corrido* has been one of the main elements of dissemination of this history and lifestyle. Theorist of cultural studies Valenzuela Arce (2014) points out that these cultural and musical productions have a historical tradition dating back to the revolutionary *corridos* in which the exploits of bandits and the revolutionaries were narrated. They were also in the contraband *corridos* where they are narrated the events that occurred in train robberies and trafficking of prohibited objects, not necessarily drugs. It is not until the 1970s that the *corridos* dedicated to drug trafficking emerged, and when metaphors were first used to talk about trafficking, the people involved, and the heads of the cartels (Valenzuela Arce, 2014).

There is a substantial difference in the production of *narcocorridos* and the so-called *sick* or *altered narcocorridos*. In these corridos, which come from *El movimiento alterado* (the Altered Movement), they speak openly and without metaphor of drug trafficking and consumption, and contain explicit descriptions of clashes, executions, and torture, mixed with hedonism and an exhibition of the culture of luxury and that can be considered *narcoglamour* (León Olvera, 2019).

The rise of *narcorap,* also occurring within the context of the Mexican Drug War, has a generational and geographical concentration that can be observed due to the fact these products have a greater consumption in the area of the states of Tamaulipas and Nuevo León. Narcorap MCs (Masters of Ceremony) use anecdotes from the people involved in drug trafficking, hired assassins, as well as the lives of the young people who make up the gangs in Mexican narcoculture. Likewise, we can observe that the altered *corridos* and narcorap share a common element not recorded in the previous narratives of the music dedicated to the narco, namely the advertising that is enunciated in the songs, as well as the advertising campaigns that are created in the diffusion of videos on the web, specifically on the YouTube platform.

> The narrative of the corrido was traditionally to account for the events that happened, but now it is used as an instrument of consumption, in addition to normalizing the violent deaths, the lyrics of the so-called altered corridos and the narcorap, distribute speeches that combine the violence and the consumption of certain brands, which seems to make of violence a brand to consume.
>
> *(León Olvera, 2019: 42)*

On the other hand, the internet also has niches that represent social movements and resistance to the logic of violence, patriarchy, and hyper-consumption. This is the case with the feminist movement that has generated social discourses, cultural elements, and products in order to demonstrate the situation of women. With the use of complaints, escraches (direct action public condemnations), and organization through groups, feminists have organized themselves globally and appropriated the networking resources and new forms of advertising generated by the algorithm, such as the use of hashtag campaigns.

> Since the 2000s, "Ni una más/Ni una muerta más" (Not one more/ Not one more death), has been the cry of activists in Ciudad Juárez in the Mexican state of Chihuahua, demanding an end to this violence; April 24th being the biggest march ever taken place in Mexico against femicides under the hashtag #VivasNosQueremos. From June 3, 2015 on, when demonstrations broke out also in the main squares of Argentina, this mourning has been reversed as a way to refute the loss. The "Ni una menos" (Not one less) movement focuses its demands on the implementation of protection measures, promoting access to justice, calling for the creation of more shelters and reporting an official count of gender-based violence crimes, apart from, of course, ending structural violence against women. The pace at which the #NiUnaMenos and #VivasNosQueremos movement has gained momentum by turning emotion, denunciation and global rage into a symbol shows that no country is immune to the problem of femicide or gender-based systemic violence against women, lesbians, transvestites, bisexuals and transgender people. The international strike with public demonstrations in fifty-four countries on March 8, 2017 (and #LaHuelgaFeminista8M in Spain in 2018 with the transnational strike of care and consumption) show a catastrophic global dimension of inequality, anger and indignation against violence.
>
> *(Villaplana-Ruiz, 2019: 115)*

Another contribution of the feminist and resistance network in Mexico is the interactive map created by geophysicist María Salguero that relates femicide to organized crime. This map, created in 2016, positions crosses where the click generates a section with the details of each case of femicide that has been documented by the media. It shows on a blue cross the femicides of 2016, in purple are those of 2017, in red those of 2018, and finally are those of 2019 in yellow. Salguero herself uses the map to generate tweets with information, which also helps to generate databases and statistics. In the following appointment we can see the recorded femicides between January and August of 2019.

> So far this year they have murdered 1835 women. The State that occupies the first place is the State of Mexico, followed by Jalisco that this year for several months is in second place, followed by Guanajuato, Chihuahua, Baja California and Mexico City (@msalguerb, August 18, 2019)

In this map (See Figure 3.1) the researcher included the element of the Huichol triangle, which identifies the activity of fuel theft, and is also associated as a new practice of Mexican cartels who have diversified their markets. Salguero enunciates the relationship between feminicide and organized crime, generating the concept of: "Feminicidio por pertenencia" (feminicide by ownership).

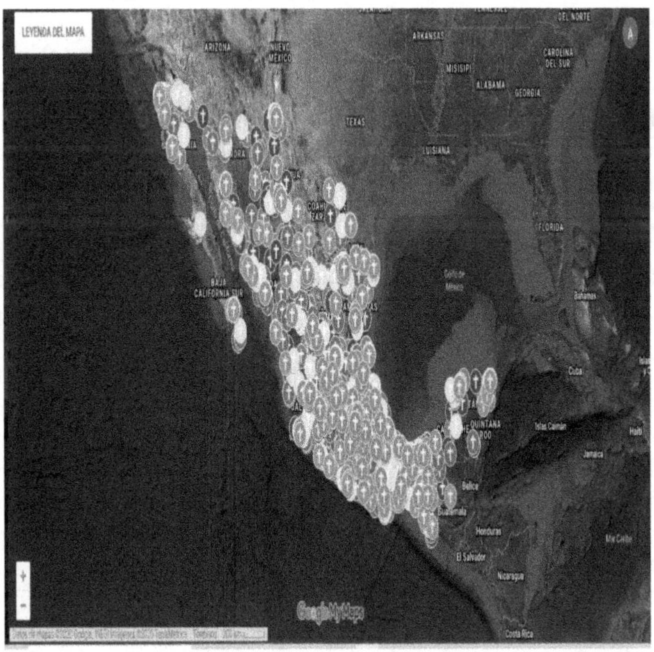

Figure 3.1 Interactive Map of feminicides in Mexico.

Screenshot Source: Interactive Map of feminicides in Mexico. María Salguero. URL: https://www.google.com/maps/d/u/0/viewer?mid=174IjBzP-fl_6wpRHg5pkGSj2egE

We consider it necessary to take an analytical approach to examining how discourses of violence and femicide are disseminated on the Internet, and how elements of opposition and resistance emerge from the same context within which Mexican narcoculture develops. Recognizing that the Internet is its most widespread platform, we propose the concept of net-narcoculture, because Web 2.0 social platforms provide access to a wide range of cultural including expressions from identities of both narcoculture and feminist resistances.

Net-narcoculture background: Gore Capitalism, narcomarketing, and social media

Net-narcoculture as a concept is the main contribution of the present work, identifying how narcoculture uses the Internet as its largest platform for distribution of cultural consumption. Online platforms are the context within which narcoculture creates, assimilates, and reproduces the imagery of lifestyles immersed in drug trafficking, as well as identities based on dynamics of hyper-consumption and the aestheticization of violence (Valencia, 2018). Secondly, it also helps to bring visibility to the normalization of femicide violence (Segato, 2016), one of the cultural products created by narcorap. The feminist rap resistance provides an ideal lens to examine narcorap aesthetics' most characteristic manifestations in music videos (Costa, 2016). Therefore, our main objective is the analysis of the representation of gender roles in narcorap music videos on YouTube.

We are going to explore the expressions and cultural consumptions from within the logic of what the Mexican philosopher Sayak Valencia has called gore capitalism (2018), which serves as a philosophical basis for understanding and explaining violence in global capitalism. Where the cultural consumption of narcorap generates cultural identity politics, specifically through aesthetic practices, we also return to the concept of narcomarketing (León Olvera, 2019), defined as:

> Commercial management of the cartels, where their advertising can be divided into two campaigns: hedonism and terror. This in order to remain current companies, where customers and employees will be captured. In this sense, social networks are fundamental for the promotion of cartels, spreading the discourse of social responsibility, of coercion and, I would add, of aspiration, where drug trafficking is seen as a way to get ahead in the capitalist world.
>
> *(León Olvera, 2019:38)*

The analysis of the discourses in the corpus of music videos from rappers within the context of Mexican narcoculture, as well as interactions with users, shows how this type of violence is normalized and attributed to the processes of sentimental breakdown in the context of romantic love, the objectification of female affections, rape, and punishment when women make decisions regarding their lives and bodies. But it also makes visible and generates confrontation processes on the part of women who are dedicated to feminist rap.

We understand YouTube as a platform that builds and consolidates the hyper-consumption logics that Valencia (2018) points out and that are used by narcomarketing to sell the experience of "being a narco." That is, YouTube is a new market where the narratives that are disseminated are appropriate to the capitalist culture of the show, which, Bañuelos (2009) describes:

> YouTube is built under the logic of the capitalist culture of the show, with interactive qualities, under the control of contents of a private administration, which responds to the rules of the market and to the dynamics of a contemporary culture, characterized by ephemerality, banality and instantaneity
>
> *(Bañuelos, 2009: 8)*

Recognizing that YouTube is a platform for the dissemination of discourses in favor of capitalist culture, we highlight the great opportunity that narcoculture has to obtain a space for the visibility and exhibition of its cultural consumption, such as narcorap MCs' songs and videos. Illescas, in his book *The dictatorship of the video clip* (2015), discusses what he calls the hegemonic video clip. Reflecting Barrientos' view, Illescas also assumes that this platform is focused on capitalist, hyper-consumerist, and individualistic culture. In this sense, we can position the narcorap videos as part of the corpus of the hegemonic videos, and even further represents the classification of Illescas, as a gangster video, the logic behind which is to sell an experience of violence.

> In this way, the dominant video clip continues the wake of the Hollywood action cinema, aimed at young people, but adds a banalization of violence through music and the desire to party that produces a representation of it, even more alienated than the one spread by the Rambo franchise and all its contemporary followers. From a significant part of videos, an alienating and dehumanizing culture is promoted where aggressiveness, violence and even torture are portrayed as something cool.
>
> *(Illescas, 2015: 257).*

In contrast, the videos of feminist MCs are counter-hegemonic videos (Illescas, 2015) that cannot be classified in the same logic of hyper-consumerism. In fact, the lyrics can be considered as more of a social claim. The message, rather than selling an experience, is denouncing events that happen day-by-day in a context where patriarchal violence is applied to the body of women, in both practice and speech, through the logic of gore capitalism. It is necessary to carry out the analysis of the net-narcoculture, since it not only helps us to show how the imagery of living within the narcoculture is generated, but because it demonstrates how other identities emerge that are socially linked by violence. This remains the case even where they are not directly inserted in the explicit violence that is lived in a capitalist culture that values individualization, success at all costs, and develops from the logic of death, where drug trafficking is the greatest example of success in a voracious economic system.

Understanding the net-narcoculture: Methodology to analyze image and discourse

Academic positioning also shows a political positioning, and it is necessary in order to make a critical analysis of discourses in net-narcoculture. Therefore, the theoretical and methodological framework for this study combines critical perspectives from gender studies (Butler, 2006), including critical analysis of visual narratives. This helps to analyze the tendencies of discourses on femicide violence in narcorap and its resistance in feminist rap within youth culture. This selected technique for this study will be netnography, in which music videos are identified on the YouTube platform (Costa, 2016) as a space for narcoculture consumption in Web 2.0. This method, of great trajectory in the field of social sciences, is considered suitable for exploratory research, especially if it addresses discursive tendencies in social networks (Fuchs, 2014). Digital netnography (Turpo, 2008)—qualitative method of partial approach without integration—is an ideal technique to address the relational processes, types of users, behaviors, and dynamics of the virtual community in the consumption of narcorap in music videos (Illescas, 2015).

In addition, a quantitative analysis is made of the number of interactions and trends using tools such as Google Trends (google.es/trends/). This quantitative approach will be essential to identify narcorap music videos in social conversation and its relationship with the imaginary of narcoculture, women and violence (Jimenez, 2014; Lizárraga, 2012), and youth culture (Rivera & Reis, 2015). Finally, the critical discourse analysis is ideal to reveal how forms of domination and/or resistance to domination are generated in concrete contexts. This approach will allow questioning the structures of discourse (Van Dijk, 1999) in Web 2.0 conversations and media texts as a social domain. The combination of various participation systems in the digital medium (Carpentier, 2007) and mechanisms for their production and understanding implies the development of a multimodal analysis.

The video collection corpus requires identification of artists that are considered typical within each selected genre under analysis, and particularly artists within Mexico. In the case of narcorap, names of groups that can be geo-located in the Mexican northeast include: Cartel de Santa, Millonario,

Santa Estilo, Cano y Blunt, Santa Grifa, and Santa Fe Klan. With respect to feminist MCs, the diffusion focuses more on female artists of various geopolitics. The names of Rebeca Lane, Tribade, IRA, Gatta Cattana are all identified with YouTube's algorithm as feminist rap. However, if a deeper and specialized search is done, we will find Mexican MCs who identify as feminists and activists, such is the case of Mare Advertencia Lirika, Masta Quba, and groups such as Mujeres Trabajando y Batallones Femeninos (Women Working and Female Battalions). We will highlight their participation in the hip-hop scene and broader music industry, which continues to be dominated by male names and where they still have to face sexists situations.

The selection of the corpus is made according to the choice of musical themes with explicit messages about gender violence. Cartel de Santa and Millonario are examples of MCs that talk about rape, psychological violence, and femicide unapologetically in their songs. Songs selected from feminist MCs were chosen based on the response they have in their lyrics regarding the same themes of gender violence. Below is a table (Table 3.1) with four songs that formed part of the corpus that serve to exemplify the way in which the methodology and analytics of net-narcoculture can generate new discussions regarding the assimilation of speeches and perform Multimodal Critical Discourse Analysis (MCDA) (Kress & van Leeuwen, 2001).

The use of tables helps us to simplify and contrast the information from the videos visually, which helps to identify and analyze the means of circulation, dissemination, and scope. This data can then be compared with the data derived by Google Trends, which allows geographical graphing the of search entries for the songs. In the subsequent images only the narcorap songs are presented.

Table 3.1 Narco Rap and Feminist Rap Songs

Examples: analyzed songs				
Song name	*Artist/s*	*Year*	*URL*	*Views*
Así era ella	Batallones Femeninos	2015	https://www.youtube.com/watch?v=ejz6Ba8TLUQ	16,548 views (October de 2019)
Autodefensa	Masta Quba & MarieV	2018	https://www.youtube.com/watch?v=1-vAtVt0MKU	28,451 views (October de 2019)
Si estuviera en Dubai	Cartel de Santa	2016	https://www.youtube.com/watch?v=9ZYc_w51zv8	30,114,610 views (October de 2019)
Rayas de Patrón	Millonario	2015	https://www.youtube.com/watch?v=4iuYwTFJpQY	27,219,620 views (October de 2019)

Source: Own development with data from our research in YouTube.

The image identify where the largest youth consumption of narcorap is concentrated. That the feminist MCs do not appear reaffirms the discourse about the lack of diffusion for female work in the Mexican hip-hop scene and emphasizes the forces behind what Illescas calls the hegemonic video clip (2015). These tools help to generate more critical analyses of the net-narcoculture because these results can be contrasted with the geopolitical maps of the Mexican narco activity and where the territories of the cartels are delineated. They can also be compared with the Salguero map, mentioned previously. Below are some of the results regarding the comparison of the selected discourses.

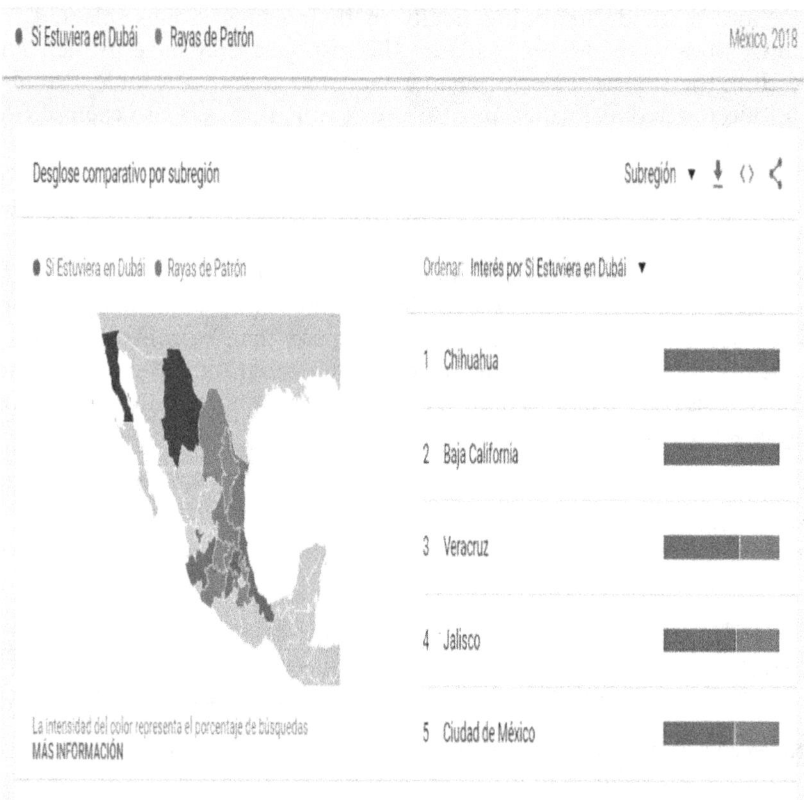

Figures 3.2 and 3.3 Locations of the most search entries of "Si estuviera en Dubai" and "Rayas de Patrón" songs.

Source: Screenshot from information in Google Trends. URL: https://trends.google.es/trends/explore?date=2018-01-01%202018-12-31&geo=MX&q=%2Fg%2F11c5wmv1f9,%2Fg%2F11bzvvkrvy

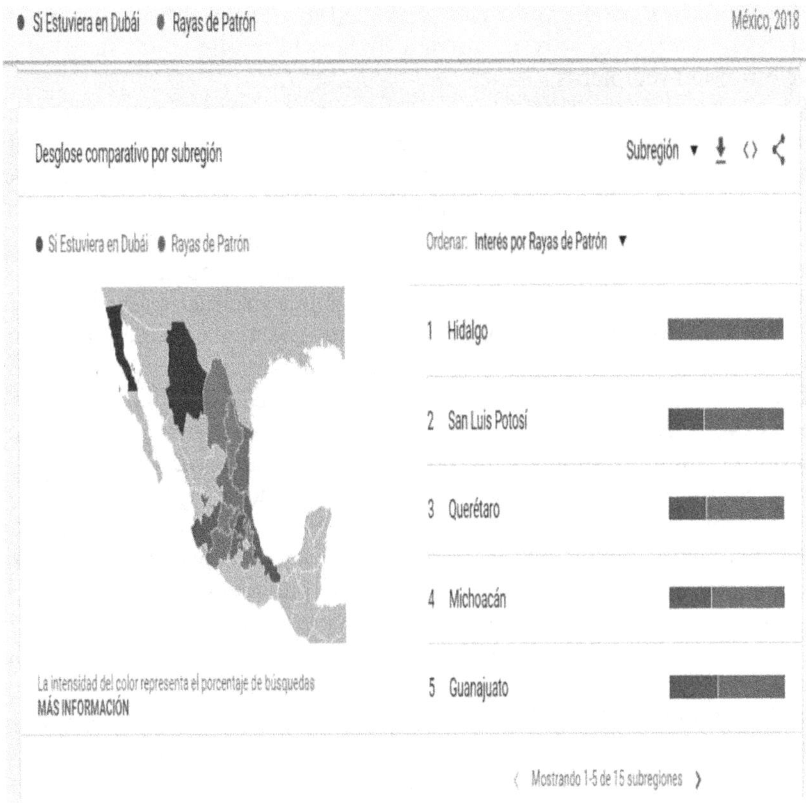

Figures 3.2 and 3.3 (Continued)

Unraveling the net: Narcorap's narratives and the feminist rap response

We must understand narcorap as a cultural production in a context of extreme violence where sexist practices and femicide are evident. We must recognize that the lyrics of these products, as well as those of the narcocorridos, form a narrative that represents the events that take place in Mexico. The criticism and analysis of these products should be more complex and should not be limited to a simplistic vision that reduces the discourses of these songs' products of consumption, due to the insertion, assimilation, and practice of violence by the recipients.

The lyrics of the songs analyzed using MCDA give us different angles on how to understand the various perspectives, interpretations, and narratives that emerge within each musical theme. In the four songs that were chosen as examples for the analysis exercise, there is a great difference in their scope of dissemination, where the lyrics produced by narcorap have a mass diffusion, while the feminist lyrics form a niche where one could say that they have bounded recipients.

We must not forget that these cultural consumptions are contextualized in an entertainment market within network culture. Therefore, it is important to point out that they become products of a digital marketing network, where they will position themselves in a better way and invest in greater publicity in the video of the song that has more demand, despite the mention of gender violence. Illescas (2015) notes that the music industry has no interest in generating a moral production, but a product to sell. The video clip that is transmitted on YouTube becomes the new commercial, without most even realizing what it is advertising.

The lyrics of the narcorap songs form part of the narcomarketing corpus (León Olvera, 2019) and generate aspirational narratives. Many of these songs describe how masculinities are practiced and assumed in a context of hyper-violence, as well as how the aesthetic of the drug dealer hitman lifestyle has been created. In this performative masculinity, reference is also made to their behavior toward women, where a macho treatment is expected. If we consider narcorap as a product of cultural consumption and recognize that its distribution has to do with the sale of an experience or an identity, rather than criticizing consumers we must unravel the system that makes violence something so marketable, and such a central part of the hegemonic video (Illescas, 2015). In the following table (Table 3.2) we can identify explicit mention of gender violence in the narcorap, which is made invisible as greater importance is placed on the discourse of belonging and identity construction. Sexual, psychological, and physical violence can be evidenced here, while the examples of feminist rap lyrics articulate a complaint regarding gender violence.

These lyrics contain constant reference to gender roles. In the case of narcorap these roles legitimize a patriarchal masculinity where women are treated as inferior. Feminist rap lyrics question these roles and even talk about organization and denunciation. In the net-narcoculture, Cartel de Santa and Millonario maintain the status quo, while Masta Quba & Marie V together with Batallones Femeninos present narratives that question the underlying system. Their absence in Google Trends may be associated with not being part of hegemony behind the consumption of video clips, not performing songs that legitimize hyper-consumption, and of course questioning the violence and machismo of the cultural context.

This research shows that feminist rap songs are not a direct response to the narcorap songs but are created to denounce the machismo and day-to-day violence toward women living in Mexico. Finally, all the lyrics in the net-narcoculture respond to the economic and social demands that are created within the logic of gore capitalism (Valencia, 2018). Both narcorap and feminist rap are means of disseminating information and representing narratives of the reality of life in Mexico, but it should be emphasized these discourses have a worldwide reach. On the one hand, the aspirational

Table 3.2 Comparison of lyrics between narcorap and feminist rap

	Identified discourse in lyrics and their counterpart	
Discourse	*NarcoRap lyrics*	*Feminist rap lyrics*
Sexual violence	Rayas de Patrón (Boss stripes) (Millonario)[1]	*Así era Ella (This was Her) (Batallones femeninos)*[2]
	She falls asleep and Mili* gets soaked Legs up I stick her with my riata (another word for a large penis) I love your cheap slut face Fucking ugly chick but she is doing good She knows what is coming, she does not stop, she does not say no The music sounds like a million (great), the mattress sounds very loud The traca (MDMA/Molly) climbs to my head and it's so crazy this trip This is a normal bad day It is mamalón (very well) This is a normal bad day	I notice that they look at me more I did not imagine that fear would catch me When I was walking alone, I saw someone approaching I accelerated my step when they pulled my hand I screamed as much as I could, everyone became deaf No one said anything, nobody looked at anything And raped, tortured, threatened, gagged With tears in my eyes I implored that this would end
Physical and psychological violence	*Si estuviera en Dubai (if i was in Dubai) (Cártel de Santa)*[3]	*Autodefensa (Self-defense) (Masta Quba & MarieV)*[4]
	What do you like to be a culera (bitch)? I know That you like to sweet-talk anyone also know That you are a rowdy Cheating bitch Poor fool who believes you. How I wish you were A sincere bitch That you will speak *al chile* (without lies) Don't lie to me Don't leave me with so much bullshit If I was in Dubai, I would blow you with stones If I was in Dubai, ay ay ay If I were in Dubai bye bye bye bye bye	Tales of princesses and soap operas To say that we are passive, that we are helpless Feel free to use force for your defense Shout out loud, put the aggressive in evidence Remove who harasses you from the road Answer who insults you, who touches you Take off the abuse, even if they tell you crazy Self-defense is necessary or if not the pit.

* Mili may refers to the singer as citation of Millionaire and also may refer to the "Mili" (Eric San Juan Palafox, condemned feminicide of the State of Mexico

1 Own transcription adapted from YouTube videoclip "MILLONARIO RAYAS DE PATRON VIDEO OFICIAL" (elcarteldesantatv channel). https://www.youtube.com/watch?v=4iuYwTFJpQY

2 Own transcription adapted from YouTube videoclip "Batallones Femeninos en Cero Decibeles—Así era ella" (Cero Decibeles channel). https://www.youtube.com/watch?v=ejz6Ba8TLUQ

3 Own transcription adapted from Youtube videoclip "Cartel de Santa—Si Estuviera en Dubái #VIEJOMARIHUANO" (elcarteldesantatv channel). https://www.youtube.com/watch?v=9ZYc_w51zv

4 Own transcription adapted from Youtube videoclip "Masta Quba & MarieV—Autodefensa (Beatprod x Ramiro Jota)" (Masta Quba & MarieV channel). https://www.youtube.com/watch?v=1-vAtVt0MKU

discourses of narcorap can be fed by other cultural consumptions of global narcoculture, such as gansta rap, rap quinqui, and trap. All of these musical genres contain examples of sexist violence. Even if they are not explicitly violent against women, many of their lyrics do not question the discourses.

On the other hand, feminist lyrics help to demonstrate the types of violence that are lived in all areas of social life. That is, these lyrics persist in net-narcoculture because they criticize it. They help identify violence as well as forms of resistance throughout the world, giving a platform to women who live within these violent contexts. In the case of Batallones Femininos, some of them come from one of the places that has been most closely associated with femicide: Ciudad Juárez.

Final thoughts, different views, and assimilation of net-narcoculture

How useful is net-narcoculture in social analyzes of violence and feminist resistance? Recapitulating the way that we have defined this cultural network first acknowledges that its largest distribution platform for cultural consumption is through the internet, where the product of cultural consumption that legitimizes the normalization of violence and youth hyper-consumption has a hegemonic element. The products of narcoculture are favored because drug trafficking is the clearest example of success within the logic of gore capitalism (Valencia, 2018).

It is necessary to do these studies to analyze, part-by-part, how the net-narcoculture is built and the niches from within which feminist rap arises. This critical analysis forms a counterpoint to the would-be assimilation of the violence of the narcoculture in the global network. The exercise of the most explicit violence is driven by the logic of transnational capitalism, where the violence will also be located in poor territories where the population is disposable. Femicide is mixed with these waves of violence leaving women invisible once more.

When using netnography in the study of net-narcoculture the most important things to analyze are the ways that aspirational discourses are mixed with hegemonic discourses that normalize patriarchy, sexism, and violence, and the way that non-hegemonic discourses enunciate complaints. With regard to the latter, in this text we exemplify feminist rap lyrics. In other words, critique should focus on how power is exercised with respect to what is disseminated on the web so that we can analyze the hegemonic discourses that build a population-network out of Web 2.0 interactivity. This form of analysis allows us to identify how we manage new interactions from identity-shaping discourses, but also allows us to be critical regarding the normalization of violence, in this case aimed at women. The study of online social interaction should be highlighted and encouraged, because it plays a significant part in daily youth culture and reveals processes and power dynamics through its distribution of hegemonic discourses.

Net-narcoculture must be seen from the perspective of gender studies, as it allows a social critique of violence in addition to identifying new forms of resistance such as feminist rap. It also helps to generate tools, such as the Salguero map that reveal specific patterns of violence, both localized in violent territories and its global aspects, contrasted with the presence of other forces such as organized crime. This work serves to define some of the specific characteristics of violent phenomena in Mexican drug trafficking, such as femicide by ownership. Understanding net-narcoculture is to understand the algorithm that is generated in social networks, but it allows us to assimilate our insertion into the cycle of consumption in a more critical way.

Notes

1. To visit the website Blog del Narco follow the following link, URL: https://elblogdelnarco.com/

References

_____________ (2016) *El movimiento alterado en la ciudad de Querétaro: el performance de una masculinidad juvenil en la narcoculture* (Master degree dissertation, Alejandra León Olvera). México: El Colegio de México.

Bañuelos, J (2009,julio-septiembre) You Tube como plataforma de la sociedad del espectáculo. Razón y Palabra (69). Recuperado de http://www.razonypalabra.org.mx/Jacob.pdf

Butler, J. (2006). *Gender Trouble*. New York: Routledge.

Carpentier, N. (2007). Participation and Interactivity: Changing Perspectives. The Construction of an Integrated Model on Access, Interaction and Participation. In V. Nightingale (Ed.), *New Media Worlds* (pp. 214–230). Oxford: Oxford University Press.

Costa, J. (2016). *Da MTV para o YouTube: a convergencia dos vídeos musicais*. Porto: Afrontamento.

Fuchs, C. (2014). *Social media: A Critical Introduction*. London: Sage.

Illescas, J. (2015). *La dictadura del videoclip*. Madrid: El Viejo Topo.

Jimenez, E. (2014). *Mujeres, narco y violencia: resultados de una guerra fallida. Región y sociedad*, *4*, 101–128.

Kress, G. y van Leeuwen, T. (2001). *Multimodal Discourse: The Modes and Media of Contemporary Communication*. London: Arnold.

León Olvera, A. (2019). *La Feminidad Buchona: performatividad, corporalidad y relaciones de poder en la narcocultura mexicana* (Doctoral dissertation, Alejandra León Olvera). México: El Colegio de la Frontera Norte.

Lizárraga, E. (2012). De Sinaloa y el narcotráfico. En Santamaría, A. (coord.) *Las jefas del narco. El ascenso de las mujeres en el crimen organizado* (pp. 53–70). México: Grijalbo.

Rivera, S. y Reis, B. (2015). Los consumos juveniles de música en la era digital: un estudio de caso en la Zona Metropolitana de Querétaro. *Cuadernos de Música, Artes Visuales y Artes Escénicas*, ^= *10*(2), 171–192.

Salguero, M [@msalguerb] (18 de agosto 2019) *En lo que va del año han asesinado a 1835 mujeres. El Estado que ocupa el primero lugar es Estado de México, seguido de Jalisco que este año por varios meses está en segundo lugar, seguido de Guanajuato, Chihuahua, Baja* [Tuit]. Recuperado de https://twitter.com/msalguerb/status/1163257116506804225

Segato, R. (2016). *La guerra contra las mujeres.* Madrid: Traficantes de sueños.

Turpo, O. (2008). La netnografía: un método de investigación en Internet. *Revista Iberoamericana de Educación, 47*(2), 1–10. Retrieved from file:///C:/Users/ComunicacionAcer/Downloads/2486Gebera.pdf

Valencia, S. (2018). *Gore Capitalism.* Los Ángeles: MIT/Semiotext(e).

Valenzuela Arce, J. M. (2014 [2002]). *Jefe de jefes. Corridos y narcocultura en México.* Tijuana: El Colegio de la Frontera.

Van Dijk, T. (1999). *El análisis crítico del discurso. Anthropos,* (186), 23–36. Retrieved from https://goo.gl/JQsyZ4

Villaplana-Ruiz, V. (2019). Transnational feminist activism to reframe femicide: the case of #NiUnaMenos and #VivasNosQueremos. In M. J. Gámez, S. Nuñez & E. Gómez (Eds.), *Re-writing Women as Victims. From Theory to Practice.* London: Routledge.

Villaplana Ruiz, Virginia, & León Olvera, Alejandra (2019). Transfeminidad viral en la cultura red.: memes, videoclips en la construcción social de la narcoestética buchona y choni. en Villegas J., Conejo S., & Panarese P. (Eds.), Comunicación, género y educación: Representaciones y (de)construcciones (pp. 290-297). Madrid: Dykinson, S.L. doi:10.2307/j.ctvktrwjp.41

4 COVID-19 confinement-related mental disorders: Morbidity and the remedial use of ICT in Hispanic societies

Sergio Yagüe-Pasamón

Introduction

The very beginning of the second decade of the 21st century has undeniably gained an unfortunately indelible place in the history of the world, attributed to the outbreak of one of the worst health emergencies in centuries. The main actor in this world-level crisis, technically referred to as COVID-19 and colloquially referred as Coronavirus due to its taxonomical classification within the realm of pathogens, was first detected in the Chinese region of Wuhan in November 2019. Ever since its outbreak in the Asian Giant, COVID-19 viral infectious pathogen managed to take over the five populated continents of the globe within a record time which is estimated not to exceed two to three months.

The massive outreach of COVID-19 comes out as one of the factors that decisively contributed to make of it an unprecedented event in history which surpasses any previous data records. Interestingly, the 2020 world pandemic is far less ineffective, in terms of lethality, than the previous greatest epidemics analyzed by Arbós and Belles (2020). According to these researchers (Arbós & Belles, 2020), the five pathogens that have decimated the human population across centuries, namely smallpox, measles, the 1918 unfairly denominated "Spanish flu," the Middle Ages Black Death, and the yet incurable Human Immunodeficiency Virus (HIV), have an unrivalled aggressiveness. Although the ongoing outbreak of COVID-19 makes impossible to produce any sort of estimation about its overall mortality whatsoever; COVID-19 geographical extension is undeniably unmatched by any other major pandemics, partially adjuvated by the contemporary phenomenon of globalization which has transformed the world into a "nation of nations."

While the lethality of the pathogen has been studied to be far more reduced than other previous pandemic episodes, its social outreach has been much more significant than any other health emergency due to the alteration of the overall principles governing social dynamics.

This chapter aims to review the extent up to which COVID-19 modified social dynamization, where physical distance formerly served as basis for communication, education, commerce, work, and socialization; and was forcefully compelled to find alternative scenarios where social dynamics may resume under safety conditions. The application of extraordinary measures for the contention of the pandemics by national governments have been evaluated according to its effectiveness in prophylactic terms, with a particular focus on confinement. To these regards, the potential psychological affectation deriving from the self-isolation policies implemented in Spain and Latin American countries will be assessed within the particular framework of contact cultures, which evidence to intrinsically require more intense face-to-face interaction, as their individuals exhibit to benefit from exposure to tactile communicative experiences. Finally, alternative means for the establishment of communicative exchanges hindered by public health measures will be reviewed. In these respects, technology-mediated socialization, which was formerly used to complement physical interpersonal interaction will be approached as a remedial resource for the temporary replacement for face-to-face communication during COVID-19 worldwide health emergency and as an active mean to counter fight mental and physioogical disorders caused by mandatory social distancing.

Context

COVID-19 pandemic record-time expansion is not only remarkable as a phenomenon by itself. In fact, its massive worldwide spread led to substantial change, in a matter of a few weeks, of the governing operativity of the great variety of society models existing in the 21st-century diverse world. Such an alteration in the social dynamics of those countries would stem from the COVID-19 exponential advancement which forced governments all over the globe to step up and suspend basic citizen rights that sustained the freedom-led ideological precepts of democracy, such as citizens' free movement entitlement, as a desperate measure to contain the advancement of the pandemic.

Hitherto, prophylactic individual-based isolation, promoting social distance to avoid infections, has evidenced to be the most effective policy to reduce the massive spread of COVID-19, which transmits through respiratory excretions suspended in the air in the form of liquid droplets as a result of the virus host's "coughs, sneezes" or vigorous breathing as noted by Wang and Du (2020: 1). Hence, most Latin American countries' governments, where COVID-19 infections stuck up to different extents, opted for the implementation of mandatory quarantines and curfews (CNN Español, 2020). Such a resolution would befit a preventive measure to minimize the deleterious effects COVID-19 previously had in "Old Continent" countries as Spain, which was forced into confinement on March 14th, 2020 due to the devastation COVID-19 caused in the Iberian Peninsula.

Notwithstanding the effectiveness of prophylactic confinement, it shall be contemplated that isolation policies are far from being innocuous instruments for pandemic control. To these regards, Brooks, Webster, Smith,

Woodland, Wessely and Greenberg (2020) warn about the harmful impact confinement may have on the citizens' psyche by defending that "the potential benefits of mandatory mass quarantine need to be weighed carefully against the possible psychological costs." The inherently social nature of human beings requires an intense interpersonal contact for the fulfilment of the emotional and communicative needs of the individuals of the species which is undeniably incompatible with isolating lockdown.

Interestingly, the relevance of interpersonal communication for the individual's well-being would be observed to be even more intense for Hispanic cultures, which lay under the basics of social operativity in Spain and Latin America. As recalled by Sorokowska, A., Sorokowski, Hilpert and Cantarero (2017: 579), "Interpersonal space, or interpersonal distance, is an essential feature of individuals' social behavior in relation to their physical environment and social interactions." According to Hall's classic proxemics theory (1966), social interactions would generally be structured into a four-fold taxonomy of social distance, namely public distance, social distance, personal distance, and intimate distance, which would be determined by the relationship between the interactors. However, Hall (1988) contemplates the influence of the society's cultural framework as an ultime factor in the delimitation of the preferred social distance, observing a set of socio-cultural settings where individuals are more prone to contact. These so-called "contact cultures" would include "Southern European, Latin American, and Arabian countries" (Sorokowska et al., 2017: 579) and would explain Spain and Latin American populations' urgency for a close interpersonal communication and a more exacerbated psychological and affective impact resulting from COVID-19-motivated prophylactic suppression of physical contact.

To these regards, there is a vast volume of research on the deleterious psychological effects of social distancing and loneliness in the human being, including anxiety and depression, which are generally acknowledged as undesired side effects of an insufficient socialization affecting individuals' health.

Provided the role of short-distance interpersonal relationships in close culture societies, forceful confinement may be assumed as a real challenge for Hispanic societies, which are not ready to cope with such an exceptionally sudden and prolonged cease of face-to-face interpersonal communication, since it demands an alteration of these populations' behavioral and socio-structural bases. Indeed, the COVID-19 outbreak became, in a record time, an inflection point in the overall operativity of Western societies, with a special emphasis on southern American and southern European social constructs. Intense interpersonal interaction is deeply enrooted in every manifestation of Hispanic cultures as a result of the confluence of the participant individuals' social essence. The inherently social factor that would motivate close culture individuals' need for consistent interpersonal relationships could be found in the individuals' own personality and, therefore, its absence could disturb the individuals' psyche.

As argued, socialization and individuals' psychological well-being may rely on a constant link that may be hindered by the novel legal constraints to social distance which were never seen before in Western countries but were occasionally implemented in Asian countries as a response to the outbreak of highly infectious epidemics such as MERS. Although COVID-19 prophylactic confinement has been defended to pose an unprecedented challenge for the maintenance of Hispanic populations' living conditions and natural behavioral trends, it shall not be overlooked that Spanish and Latin American citizens who may see their routine socialization altered by these extraordinary circumstances may rely, as a novelty which was not available in any previous world-scale pandemics, on technological resources to meet their interactive needs.

To these regards, it is undeniable that the current societies' possibilities for a proper management of the inevitable social distancing is far more effective than it ever was. In the contemporary, technology-based, globalized world, Information and Communication Technologies (ICT) may play a fundamental remedial role for contact cultures as the Hispanic ones to fulfil their close social interaction needs, avoiding thus, the morbidity of mental disorders which have commonly been documented to co-occur with COVID-19 preventive confinement.

Clinical repercussions of social isolation within COVID-19 confinement

The pernicious effects of physical social isolation and perceived loneliness in health in regular contexts

As mentioned above, one of the most substantial elements of human nature befits the social needs of the species. According to Cacioppo and Patrick (2008: 5) "transient loneliness" is assumed as a natural part of life. However, as Cacioppo and Patrick (2008: 5) proceed, social connection is valued as one of the factors that contribute most definingly to happiness. To Cacioppo and Patrick (2008: 5), "the importance of social connection to our species" would be evidenced in the correlation they establish between a "sufficient isolated feeling" and "a major source of unhappiness." Such would be the detrimental effects of an excessive social distance in health that these researchers (Cacioppo & Patrick, 2008: 5) equate its negative consequences "the effect of high blood pressure, lack of exercise, obesity or smoking." Either subjective or objectified on concrete facts, long-lasting loneliness perception is studied to have a potential to "accelerate the ageing process, [...] alter behavior [...]" and modify the physiological processes of the organism, as observed "in measurements of stress hormones, immune function and cardiovascular function" (Cacioppo & Patrick, 2008: 5) and the activation of the brain areas that have traditionally been associated to experimentation of physical distress in MRI clinical testing (Cacioppo & Patrick, 2008: 8).

In the light of the negative impact social isolation feeling has in health, loneliness shall be contemplated, by itself, as a serious threat to the well-being of the species, on the ground of the estimations made by Hawkley and Cacioppo (2010: 218), who attribute loneliness as a common feeling to 80% of the underage population, a trend that would persist throughout adulthood in a decreasing tendency until early old age, when loneliness feelings intensify.

Currently, the high rate of incidence of social distance and its link to loneliness as a socio-sanitary defiant phenomenon remains unsolved despite the social and political initiatives implemented to tackle its harmful effects. However, COVID-19 health emergency may be expected to contribute to nothing, but an alarming escalation of the morbidities associated to social distance. Undeniably, such an exponential morbity growth shall be examined as an undesirable consequence to the extension of social distance to all the population with prophylactic purposes.

Cultural sensitivity to social distance and relative tolerance to COVID-19 confinement

Interpersonal relationships within the socio-political framework of the multiple types of communities that exist have been asserted to be inherent to human species' inclinations to sociability and behavioral trends in social interaction. The environmental sphere where interpersonal relationships would typically take place was delimited by Hall (1988) in his proxemics theory. According to Hall's (1988) precepts, physical distance between the interactors' bodies was fundamental to both establish and alter the interactive possibilities of interlocutors in communicative exchanges. Thus, physical distance between the agents taking part in interaction could compromise, either by excess or by defect, the successful development of a mutually satisfactory relationship.

Provided the infinite interactive possibilities that may occur within the framework of socialization in the multiplicity of models of communities and societies that exist, Hall (1988) contemplated a four-fold taxonomy to regard the degree of interpersonal space within communication as a modulator for privacy through the regulation of sensory exposure. Thus, Hall (1988) would classify interpersonal relationship manifestations according to the expected distance in the different communicative situations that may occur between interactors depending on the degree of closeness bounding speakers.

The first modality of interpersonal communication, public distance, considers wide physical spacing, ranging from 3.65 to 7.62 meters, between participants with merely intentional and sporadic communication. Besides, for those situations where interaction is conditioned by a mutual interest of agreement between interactors but there is a lack of personal bounds, as in trading or hierarchy-based formal interactions, Hall (1988) previews a social distance ranging from 1.20 to 3.65 meters roughly. The third classification within Hall's (1988) taxonomy would befit personal distance, which is estimated to range from nearly 0.5 meter to 1.20 meters and is considered to be the ideal setting for interpersonal relationships connected by close personal bounds while preserving the individual's right to keep their personal space, allegorically represented by a soap or an oxygen bubble, unaltered. Finally, the shortest interpersonal communication would occur between interactors who are bounded by a mutually agreed concession of a trespass of the aforementioned personal space bubble in favor of an access to the most private sphere of the individuals involved. Such an intimate distance is calculated by Hall (1988) to range from 0.45 meters to full physical contact.

In the light of the classifications established by Hall (1988), recommendations made by world-leading authorities in health matters, such as the Centers for Disease Control and Prevention (2020), which prescribes a social distancing of, at least, 6 feet (approximately 1.8 meters), would reveal a correspondence between the social distance to respect for prophylactic purposes and the impossibility to hold a clearly satisfactory physical interpersonal relationship while COVID-19 pandemics episode is in force. Such a distance would impede all those interpersonal interactions based on personal and intimate relationships.

Provided the general classification by Hall (1988) to quantify the ranges for communication within the conception of satisfactory social interpersonal relationships, it shall be expected to apply unequally on different social groups. According to Sorokowska et al. (2017: 579), one of the most defining factors that Hall contemplated for the adaptation of social distance for pleasing social contacts to the vast multiplicity of human groups existing all over the globe would be, by far, "cultural norms." These so-called cultural norms would befit all those conventions that contribute to the recreation of a sense familiarization of the individuals within the cultural framework they identify with. Taking into account the divergent cultural norms which govern the distinct social systems, Hall may have invoked the traditional contrast between "the North" and "the South," as distinguished social entities and opted for a fairly simplistic two-fold categorization. Hence, social distances may be understood to reduce in contact cultures, which would show a clear preference for "closer interpersonal distances and engage in more touching" (Sorokowska et al., 2017: 579) and, therefore, benefit from shorter social distances than initially estimated by Hall (1988). By contrast, those distances may be amplified in non-contact cultures, which would exhibit "opposite preferences and behaviors" (Sorokowska et al., 2017: 579).

Considering Centers for Disease Control and Prevention's (2020) two-meter minimum prophylactic distance recommendation to implement for the prevention of the COVID-19 spread through saliva droplets, which have been confirm to work like bio-aerosols (Wang & Du, 2020), it may be concluded that the impact of a lack of fully satisfactory social relationships may be certainly greater in contact cultures, which would include the cultural frameworks of "Southern European, Latin American and Arabian countries" (Sorokowska et al., 2017: 579). Such a trend is accounted by Andersen,

Hecht, Hoobler and Smallwood (2002: 91), who, defend that "people in these countries stand close, touch more, and prefer more sensory stimulation than do people in lower-contact cultures," where, according to Ting-Toomey (1999: 129) individuals' socialization is satisfied by more visual needs than olfactory or tactile.

Consequently, the exceptional government-led confinement for the prevention of COVID-19 expansion could be noteworthily insidious for a great extent of Latin America and Spain's population. Specifically, an inadequate sensory exposition to tactile experiences which naturally occur in social interaction and close interpersonal communication shall be regarded as a catalyser for the occurence of those morbidities in these Hispanic populations.

To these regards, the exploration of the consequences of prophylactic confinement in non-contact Wuhan's population, the epicenter of the COVID-19 health emergency, may give a mild impression of the potential mid- and long-term repercussions mandatory lockdown may have in close-contact culture countries such as Latin America and Spain. By the end of the sanitary crisis caused by the first wave of COVID-19 in China, marked by Wuhan's lockdown lift on April 8th, 2020 (Gan, 2020), individuals living in the area reported to feel trapped, rejected, and terrorized (Vidal, 2020). Additionally, emotions such as culpability, panic, and confusion brought about by an unknown situation, as well as episodes of uncontrollable anger and sadness were also common, according to Vidal's (2020) research. Such feelings were experienced throughout the 10-week confinement of the country, a period that is fairly shorter than the initial duration of the 14-week lockdown in Spain or the 9-week confinement in Argentina.

Interestingly, the aforementioned interactive difference between non-contact Chinese population and high-contact Spain and Latin America, along with an extended mandatory confinement, predicts more severe psychological morbidities in the Hispanic countries' population as a side effect of the lockdown. Precisely, that is the reason behind (Brooks et al., 2020: 912) recommendation to "weight carefully [...] the possible psychological costs" against "he potential benefits of mandatory mass quarantine," provided the impact the disturbing "separation from loved ones, the loss of freedom" and the "uncertainty" quarantine entails.

In general terms, Fariña (2020) estimates that the psychological impact of isolation is substantial and long-lasting. As noted by Fariña (2020), the stressing factors associated to an extended confinement to be considered by psychology and mental health professionals would be linked to routine disruption boredom, frustration, and fear of getting infected by COVID-19 as a consequence to an inevitable exposition to the potentially risky situations related to the fulfilment of professional duties or basic needs, a mental disorder known as nosophobia. Additionally, the existence of a pandemic as catalyzer for the forceful confinement of the population is highlighted by González (2020) as one of the main stressing factors of lockdown.

While the aforementioned boredom, frustration, and fear sensations would lead to some sort of anguish and anxiety in a great percentage of the population subject to confinement, as confirmed by studies conducted by Universidad Complutense de Madrid (Agencia EFE, 2020), acute clinical manifestations reported by Brooks et al. (2020: 913), involving low mood, nervousness, grief, numbness, and emotional exhaustion, would be rarer. Likewise, González (2020) declared that physiological disorders such as high blood pressure or immune system depression enhancing organic proneness to infections may derive from the social isolation inherent to prophylactic lockdown. These rare manifestations of confinement-related symptoms could require professional attention since prolonged insomnia and depression symptoms has a potential to lead to the appearances of suicidal thoughts, as reported by González (2020).

It is noteworthy that the importance of acute clinical manifestations shall not be assessed as isolated, transitory events by themselves. Indeed, Bai, Lin C. C., Lin, Chen, Chue and Chou (2004) established a correspondence between this sort of acute disorder and emotional and behavioral changes that could outlast the clinical episode itself. Similarly, Marjanovic, Greenglass and Coffey (2007) linked distressing confinement experiences with burnout syndrome and avoidance behavior within the SARS outbreak in Canada.

The occurrence of a post-traumatic stress following up the appearance of lockdown-related psychological disorder referred by Hawryluck, Gold, Robinson, Pogorski, Galea and Styra (2004) would be specifically intense in those confinement periods which are subject to a duration superior to 10 days, as upheld by Brooks et al. (2020). Alarmingly, COVID-19 confinement-related post-traumatic stress, which stems from the lack of close social relationships and the aforementioned exposure to tactile person-to-person stimuli deprivation, would have highly pernicious effects during the pandemic crisis within the Latin American and Spanish population. This is acknowledged by Universidad de Alicante (2020), which defends that the Coronavirus is causing a social crisis in Spain due to the Spaniards' need for constant socialization. Similar effects are expected to apply to Latin America, where "millions of inhabitants" would be "under quarantine to control viral spread" (CNN Español, 2020) and, thus, disturbed by social deprivation. The outreach of post-traumatic depression would be even greater in those social collectives which evidenced to be especially vulnerable during the COVID-19 pandemic, such as children and teenagers, whose anxiety is fostered by a confinement-induced sense of inner chaos (González, 2020) and are examined to suffer post-traumatic stress four times as often as regular adult groups (Brooks et al., 2020). Hence, children and teenagers up to 14-years-old were the first group of population proposed for partial de-confinement by the government of Spain from April 26th onwards (TeleSur, 2020). Similarly, the elderly, who are estimated by González (2020) to account for more than 2 million only in Spain, is a collective which typically suffers from a situation of loneliness which was inevitably increased by enforced lockdown and the institutional recommendation of self-isolation from the overall population, as they constitute the main target of COVID-19.

The remedial role of ICT of social distance in COVID-19 confinement and related psychological disorders

As hereby analyzed, mandatory confinement has been implemented all over the globe as a rather emergency measure to slow down the expansion of the COVID-19 pathogens in an attempt to reduce the overall impact in the population. The social distancing that sustains the application of generalized lockdown has been justified as a necessary initiative to control the exponential growth of COVID-19 infections. However, an inadequate socialization stemming from tactile stimuli deprivation has been examined to cause psychological side effects in contact countries like Latin America, where millions of inhabitants are subject to lockdowns or curfews (CNN Español, 2020), and Spain, under an initial massive three-month and a half confinement.

The negative psychological impact attributed to confinement, which has been listed to include short-term anxiety (Agencia EFE, 2020), "low mood [...] and emotional exhaustion" (Brooks et al., 2020: 913), insomnia and depression symptoms (González, 2020); and long-term post-traumatic syndrome (Fariña, 2020, González, 2020, Hawryluck et al., 2004), would require, as some sort of antidote, the compensative resumption of socialization.

While the establishment of alternative means for interpersonal relationships was not feasible in prior great pandemic episodes suffered by humankind in the last centuries, as the Spanish flu caused by H1N1 Influenza virus, the rapid advancement of technology and its progressive democratization across the last decades of 20th century has allowed its disposition in different formats by a great part of the social spectrum in Spain (La Vanguardia, 2017) and Latin America (Silva, 2018). As a novelty, devices that were formerly used for the complementation of face-to-face interpersonal communication throughout the routineer activities of the individuals, namely landline, mobile phone, or internet-based instant messaging and video call applications for smart devices with data and personal computers with access to internet forcefully gained a new role in Hispanic societies. Thus, these resources which did not exist in previous epidemic crises would become the main tools for Hispanic and other contact countries' populations to prevent a total disruption of their social bounds with relatives, friends, and acquaintances whose entitlement to participate in social gatherings were temporarily suspended by governments through prophylactic confinement. Hence, Information and Communication Technologies, commonly referred by the acronym ICT, have become a novel factor to be taken into account in the complex equation to account for the socio-sanitary consequences of the epidemic in the citizens.

As lockdown duration was reiteratively extended to fulfill its prophylactic purposes, ICT remained as the only mean for socialization and became a sort of refuge for those cultural backgrounds that were naturally inclined to intense interpersonal relationships. The canalization of Latin American and Spanish individuals' communicative needs by ICT resources, as a temporary substitute of physical interaction, may clearly be observed in the significant alteration of ICT user trends in these two high-contact cultural backgrounds. As noted by El Publicista (2020) journal, consumption trends have changed during COVID-19 pandemic crisis globally, on the ground that 86% of the worldwide population contributed to an exponential increase of the activity in the most reputed social networks. Specifically, data traffic has been reported to rise sharply in Latin America, where internet network has been confirmed to overload by Oliveira (2020). By countries, Perú would be the country leading with the most increase of internet traffic use. Carreño (2020) estimated a rise in a range of 30% to 36%. Such an increase in internet use was followed by Argentina, where data traffic grew by 25% (Tomoyose, 2020), and México, which witnessed a rise in Internet use of 20% (Gutiérrez, 2020). Similarly, according to Sánchez (2020a), the internet service in Spain has been subject to data speed slow-down since the State of Alarm, which implemented massive population confinement in all the territories of the country, was approved by the Spanish Government on March 14th, 2020.

Within the abovementioned consumption trends, which highlight the essential role of the combined deployment of ICT with internet and data services, mediated communication and interaction appear to account for a great percentage of the Hispanic participation in the cyberspace. On the one hand, interaction through social networks has had a prominent place, especially evident in countries like Perú, where Facebook has concentrated half of the internet traffic these days (Carreño, 2020). Social network use also intensified during the COVID-19 pandemic episode in Spain, where Twitter, Facebook, Instagram, and LinkedIn increased their usage rates to 55% as opposed to an 18% rise which was experienced in non-contact cultural frameworks like the United Kingdom (Sánchez, 2020b). On the other hand, instant messaging platforms played a fundamental role in private communication within high-contact countries, due to its dual messaging and video call possibilities, as exhibited by WhatsApp consumption rate, which acutely grew in Spain to 76% (Marketing Directo, 2020) and Perú, where Carreño (2020) estimates that WhatsApp use increased to 61%. Other major instant messaging apps, such as Skype (Sánchez, 2020a), Hangouts (Sánchez, 2020b), ZOOM, and Slack (Angulo, 2020) have also been reported to register high transference rates in Spain, where SmartME Analytics consultant (Sánchez, 2020b) revealed that the average time spent by Spaniards in these apps has gone up from 2 hours and 40 minutes to 3 hours and 24 minutes.

Regarded the high affluence of social network and instant messaging applications in the Internet use growth during the COVID-19 epidemic in Spain and Latin America, it is undeniable that ICT tools at the disposition of the great majority of the population assisted invaluably the intense communicative needs of Hispanic populations. Therefore, ICT would have been an instrument for high-contact individuals under confinement to tackle, even if just partially, the lack of face-to-face interaction and the morbidities, both mental and physiological, associated to it. As indicated by López (2020), individuals need to socialize, feel the company of their fellows, and rely on the reassurance that there are other people beyond their own home walls. Thus, ICT tools would reveal to play a remedial role in the pathological impact of social distance in those cultural frameworks where communication is rather a necessity for the well-being of Latin American and Spanish citizens and, therefore, should be considered for the provision of acknowledgement and support by the corresponding health administrations. Agencia EFE (2020) defended the operativity of technologies to mitigate confinement side effects in order to preserve the social bounds that already exist and an extroverted attitude to aspire to keep connected with acquaintances, friends, and relatives. Moreover, González (2020) alluded to ICT's role to diminish isolation sensation and attributed therapeutic features to the use of new technologies for socialization with the closest environment of the individual during the COVID-19 health crisis. Such a functionality would be complemented by ICT-mediated social networks, which have been stated to assist individuals' relationships with those people outside their immediate environment (Brooks et al., 2020). In addition to its social purposes, ICT would exhibit a potential for enhancing citizens' health care assistance by serving as a bridge which would allow the performance of telematic appointments with general practitioners and specialist doctors (González, 2020).

The significance of the substitutive communicative purposes performed by ICT to compensate the inadequate interpersonal interactions after lockdown measures that were implemented is depicted by Universidad de Alicante (2020), which insists in the fact that social isolation does not necessarily imply an effective distancing anymore due to the remedial role of technology to prevent social distancing, when desired. Nevertheless, the vehiculation of communication through social networks and instant messaging software shall not be dismissed, as it poses a new paradigm of communication, based on technology, to canalize those interactive needs which would otherwise be suppressed due to the impossibility to establish a safe face-to-face communication within the framework of the highly infectious COVID-19 health emergency.

Concluding remarks

The beginning of the second decade of 21st century will definitely break into the history of the world due to the outbreak of one of the worst health emergencies in centuries. The highly infectious pathogen behind the crisis,

COVID-19, was first spotted in Wuhan in the last term of the previous decade and managed to take over the globe within three months.

Such an unprecedented event forced the different models of societies all over the world to undergo significant structural alterations that affected the living conditions of the citizens, modifying their daily routines, rights, and obligations in favor of emergency measures which suspend individuals' basic entitlements, as the massive confinement of the population into their residences to prevent the spread of the pandemic.

Scientific research on the evolution of the epidemics in different places all around the globe evidenced that confinement is an effective policy for the contention of the pathogen expansion throughout the population. Notwithstanding the effectiveness of the lockdown measures implemented by the corresponding governments, the need for enforced confinement must be assessed thoroughly due to the negative impact it has been examined to have in the *psyche* and the overall well-being of the individuals subject to prescriptive self-isolation. The human has been acknowledged to have an inherently social nature deeply enrooted in all the facets of its behavior, personality, and inclination to interaction with its fellows.

Even if socialization has been deemed as a universal need for the species, Hall's classic proxemics theory recognizes the weight of cultural frameworks in the individuals' communicative and interactive trends. Thus, Hall (1988) classifies human communities into contact, which give priority in close-distance interpersonal relationships providing tactile experiences, as in Latin American, Arab, and South European countries; and non-contact cultures, which would benefit from the existence of a personal space to respect, usually compared to a soap bubble, as in Northern European countries, North America, and Asia.

According to Hall's theory, Latin American and Spanish contact cultures would require a more intense face-to-face interaction and suffer more powerfully the deleterious psychological and physiological effects of prophylactic social distancing due to an inadequate exposure to physical interpersonal contact, which would impede all those interactions based on personal and intimate relationships.

Undeniably, confinement-related disorders come across as a threat to Latin American and Spanish populations, as the psychological impact of isolation has been studied to have long-lasting effects that surpass the sensation of boredom, frustration, and fear that typically occur as acute clinical manifestations and the rare but worrisome low mood, emotional exhaustion, insomnia, and depressive syndromes which could lead to the rise of suicidal thoughts. Post-traumatic stress episodes have exhibited to be of common occurrence within confinement, being particularly sharp in vulnerable groups such as children and teenagers up to 14 years old, who were observed to suffer post-traumatic stress four times as often as adults, and elderly, who have been studied to be especially prone to loneliness, even before COVID-19 crisis, and are the population group where the pathogen has most devastating effects.

In such a pessimistic panorama for Hispanic populations, ICT tools which formerly complemented face-to-face interaction, such as the landline, mobile phone, or internet-based instant messaging and video call applications for smart devices vectorized communication and assisted individuals to counter-fight the effects of confinement and social distancing. Such a phenomenon may be observed in the alteration of the consumption trends in Spain, where internet services have been perceived to slow down due to the massive demand, and Latin America, where internet traffic rise has been particularly noteworthy in Perú, Argentina, and México. Such an increase in internet consumption is attributed to the intensification of social networking in Facebook, Twitter, or Instagram, which grew 55%; and instant messaging apps with video call features such as WhatsApp, Skype, Hangouts, ZOOM, or Slack.

Thus, the aforementioned ICT tools may be deemed to have become rather a necessity for Latin Americans and Spaniards to mitigate isolation sensation, and preserve social bounds, besides its potential to enhance professional health care assistance through telematic means.

Consequently, it may be asserted that the remedial use of ICT for individuals to tackle the social distancing imposed by the unprecedented massive confinement during the COVID-19 health emergency may leave a message for hope amidst the disgrace. Social isolation does not entail a factual distancing anymore thanks to the assistance of technology, which has posed a new paradigm of communication by fulfilling those communicative needs that would otherwise be impossible to satisfy.

References

Agencia EFE. (2020, March 26). Ya se notan los efectos del confinamiento: depresión, estrés, insomnio y ansiedad. Retrieved from https://www.elconfidencial.com/espana/2020-03-26/estres-pandemia-depresion-coronavirus_2520347/.

Andersen, P. A., Hecht, M. L., Hoobler, G. D., Smallwood, M. (2002). Nonverbal Communication Across Cultures. In M. K. Asante, W. B. Gudykunst, B. Mody (Eds.), *Handbook of International and Intercultural Communication*. London: Sage Publications, Inc.

Angulo, F. (2020, April 1). Impacto económico del coronavirus: mercados ganadores y perdedores por COVID-19.

Arbós, D., Belles, M. (2020). *14 maneras de destruir la humanidad*. Pamplona: Next Door Publishers.

Bai, Y., Lin C. C., Lin C. Y., Chen J. Y., Chue, C. M., Chou P. (2004). Survey of Stress Reactions among Health Care Workers Involved with the SARS Outbreak. *Psychiatric Services*, 55(9), 1055–1057.

Brooks, S. K., Webster, R. K., Smith, L. E., Woodland L., Wessely, S., Greenberg, N. (2020). The Psychological Impact of Quarantine and How to Reduce It: Rapid Review of the Evidence. *Lancet*, 395, 912–920. Retrieved from https://doi.org/10.1016/S0140-6736(20)30460-8.

Cacioppo, J. T., Patrick, W. (2008). *Loneliness: Human Nature and the Need for Social Connection*. New York: Norton Paperback.

Carreño, I. (2020, March 24). Video provoca aumento en el tráfico de datos durante aislamiento social en Perú. Retrieved from https://digitalpolicylaw.com/video-provoca-aumento-en-el-trafico-de-datos-durante-aislamiento-social-en-peru/.

Centers for Disease Control and Prevention (2020, May 6). Coronavirus Disease 2019: Social Distancing. Retrieved from https://www.cdc.gov/coronavirus/2019-ncov/prevent-getting-sick/social-distancing.html.

CNN Español (2020, March 25). ¿Qué están ofreciendo los países de América Latina para aliviar la crisis económica por la pandemia de coronavirus? Retrieved from https://cnnespanol.cnn.com/2020/03/25/que-estan-ofreciendo-los-paises-de-america-latina-para-aliviar-la-crisis-economica-por-la-pandemia-de-coronavirus/.

El Publicista. (2020, April 15). ¿Cómo han cambiado las costumbres y el consumo en España ante el COVID19? Retrieved from https://www.elpublicista.es/investigacion1/como-han-cambiado-costumbres-consumo-espana-ante-covid19.

Fariña, E. (2020, March 20). El confinamiento produce efectos psicológicos negativos, como estrés postraumático, confusión y enfado. Retrieved from https://elmedicointeractivo.com/el-confinamiento-produce-efectos-psicologicos-negativos-como-estres-postraumatico-confusion-y-enfado/.

Gan, N. (2020, April 8). China lifts 76-day lockdown on Wuhan as city reemerges from coronavirus crisis. Retrieved from https://edition.cnn.com/2020/04/07/asia/coronavirus-wuhan-lockdown-lifted-intl-hnk/index.html.

González, V. (2020, March 16). Los efectos psicológicos del aislamiento social. Retrieved from https://www.muyinteresante.es/salud/articulo/los-efectos-psicologicos-del-aislamiento-social-861584361450.

Gutiérrez, A. L. (2020, March 27). Aumenta 20% tráfico de la Red Compartida en México por COVID-19. Retrieved from https://www.elfinanciero.com.mx/empresas/aumenta-20-trafico-de-la-red-compartida-en-mexico-por-covid-19.

Hall, E. T. (1988). *The Hidden Dimension*. New York: Bantam Doubleday Dell Publishing Group.

Hawkley, L. C., Cacioppo, J. T. (2010). Loneliness Matters: A Theoretical and Empirical Review of Consequences and Mechanisms. *Annals of Behavioral Medicine: A Publication of the Society of Behavioral Medicine*, *40*(2), 218–227. https://doi.org/10.1007/s12160-010-9210-8.

Hawryluck, L., Gold, W. L., Robinson, S., Pogorski, S., Galea, S., Styra, R. (2004). SARS Control and Psychological Effects of Quarantine, Toronto, Canada. *Emerging Infectious Diseases, 10*(7), 1206–1212. https://doi.org/10.3201/eid1007.030703.

La Vanguardia. (2017, November 15). España se mantiene en el puesto 27 de países con las TIC más desarrolladas. Retrieved from https://www.lavanguardia.com/vida/20171115/432903450954/espana-se-mantiene-en-el-puesto-27-de-paises-con-las-tic-mas-desarrolladas.html.

López, N. (2020, March 17). El coronavirus y la necesidad de comunicarnos. Retrieved from https://cadenaser.com/emisora/2020/03/17/ser_madrid_norte/1584462508_507021.html.

Marjanovic Z., Greenglass E. R., Coffey, S. (2007). The Relevance of Psychosocial Variables and Working Conditions in Predicting Nurses' Coping Strategies during the SARS Crisis: An Online Questionnaire Survey. *The International Journal of Nursing Studies*, *44*(6), 991–998.

Marketing Directo. (2020, March 27). El uso de WhatsApp aumenta un 40% en plena crisis del COVID-19. Retrieved from https://www.marketingdirecto.com/digital-general/social-media-marketing/el-uso-de-whatsapp-aumenta-un-40-en-plena-crisis-del-covid-19.

Oliveira, R. (2020, March 25). Coronavirus sobrecarga tráfico de datos en América Latina. Retrieved from https://www.scidev.net/america-latina/salud/noticias/coronavirus-sobrecarga-trafico-de-datos-en-america-latina.html.

Sánchez, J. M. (2020a, April 2). El uso de las redes sociales en España aumenta un 55% en la pandemia de coronavirus. Retrieved from https://www.abc.es/tecnologia/redes/abci-redes-sociales-espana-aumenta-55-por-ciento-pandemia-coronavirus-202003241257_noticia.html.

Sánchez, J. M. (2020b, March 31). El estado de alarma dispara el consumo de internet en España pero provoca una ralentización. Retrieved from https://www.abc.es/tecnologia/redes/abci-estado-alarma-provoca-record-consumo-internet-madrid-202003171241_noticia.html?ref=https%3A%2F%2Fwww.google.com%2F.

Silva, A. (2018, December 17). Una mirada regional al acceso y tenencia de tecnologías de la información y comunicaciones—TIC, a partir de los censos. Retrieved from https://www.cepal.org/es/enfoques/mirada-regional-al-acceso-tenencia-tecnologias-la-informacion-comunicaciones-tic-partir.

Sorokowska, A., Sorokowski, P., Hilpert, P., Cantarero, K. (2017). Preferred Interpersonal Distances: A Global Comparison. *Journal of Cross-Cultural Psychology*, *48*(4), 577–592.

TeleSur. (2020, April 26). España alivia medidas de confinamiento por Covid-19. Retrieved from https://www.telesurtv.net/news/espana-alivio-confinamiento-paseos-menores-coronavirus-20200426-0003.html.

Ting-Toomey, S. (1999). *Communicating Across Cultures*. New York: The Guilford Press.

Tomoyose, G. (2020, March 17). Cuarentena online: cómo es el estado actual de las conexiones a internet en la Argentina. Retrieved from https://www.lanacion.com.ar/tecnologia/cuarentena-online-como-es-estado-actual-conexiones-nid2344334.

Universidad de Alicante. (2020, March 20). El coronavirus está provocando una crisis social. Retrieved from https://web.ua.es/es/actualidad-universitaria/2020/marzo2020/16-22/el-coronavirus-esta-provocando-una-crisis-social-digna-de-estudio-para-los-sociologos-afirma-la-experta-de-la-ua-alba-navalon.html.

Vidal, M. (2020, April 10). Coronavirus: todo el mundo en Wuhan padece un trauma. Retrieved from https://elpais.com/sociedad/2020-04-10/todo-el-mundo-en-wuhan-padece-un-trauma.html.

Wang, J., Du, G. (2020). COVID-19 may transmit through aerosol. Irish journal of medical science, 1–2. Advance online publication. https://doi.org/10.1007/s11845-020-02218-2.

5 Speaking for communities and against oppression

Digital media responses to COVID-19 within marginalized communities of Brazil and Mexico

Stuart Davis and Melissa Santillana

Introduction: The Coronavirus versus digital community activism

Since December 2019 the novel COVID-19 virus has created unprecedented challenges for public health infrastructures. Along with the unpredictability of the mutating virus and the economic and social costs of imposed distancing, one of the most pressing issues has been addressing its impact on marginalized communities. For areas that are already experiencing economic marginality, infrastructural precarity, and lack of public investment the Coronavirus compounds and intensifies pre-existing problems. Following Mike Davis (2020) in arguing that rapidly diffusing contagious diseases like COVID-19 provide an existential challenge to marginalized communities, we note that across Latin America, this virus is disproportionately detrimental to the poorest and most vulnerable communities. As such, a pressing demand for digital media activism within Latin America becomes how to harness these channels in service of disease abatement and community survival.

Combating neglect and indifference, we argue that digital media activist projects working in favelas (urban slums), quilombos [protected autonomous communities of ancestors of Afro-Brazilian freed slaves], and indigenous regions in Brazil and Mexico are acting as de facto health communication sources in powerful ways as they provide *community-building* and *community-based advocacy*. We will develop this position by examining how digital media channels facilitate the sharing of medical advice and resources, disseminate information about the distribution of free food and medical supplies, and (perhaps most crucially) provide a space for residents to voice their concerns about how their societies have failed to address their human rights and needs. Drawing on a qualitative content analysis of five digital media projects (three from Brazil and two from Mexico), we offer an analysis of how digital media activism acts as a community resource for marginalized communities to fight for their own existence against COVID-19 and the structural inequalities onto which it grafts.

COVID-19 and the Fourth World: Background from Brazil and Mexico

As of June 2020, Brazil and Mexico have been recognized by the World Health Foundation and other monitoring organizations as two of the fastest growing national hotspots for COVID-19. In late May Brazil was deemed the nation with the second highest exponential growth curve of new cases and the highest exponential growth curve in terms of daily deaths in the world (Rodrigues and Cancian, 2020). Though projections are too preliminary to generalize, initial data shows that, following similar patterns to other nations with large outbreaks, the most sizable concentrations of these cases in Brazil have been in areas with poor existing health infrastructure (Rummler, 2020). Though the virus has not penetrated Mexico to a comparable degree, available indicators suggest that similar patterns are likely. As the virus spreads, the cost will be borne by those with the least resources to handle it.

The comparative aspect of this chapter is built around two shared characteristics. The first is the active attempt on the part of national, state, and local leaders to minimize health concerns. Brazilian president Jair Bolsonaro has received global criticism as the leader most opposed to imposing public health interventions to stem the spread of the Coronavirus. Since initial cases manifested, he has repeatedly engaged in activities aimed to minimize the severity of both the breakout and the virus's impact on individuals. From calling the Coronavirus "a little cold" (Vasconcelos, 2020) to arguing that left-wing activists are burying empty coffins to amplify the mortality rate (Lemos, 2020), he has consistently downplayed the danger of COVID-19. In Mexico, President Andrés Manuel López Obrador ("AMLO") has also been accused of minimizing the impact of the Coronavirus. The perceived lack of interest in heeding scientific expertise in the face of the Coronavirus has led some journalists and pundits in the United States to declare both "populist dangers to their own populations." While it is outside the ambition of this chapter to address the presidential rhetoric and politics of COVID-19 in Brazil and Mexico, it seems clear that neither is adopting a proactive approach.

The quasi-official disregard becomes especially dire in light of the second shared characteristic: the presence of marginalized communities already experiencing economic and political suffering. Both countries are home to large numbers of "Fourth World" communities, spaces facing un- or underfunded infrastructure, failing public security, and the sense that everyday residents have very little control over their lives (Castells, 1996). Even in the absence of a public health crisis these communities face health challenges. During the COVID-19 outbreak these challenges in Brazil have intensified due to a combination of already precarious living conditions (overcrowding, lack of regularized health care, geographical isolation, etc.) and recent policy changes. Within Brazil, numerous state and federal policies have been changed during Bolsonaro's tenure to dismantle the social safety net programs created by previous administrations to provide free health care and food subsidies for lower lower-class populations. Reports from early June indicate that the public hospital system within Mexico has begun to become overtaxed by COVID-19 (Sheridan, 2020) reinforce concerns expressed early in Chiapas that protective equipment and palliative medications will not be available at the levels necessary for community safety (Partners in Health, 2020).

Our central contention is that the widespread minimization of COVID-19's impact by national governments and other "official actors" combined with chronic public health problems facing marginalized communities has created a situation that makes public health communication a priority. Arguing that alternative media producers have played and will continue to play a pivotal role, we raise two questions:

1 How can digital media be mobilized as tools for "speaking with" marginalized communities through providing informational resources and capturing perspectives of residents?
2 How can digital media act as advocacy tools for marginalized communities by "speaking against" engrained structures of oppression (including negligent governments and underfunded public health infrastructure)?

Theoretical Issue 1: Alternative media as a community tool and advocacy resource

Addressing these questions entails a brief foray into the debate on the role of alternative media in relationship to marginalized communities. At its core this debate focuses on the distinction between "speaking *with* marginalized populations" and "speaking *against* hegemonic actors." On one side are those who argue that alternative media's primary mission is to provide a communication outlet for marginalized populations. This argument, rooted in the pivotal work on community-media and the oppositional role of traditional and popular culture, claims that alternative media's central function is to capture the culture, customs, politics, and other facets of life within marginalized communities. On the other side, political economy-oriented approaches define alternative media through its oppositional stance against hegemonic political elites and/or mainstream culture. From this perspective, underground magazines, pirate radio stations, or decentralized activist news sites are "alternative" because they attack the status quo–even if they do not provide a voice for marginalized constituencies.

Within the Latin American context, we see this debate over how to define the function of activist media within marginalized communities largely couched around how to understand the revolutionary or emancipatory potential of "popular culture." Summarized by Gomez-Rodriguez et al. (2017) and others, the debate might be best expressed in the division between those who valorize popular culture as a means of everyday resistance to "official" culture (Beltrão, 1988; Murphy and Rodriguez, 1997) and those who view popular culture as simultaneously a reflection of the class values of political elites and those in control of media industries and as a tool for maintaining pacification (Walsh, 2002). While the popular culture approach places perhaps too much faith in the embryonic (proto)-politics embedded in the cultural practices of marginalized populations, in parallax fashion the critical approach holds a dystopian view of popular culture—emphasizing the burgeoning creation of a consolidated capitalist cultural hegemony. As Chaffee, Gomez-Palacio, and Rogers reflect in one of the few English-language attempts at a comprehensive account of communication theory in Latin America, critical theory's rejection of the "popular classes" remains one of the longest enduring traditions within scholarship in the region (Chaffee et. al., 1990, p. 1020).

Updating this position, Claudia Magallanes-Blanco's work on the role of documentary film and television production within the Zapatista uprising simultaneously acknowledges that corporate/mainstream media exercises hegemony over the kinds of representations audiences consume while examining how alternative media producers from subaltern populations can "hack" that system (Magallanes-Blanco, 2008). Furthermore, Trere (2012) and others have argued that the growing availability/affordability of digital media has lowered barriers to participation within marginalized communities. For the purposes of this chapter, we will adopt an ecumenical conceptualization of alternative media that draws on both traditions by simultaneously valorizing the perspectives of subaltern groups and recognizing the power asymmetries that cut through Brazilian and Mexican society.

Theoretical Issue 2: Public health communication

A logical question arises at this point: What does the debate over the role of alternative media in Latin America have to do with the COVID-19 outbreak? It takes on key pragmatic dimensions when addressing how technological channels might be utilized to help residents combat widespread public health threats. In particular, non-mainstream media channels (particularly digital channels) address two pressing issues: the difficulty of widely circulating reliable health information within marginalized areas due to lack of established communication channels and the pressing need to create avenues for public health advocacy that are readily available to and welcome the participation of residents within these communities (Davis, 2017).

The first aspect of public health communication addressed by alternative digital media producers is the question of information distribution. All of the cases we will discuss at the very least aim to spread both medical information disseminated by sources perceived as trustworthy and to share the experiences of COVID-19 among the populations they serve. This strategy is built around leveraging social ties already developed within communities. As Everett Rogers famously learned in later editions of *The Diffusion of Innovations,* the dissemination of public health information is doomed if local buy-in is not considered (Rogers, 2003, pp. 4–5). More recent work on responses to Hurricane Katrina within African-American communities finds that the effectiveness of public health-related messages among affected communities is directly linked to interfacing with established social networks (Aldrich, 2012, pp. 2–3).

The second and more complex task is the development of a powerful advocacy strategy on behalf of community residents. As historical injustices undergird the foundations of these parts of Latin American society, an effective public health communication strategy cannot ignore them. This strategic combination of bringing residents into the formation of health messages and acting as an advocate on behalf of them finds expression within public health communication in Minkler and Wallerstein's "community organizing model" (2012). In this model we see a direct analogy to "speaking with" versus "speaking for." Specifically, this approach combines "community capacity building (creating *power with*)" and "empowerment-oriented social action (challenging *power over*)" (2012, p. 43, italics in original). This model pushes for first creating an environment where community members feel safe and empowered to talk about the unique health difficulties they have to live with while at the same time using these narratives to help collectively sculpt a critique of the systems of neglect and oppression that exacerbate collective medical issues.

Introduction to case studies

In this chapter we will discuss three different types of projects that have worked in marginalized communities to fight the COVID-19 outbreak: a Facebook-based community health program in Rio de Janeiro's favelas; two citizen journalism projects, MídiaNINJA and Alma Preta Jornalismo, active across Brazil; and Radio Zapatista and Radio Pozol in Southern Mexico.

Brazil Case Study Type 1: CMS/CAPS Facebook outreach

Our first Brazilian case study consists of Facebook-based public health pages launched in the early 2010s through the non-governmental organization Viva Rio (Viva Rio, 2013). Through the partnership, there are two active types of centers within favelas: "Centros Municipal de Saude" [Municipal Health Centers], which focus on triage and urgent care; and "Centros de Atenção Psico-social" [Centers of Psychosocial Attention], or CAPS, which focus on mental health or behavioral issues like eating disorders or drug abuse. These centers were launched in the early 2010s as part of a larger program for building community health infrastructure in favelas. The logic behind the project was that community members within favelas would be more easily able to approach health workers from their own neighborhoods (Davis, 2017). This in turn would strengthen the connections between the municipal public health apparatus and these historically underserved communities.

Perhaps the most unique element of this project and the Facebook pages it launched was that it explicitly hired favela residents. The CMS/CAP Facebook pages were started by each center within the municipality of Rio de Janeiro with designated staff members covering them. In total, there have been 98 since 2014. However, we will focus on the 21 that have been posting more than once a week since March 22. As profile pages run by staff members, the content of the CMS/CAP Facebook profiles is highly variable. Hence, frequency of posting varied wildly between pages with some posting every day during the pandemic and others posting less than five times. Furthermore, the topics of the posts displayed variation as well. However, as we hope to illustrate, by and large these profiles focused much more on practices associated with "speaking with" the community through information provision and sharing experiences of residents dealing with the public health crises. In total 107 posts were included from the 21 active profiles. The following sections will briefly address major themes as they relate to the notions of "speaking with" and "speaking for." Our analysis of these 21 CMS/CAPS profile pages is neither systematic nor exhaustive. Instead it creates a preliminary picture of the way public health centers' attempted to utilize social media as a tool for information dissemination and (less so) advocacy.

Examining the thematic trends in posts since March 22 shows that the most commonly occurring topics by a significant margin were those related to the *distribution of information* about the virus, how to prevent its spread (including information about social distancing and reminders to wear masks in public), and prophylactic countermeasures (frequent washing of hands, potential contraindications with ibuprofen, etc.). The second most common theme in this group was clarification, which we define as answering community questions including clearing up rumors and potentially false statements about COVID-19. Fourteen of the profile pages had at least one post or video post from April to May 2020 dedicated to addressing queries submitted via Facebook or email. Most of these posts displayed a visage of decorum and generally cheerfulness. However, on a few occasions the cracks in the public-facing depiction of the city public health infrastructure's fight against COVID-19 began to show. For example, on May 12, 2020, CMS Cesar Pernetta posted in celebration of the "Day of Health Workers" and to invite questions. In the post's comments, individuals first praised the workers' efforts and then began to reference mishandling of the COVID-19 crisis by the city and national governments. A health worker from the CMS commented in response, writing triumphantly: "We continue our work even though Crivella [the current mayor] tried to shut us down!!!" This exchange was in direct response to a decision by the evangelical Christian mayor to have COVID-19 diagnostic tests conducted within favelas in evangelical churches instead of in community health centers (Chaves, 2020). In a few instances like this, the act of clarification sparked small instances of frustration leaking out of the overall cheery and heavily instructive nature of the profile pages.

While not occurring frequently, there were a few directly oppositional posts. Stances that either directly critiqued governmental figures or policies or mentioned larger structural inequalities were mentioned in only seven posts in 20 of the 21 profiles. However, the 21st profile, CAPS Miriam Makeba, posted almost exclusively oppositional content. While most of the CMS and CAPS centers were named after notable doctors from Brazilian history, this center, located in the enormous and oft-embattled Complexo de Alemão favela, was named in honor of Miriam Makeba, a South African civil rights leader. Of 17 posts between March 22 and June 04, 13 focused on larger public health or political issues. Topics included: Bolsonaro's mishandling of the COVID-19 outbreak; public health issues in favelas exacerbated by COVID-19 (lessened trash collection, public transportation availability, etc.); and the amplification of community perspectives through collaboration with or sharing posts from digital media projects in Alemão. Nine posts attack either Bolsonaro or the city government. Another notable aspect of the CAPS Miriam Makeba page was the sharing of posts from other favela-based community media and advocacy projects. On June 02, the profile posted a video from Voz da Communidades, an Alemão-based project that has become the most widely followed favela-based social media projects in Brazil. This video was part of a series called "Relief for Favelas" where public health agents talked about issues with tracking the spread of the Coronavirus and providing protective equipment, medical supplies, and even foodstuffs to certain communities. A significant portion of the video focused on how social movement organizations like the Landless Workers Movement are collaborating with communities to create alternative networks for giving residents supplies. A final video shared on June 2 from another local media producer addresses racial profiling and how to document police abuses (including arbitrary stops or entrance into domiciles) that might intensify during the COVID-19 crisis. By sharing posts that attack Bolsonaro and amplifying alternative networks for providing community support to the insufficient ones provided by the state, CAPS Miriam Makeba shows the clearest example of a community health Facebook profile attempting to offer both support and advocacy.

Reading the activity of the 21 CMS/CAPS Facebook profiles through the literature on alternative media and community-based public health communication, we see that the Facebook groups within favelas run by medical centers focus much more extensively on the "speaking with" function—explicitly in the form of information sharing. However, there exist embryonic attempts at structural critique as public health workers to speak their own frustrations with larger issues related to the treatment of health in poor communities.

Brazil Case Type 2: Alternative digital journalism

The second Brazilian case consists of explicitly political community-oriented digital media projects. The first organization to be analyzed is Narrativas Independentes, Jornalismo e Ação [Independent Stories, Journalism, and Action] (NINJA), a nationwide network that blossomed while covering the 2013 nationwide protests. Through its work covering public demonstrations in 2013, the group received international recognition and quickly grew to become one of the largest and most followed projects nationwide with over two million followers on Facebook and 775,000 on Twitter (Davis, 2016; Saad Filho and Morais, 2014). The other project we will discuss is Alma Preta, a blog and social media-based project started in 2015 by Afro-Brazilian students from the State University of São Paulo to "create content that acts as a public utility for Afro-Brazilians, addressing their aspirations and anxieties" ("Sobre Alma Preta," 2020). During the COVID-19 crisis, both of these projects have taken to posting at least daily regarding structural issues exposed by the Coronavirus from lack of investment in infrastructure within favelas and indigenous communities to lack of resources provided to the explicit racism in the ways Bolsonaro addressed the crisis. Unlike the public health centers' Facebook profiles, COVID-19-related posts from these groups focus extensively on public health inequalities arising with or exacerbated by the crisis.

Beginning on March 22, 2020 (matching the other Brazilian cases), we look at how MídiaNINJA and Alma Preta offer an avenue for advocacy among not just Rio's favelas but also quilombos and autonomous indigenous communities. The first, MidiaNINJA, is a young but well-established network of digital media activist centers and with over six million followers or subscribers between Facebook, Instagram, Twitter, and YouTube. The second, Alma Preta Jornalismo, is a newer and smaller blog project with a specific focus on Afro-Brazilian communities. This section will discuss how both attempt to create grassroots advocacy campaigns to "speak against" the larger structural issues embedded in the COVID-19 crisis.

MídiaNINJA

MídiaNINJA was launched during the 2013 "Brazilian Spring" protests as a nationwide network of local citizen journalism projects organized through a number of collective workspaces called "NINJA houses" that are reminiscent of the IndyMedia centers that grew up in the early 2000s

(Davis, 2016). As the number of NINJA-affiliated centers expanded, the project's output has followed suit to the point where there are often multiple live videos streaming simultaneously and up to 100 posts daily on Facebook. Due to this enormous volume of output, we limited our discussion to posts with an explicit focus on the COVID-19 crisis.

The most dominant trend within NINJA's COVID-19 coverage is to link the Coronavirus crisis to larger narratives about the exploitation of marginalized areas and the larger impact of COVID-19 on poor people. As of December 2019, developing journalistic projects in the Amazon region has been one of NINJA's main priorities. An entire episode of the NINJA YouTube documentary series "Paradise Robbed" posted on May 28 focused on COVID-19 outbreaks within indigenous communities in the Amazon region. The episode focused on longstanding problems within the area like the lack of sanitation and underfunded public health infrastructure along with COVID-19-related issues like the total lack of testing and contact tracing. In the same vein, stories posted by NINJA on May 02 and May 05 offered interviews about extractive workers coming into the region. The May 05 post discusses how the federal government's classification of timber harvesting as an "essential service" increased the spread of COVID-19 cases due to the lack of social distancing and precaution on the part of loggers moving back and forth from the region. Connectedly, a May 15 Facebook post presented a story about how the COVID-19-related redeployment of national guard soldiers stationed in the region to prevent illegal logging and mining has led to higher reports of illegal extraction in the area by indigenous communities. These stories point to a unique element of NINJA's coverage: though based in the Amazon the stories create linkages with corruption and tolerated illegality at the national level.

Along with offering an advocacy channel for marginalized communities, NINJA also created posts and videos about the larger socioeconomic strain of COVID-19 on social programs for the most impoverished sectors. The most substantial example of this focus was a series of posts in April–May about the virus's impact on Bolsa Familia, a conditional cash transfer and social welfare program started in the 2000s to provide both cash payments and subsidized access to purchasing staple foods and school supplies to families under the poverty line that was drastically cut after Dilma Rousseff's impeachment. Through these posts NINJA tracks efforts by various progressive state governments to divert money from other federal sources to restart programs started under Bolsa Familia. In a similar vein to the Bolsa Familia story, on June 02 NINJA published a story on its blog and Facebook page about the lack of personal protective equipment and unsafe working conditions of gravediggers in the rural northeastern state of Ceará who contracted to inter the bodies of virus victims. Written through interviews with representatives of the Union of Municipal Public Servants—the union that represents the gravediggers—MídiaNINJA documents a litany of safety issues ranging from lack of ventilation to lack of drinking water to 18-hour daily shifts.

Alma Preta Jornalismo

Founded in 2015 in São Paolo, Alma Preta was explicitly designed for two specific purposes: to cover issues within Afro-Brazilian communities that had been traditionally left out of mainstream media coverage and to train residents within Afro-Brazilian marginalized communities to create stories about major issues facing their communities. The name of the group, "Alma Preta" ["Black Soul"], invokes a slogan from the Movimento Negro related to the need to mobilize Afro-Brazilian activists both intellectually and spiritually. Since 2015 the group has worked explicitly on creating a nationwide network of producers in order to represent political issues and struggles facing communities across Brazil.

Alma Preta's previous attention to network-building created an infrastructure that helped it address the COVID-19 outbreak from early stages. Accordingly, the project has been able to produce at least two stories daily on the Coronavirus. Geographically focusing on the Northeast of Brazil, many of its stories examine the impact of COVID-19 on favelas and quilombos. These stories are created in collaboration with community members who act as co-authors. In a story from May 28, the project took this collaborative approach to an extreme degree by partnering with two NGOs to provide testing and contact tracing in seventeen quilombos (Ribeiro, 2020). This story illustrates the interconnectedness between Alma Preta and on-the-ground struggles against COVID. The "speaking for" element comes out in Alma Preta's discussion on the discriminatory elements of both the COVID-19 outbreak and the national response. The most striking example of this position was a May 19 story that attacked the national Ministry of Health for refusing to share race-related data for morbidity rates. Alma Preta was the first news-site to critique the ministry and sparked a mini-avalanche of coverage by larger media outlets.

The discussion of these organizations shows how alternative media producers serve an important role in educating larger audiences about how Fourth World communities are disproportionately affected by COVID-19 while also "speaking against" the social order that creates these spaces. Unlike the CMS/CAPS Facebook profiles, these projects are less interested in reaching audiences within these communities, but more interested in the amplification of marginalized experiences in the service of a larger political and institutional critique.

Case studies from Mexico: Radio Zapatista and Radio Pozol

This section focuses on how two radio- and social media-based radical activist projects in Chiapas, Mexico, worked with local indigenous communities to fight against the disease spread, the narratives that emerge about it, and the State oppression. The two case studies from Mexico are linked to the Zapatista movement and Medios Libres (Free Media). Radio Zapatista is a self-described alternative media collective created to foster "the possibility of building a Mexico outside of the capitalist logic of profit and competition." The group adopts a perspective from below, based on information created and produced by local communities. The collective was founded in 2006 in San Francisco; initially it was a monthly program broadcast organized by a committee in solidarity with the Zapatista communities in Chiapas. A group consisting of mostly migrants and Chicanos created the collective in response to the alter-globalization challenges and provocations posed by the manifesto (La Sexta) issued by the Zapatista Army of National Liberation (EZNL) in 2005. Radio Pozol, on the other hand, is a non-profit organization within the Network of Free Media (Red de Medios Libres Chiapas) that started operating in 2007. In 2010 the FM broadcast signal of Radio Pozol was interrupted when the state government intervened the building where the organization had their transmitter. Since then the project moved online as part of a network of free media producers (Ojeda de la Torre, 2020).

Both of these projects are closely linked to the community radio movement in Chiapas. One of the effects of the 1994 EZNL insurgency was the creation of community radio projects that acted outside of the government purview and without official permits. These projects are committed to an ideology of "free media" that is based on solidary and the social accumulation of knowledge, sharing information with other social movements and organizations to promote the use of information to fight oppression (Pineda, 2013). With this brief introduction to the historical and ideological background of Radio Zapatista and Radio Pozol laid out, the remainder of the section will look at how these projects attempt to fulfill the "speaking with" and "speaking for" functions for the population of Chiapas.

Speaking with: Radio Zapatista and Radio Pozol as alternative forms of disseminating health news

As one of the most critical needs during the early stages of the pandemic was access to information about COVID-19, what the symptoms look like, and how to prevent contagion. Both social media pages shared health material from various sources. One of the ways in which Radio Pozol worked to disseminate health news and health advice was by sharing PDF links to guides, books, and pamphlets, most of them illustrated. The collective posted two different anarchist guides to survive COVID-19. The first was a Google Doc with information translated from the English *An Anarchist's Guide to Surviving Coronavirus COVID-19 a.k.a 2019-n-CoV* by Four Thieves Vinegar Collective, an anarchist bio-hacking group. The guide, translated into Spanish by a collectively owned bookstore in Chiapas, contains information about what the virus is, how it spreads, how to prevent contagion, and what to do if sick. The collective shared a second anarchist guide called *Rebelion en cuarentena: Una guia anarquista de acción en tiempos de pandemia* (Rebellion in quarantine: An anarchist action guide for pandemic times) by Jorge Enkis, an illustrated guide with information from Thieves Vinegar and CrimethInc. that contains advice on creating a support network. Radio Pozol also shared a post with a link to *Where There Is no Doctor: A Village Health Care Handbook* by David Werner. The book was originally written in 1970 based on Werner's health care work on Mexican villages and it is aimed at community health workers (Saloojee, 1998). Radio Pozol's Facebook post shows the cover of the book and a PDF link and a few caveats:

> 1) Healthcare is not only everyone's right, but everyone's responsibility; 2) The main goal of every single health activity or program should be to train every person to take care of their own health; 3) If people receive clear and simple information, they can avoid and treat at home the most frequent health issues. Many times people can act faster, cheaper and more effectively than doctors; 4) Medical knowledge should not be a secret known amongst a few people, it should be general knowledge; 5) People who do not have formal education are just as responsible and intelligent as those with college degrees; 6) Basic healthcare should not come from outside, it must be fostered within the community."

These practices reflect what DIY activism scholars indicate as alternative forms of activism and resistance that do not rely on hierarchical structures: "By creating your own non-hierarchically organized community together with others and by working on alternatives … you can look for solutions to problems yourself and change things" (Nijsten, 2007, p. 28). Moreover, the concept of radical media as a form of democratic communication where those who are denied access to mainstream media are able to share their perspectives is apparent in the ways these collectives make visible marginalized communities.

Speaking with: Providing tools for marginalized groups to capture and share their own perspectives

Reflecting ideas of anarchist media as spaces that value the diversity of ways of contemplating the living world and challenging established ideas/institutions, Radio Zapatista was more concern with creating cultural resistance to fight the health crisis. The collective created a document called "Hackeando la Pandemia" (Hacking the Pandemic) and shared it to their Facebook page. Radio Zapatista asked fellow activists to take a moment to reflect on what is needed from them amid pandemic: "How do we as narrators, artists, communicators, radio hosts, journalists, cultural hackers have to respond during this extended crisis? The goal of these reflections is to share them with those who find them useful for their work as narrators; they do not attempt to be absolute truths or to indoctrinate anyone. Take what works for you and question what doesn't … These ideas are not ours, you can share them freely, misinterpret them, remix them, or suggest changes." The collective defines cultural hacking as making the radical common sense, using insurrectionist narratives of open code, and defending life and territory. This document delineates that to hack the systems of oppression such as colonialism, patriarchy, capitalism, and racism means to create narratives that do not render invisible, victimize, or further threaten the diversity of individuals and geographies. They ask activists "to narrate from dignity."

While the idea of hacking the pandemic seems to rely on ideas from anarchist and alternative media, it is also calling for community participation and the idea that citizens need to represent themselves and their needs. In that sense the Zapatista collectives reflect a use of social media that goes beyond disseminating information to push for community collaboration.

Speaking for: Providing a powerful advocacy tool for marginalized communities

Both Radio Pozol and Radio Zapatista were concerned with exposing and documenting one particular form of state oppression that the indigenous communities of Mexico were facing during the COVID-19 pandemic. This refers to the continuation of infrastructure projects such as the Mayan Train and the highway toll Toluca-Naucalpan. These two particular projects do not affect the communities in Chiapas directly, but do set a precedent for the treatment of indigenous groups and territories. Moreover, it involves denouncing possible forced displacement of marginalized indigenous people out of their homes at a time when the entire globe is following stay at home orders.

Radio Zapatista shared a blog entry in which they published a letter from the Otomi indigenous community where they manifested their opposition to the construction of a highway toll that would invade sacred territory and would interfere with the flow of water to their community. The project is now being reviewed by the Supreme Court since it was not consulted with the indigenous community (Murillo, 2020). The post indicated Ivan Gonzalez, an indigenous advocate, had been beaten and illegally detained by the State Police. The social media account denounced Mexican authorities for not following the social distancing recommendations to stop the spread of the pandemic. They claim the people working on the project come from different parts of the country and that State police officers are entering their community putting the vulnerable Otomi people at risk of contagion: "In the times of #StayHome they are taking advantage to continue the construction of the Toluca-Naucalpan Highway."

Several posts from Radio Pozol link to news and blog posts with information about the Mayan Train and asking for the project to be suspended during the Coronavirus pandemic. One of the posts was shared from the Facebook page of Múuch Xíinbal, a group of advocates for the Mayan territory in

Yucatan. The post linked to a news article about how the Mexican government was taking advantage of the stay at home order to continue the construction of the Mayan Train. Indigenous communities, activists, collectives, and non-profit organizations denounced that the people and communities who have manifested their opposition to the project are in a state of defenselessness. Another post from Radio Pozol linked to an editorial in a Yucatan newspaper penned by UNAM anthropologist Rodrigo Llanes. Llanes stated that the biggest concern with the construction of the Mayan Train was that it risks the health and life of the workers who will have to continue with the project. He echoes the idea that the communities in opposition are in "state of vulnerability." Moreover, due to the health crisis it has become materially impossible to request official information about the environmental, economic, and social impacts of the project and its progress. Llanas refers to the letter signed by different indigenous organizations asking the Mexican president to stop the project and return to it once the COVID-19 pandemic is under control. Another post linked to a blog entry from Enlace Zapatist, the website of EZNL. The post called for a live transmission of a virtual forum to discuss the Mayan Train called "Capitalism in the times of pandemic does not stay in quarantine." The EZNL claims that the imposition of the Mayan Train signifies displacement, death, and destruction of the indigenous people and their communities.

Conclusion: Speaking with and for the Fourth World

These case studies introduce activist projects in Latin America attempting to employ digital media as tools not just for raising awareness of COVID-19 but more crucially to empower local residents to fight the virus themselves. They are also creating powerful advocacy campaigns on behalf of communities in the attempt to force negligent governments to pay attention. The ideological positions of the groups vary: some like Radio Zapatista espouse a radical anti-capitalist position while others like the CMS/CAPS projects explicitly try to adopt a non-political stance (though it doesn't always work). Despite variations in location, politics, and type of media platform employed, the Brazilian and Mexican cases are similar in profound ways. They all have roots within communities that existed before the Coronavirus crisis began in Brazil. Furthermore and *pivotally*, all of these projects engage in what we have called the two central components of alternative media and community-based public health: "Speaking with" and "Speaking for" favelas, quilombos, or rural indigenous communities. All projects foster engagement within local communities (through providing information and by incorporating community perspectives) while also offering an advocacy stance aimed at illustrating larger public health issues facing neighborhoods.

Ending by returning to the beginning, we reiterate that the COVID-19 crises in Brazil and Mexico remain open wounds for the entire population and especially for the most marginalized. The cases presented in this chapter hope to point to ways that media producers, activists, and concerned medical workers can employ digital technologies to combat an unprecedented and perhaps even apocalyptic scenario that governments have at this point chosen to ignore or downplay. The future is unwritten, but we hope the kinds of media practices discussed in this chapter will mitigate the virus's damage. This is a faint hope: these are all small projects working on behalf of communities that have for decades if not centuries been structurally excluded. Nonetheless, we believe that documenting their work might offer some powerful ideas for re-conceptualizing health communication including outreach to underrepresented communities, collaboration with community media producers, and a consistent commitment to tying COVID-19-related health issues to larger structures of oppression.

References

Aldrich, S. (2012). *Building Resilience: Social Capital in Post-Disaster Recovery*. Chicago, IL: University of Chicago Press.

Beltrão, L. (1988). A folkcomunicação não é uma comunicação classista. *Intercom: Revista Brasileira de Comunicação*, 57, 5–15.

Castells, M. (1996). *The Information Age, Volume I: The Rise of the Network Society*. Malden, MA: Blackwell Publishing.

Chaffee, S.H., Gomez-Palacio, D.C. and Rogers, D.E.M. (1990). Mass communication research in Latin America: Views from here and there. *Journalism Quarterly* , 67(4), 1015–1024.

Chaves, R. (2020). Prefeitura do Rio entrega tomógrafo para combater covid-19 na Rocinha. *Noticias R7*, May 07, 2020. Available at https://noticias.r7.com/rio-de-janeiro/prefeitura-do-rio-entrega-tomografo-para-combater-covid-19-na-rocinha-03062020 (Accessed 04 June 2020).

Davis, M. (2020). Coronavirus: In a Plague Year. *Jacobin*, March 10, 2020. https://jacobinmag.com/2020/03/mike-davis-coronavirus- outbreak- capitalism-left-international-solidarity (Accessed 10 April 2020).

Davis, S. (2016). MídiaNINJA and the rise of citizen journalism in Brazil. In *Civic Media: Technology, Design, Practice* (Eric Gordon and Paul Mihaildis (eds.)). Cambridge, MA: MIT Press, pp. 527–532.

Davis, S. (2017). Citizen health journalism: Negotiating between political engagement and professional identity in a media training program for healthcare workers. *Journalism Practice* 10(8–9): 319–335. DOI:10.1080/17512786.2016.1230022

Gomez-Rodriguez, G., Morrell A.E. and Gallo-Estrada, C. (2017). A 30 años de *Comunicación y Sociedad*: Cambios y permanencias en el campo académico de la Comunicación. *Comunicación y Sociedad*, 30, 17–44. Available at: https://www.redalyc.org/pdf/346/34653156003.pdf (Accessed 12 April 2020).

Lemos, V. (2020). A farsa dos caixões vazios usados para minimizar mortes por covid- 19. BBC News: Brasil. May 08, 2020 Available at https://www.bbc.com/portuguese/brasil-52584458 (Accessed 01 June 2020).

Magallanes-Blanco, C. (2008). *The Use of Video for Political Consciousness-Raising in Mexico: An Analysis of Independent Videos About the Zapatistas*. London, UK: Edwin Mellen Press.

Minkler, M., and Wallerstein, N. (2012). Community-Based Participatory Research for Health: From Process to Outcomes. New Brunswick, NJ: Rutgers University Press

Murillo, E. (2020, April 22). *Revisará SCJN legalidad de autopista Toluca-Naucalpan—Política—La Jornada*. Retrieved from https://www.jornada.com.mx/ultimas/politica/2020/04/22/revisara-scjn-legalidad-de-autopista-toluca-naucalpan-559.html

Murphy, P. and Rodriguez C. (1997). The study of communication and culture in Latin America: From laggards and the oppressed to resistance and hybrid cultures. *Journal of International Communication,* 4(2), 24–45.

Nijsten, N. (2007). *Different Worlds, Same Heartbeats* 1. Hasselt: Self-published.

Ojeda de la Torre, I. (2020, June 1). Radios comunitarias luchan (con Fox, FCH, EPN y AMLO) en contra de censura, agresión y escasa señal. *Zona Franca.* Retrieved from https://zonafranca.mx/politica-sociedad/radios-comunitarias-luchan-con-fox-fch-epn-y-amlo-en-contra-de-censura-agresion-y-escasa-senal/

Partners in Health. (2020). Mexico. Retrieved from https://www.pih.org/article/fighting-growing-covid-19-pandemic-mexico

Pineda, N. (2013, Oct. 7). El camino de los medios libres en Chiapas. *Chiapas Paralelo.* Retrieved from https://www.chiapasparalelo.com/opinion/2013/10/el-camino-de-los-medios-libres-en-chiapas/

Ribeiro, F. (2020). Plataforma online monitora casos de Covid-19 entre quilombolas do Brasil. Jornalismo Alma Preta, May 28, 2020. Available at https://almapreta.com/editorias/realidade/plataforma-online-monitora-casos-de- covid-19-entre-quilombolas-do-brasil (Accessed 30 May 2020).

Rodrigues, A. and Cancian, N. (2020). Brasil ultrapassa França e se torna o 4° país com mais mortes por coronavirus. *Folha de São Paulo,* May 30, 2020 Available at https://www1.folha.uol.com.br/equilibrioesaude/2020/05/brasil-ultrapassa-franca-e-se-torna-o-4o-pais-com-mais-mortes-por-coronavirus.shtml (Accessed 02 June 2020).

Rogers, E. (2003). *The Diffusion of Innovations,* 5th Edition. New York: Free Press.

Rummler, O. (2020). Confirmed coronavirus deaths in Brazil's largest cities spike by over 400%. Axios, May 22, 2020. Available at https://www.axios.com/coronavirus-brazil-deaths-y79e2d09-6e73-4376-995c-461014664c3e.html (Accessed 30 May 2020).

Saad Filho A. and L. Morais (2014). Mass protests: Brazilian spring or Brazilian malaise? In *Socialist Register 2014* (Leo Panich, Greg Albo and Vivek Chibber (eds.)). New York: Monthly Review Books.

Saloojee H. (1998). Where there is No doctor: A village health care handbook for africa. BMJ (Clinical research ed.), 317(7171), 1532. https://doi.org/10.1136/bmj.317.7171.1532

Sheridan, M. (2020). Mexico's hospitals strain to treat coronavirus as officials say cases are peaking. *The Washington Post*, June 02, 2020 (Print Edition).

Trere, E. (2012). Social movements as information ecologies: Exploring the coevolution of multiple Internet technologies for activism. *International Journal of Communication,* 6, 2359–2377.

Vasconcelos, R. (2020, April, 02). Coronavírus: relembre o que Bolsanaro já falou sobre a pandemia. Estadão. Retrieved from https://politica.estadao.com.br/noticias/geral,coronavirus-o-que-bolsonaro-ja-falou-ate-agora-sobre-a-pandemia,70003234776

Viva Rio (2013). "The Third Generation of Viva Favela Website is Online.http://vivario.org.br/en/third-generation-of-viva-favela-website-is-online/. Accessed 10/01/2014

Walsh, C. (2002). Prólogo. In *Para leer al Pato Donald desde la diferencia comunicación, desarrollo y control cultural* (A. Aillón (ed.)). Caracas, VZ: Universidad Simón Bolívar.

Part II

Information technologies and civil engagement

6 Social media as an instrument of activism for feminist university students in Mexico

The cases of MOFFyL and Uni Unida

Yunuen Ysela Mandujano-Salazar and Luis Antonio Becerra-Soria

Introduction

During the 21st century, as digital technologies and social media have become part of everyday life, online activism, also called hashtag, internet, or digital activism, has gained relevance for political and civil engagement. Particularly, social media has allowed for a greater exposure of citizens' voices than traditional media. In this sense, activists rely on the fact that they can engage directly in dialogue regarding the issues of their interest, voice their demands, unmask power, challenge misrepresentation in traditional media, and so on. Digital activism has been especially important in the development of the Fourth Wave Feminism. Although its ideological bases are similar to those of the Third Wave—a clear opposition to gender violence, inequality, and patriarchal hegemony—it differentiates for the employment of digital media to express and to call for public demonstrations. In the case of Mexico, feminism has gained notoriousness precisely with the use of social media to make visible the systemic violence against women in the country.

Two cases are relevant because of the concentration of gender violence and the use of social media as means of communication for feminist collectives: Ciudad Juárez and Mexico City—hereafter Juárez and CDMX. Juárez is a city with a history of femicides and disappearances since the 1990s. The prevalent impunity around these cases and the increasing violence against women in the city has been the context of the onset of many protests from the victims' families, as well as the starting point of scholar research concerning gender violence in Mexican society. However, social outrage has been mostly lacking. Until 2019, inside the Autonomous University of Ciudad Juarez (UACJ) feminist students had not been able to obtain the recognition of the community. On the other hand, at the National Autonomous University of Mexico [UNAM] the murder of a young woman in the university grounds, in April 2017, provoked the discontent of students and originated a series of public protests at the university with the creation of different feminist collectives.

Thus, in this chapter, we analyze the use of social media in the development of two Mexican feminist university collectives—UNAM's Mujeres Organizadas de la Facultad de Filosofía y Letras [MOFFyL] and UACJ's Uni Unida. We relied on digital and regular ethnography, as well as on documental research to rebuild the history of the collectives and to analyze the role of social media in their formation, consolidation, and their activities online and offline.

Feminist digital activism in the 21st century

Castells (2015) has observed how alternative digital media—e.g. Facebook, Instagram, and Twitter—allowed the general public to create and to communicate information beyond the control of governments and corporations. By sharing sorrow, anger, and hope, through a medium which is a fast way to circulate images and opinions, they have created a sense of togetherness that allows users to overcome fear, connect practices, and initiate social movements that have begun social transformation.

As it is defined by Adler and Goggin (2005), civic engagement refers to the involvement of the members of a community in activities orientated to improve their surroundings in order to construct a better future. Social media is a space of socialization particularly sought by young people who begin to define themselves as citizens. Accordingly, digital technologies and social media are becoming a space for interaction and participation for youngsters, who may also be involved in offline civic engagement (De-la-Garza-Montemayor et al., 2019). Contrary to the so-called *slacktivism*—a neologism resulted by combining *slacker* and *activism*—online civic engagement has, indeed, contributed to raise consciousness through graphical and written testimony, toward social issues, resulting in a wider coverage by mainstream media and attracting public attention (Brimacombe et al., 2018). Castells (2015) and Gerbaudo (2012) consider that, for example, the Arab Spring in 2011 originated in Facebook and Twitter, which facilitated the organization of protests and the uprising, as well as global visibilization.

Fourth Wave Feminism has been particularly vocal in digital media. According to Kowalska (2017), its beginning has a direct correlation with the popularization of social media around 2008. Using alternative digital media, feminist organizations and individuals have denounced sexism, misogynistic acts, gender discrimination, rape culture, mediated abuse, and trolling in the discourse of mainstream media and other users. Feminist digital activism is molded by the Foucauldian idea of visibility. In digital culture, being seen, read, and shared is equal to claiming their existence. In opposition to other forms of activism, these feminist groups define themselves as *collectives* and are characterized by the pursuit of a horizontal structure, instead of a hierarchical one. As a result, they promote the idea of *sorority* among women concerning gender issues. Feminist collectives around the globe have employed the use of hashtags in social media to promote online campaigns, such as #MeToo, #HeForShe, etc. In consequence, social media has provided a space of encounter for further engagement, cross-referencing with other movements, and for inviting members and followers to support other feminist groups (Turley & Fisher, 2018).

In Mexico, feminist digital activism has been present since 2011, when #mujeresenlacantina was created to make visible the inequality of treatment for women in Mexican restaurants and cantinas, where they were, by tradition, denied service and even asked to leave the premises. This hashtag eventually functioned as a way of calling for a public manifestation to confront the owners of these restaurants in CDMX (De la Cruz, 2011). In 2015, #RopaSucia appeared on Twitter. This movement was created by female poets to expose the inequality in the Mexican academic and cultural sectors, as well as their misogynist and sexist behavior. The users shared their personal anecdotes about personalities such as Octavio Paz. Furthermore, this digital project was followed by a demonstration in which artists created a *tendedero* [a clothes line] constituted by different garments on which the best tweets were printed and "washed" with a mixture of water, ink, wine, and coffee to symbolize that those actions cannot be cleaned (Suárez Gómez, 2016).

In April 2016, Mexican feminist activists followed the #MiPrimerAsedio movement of Brazil, which invited women to share their first experience being sexually harassed to expose that women are victims of sexual violence on a daily basis (Silverstone, 2017). The Mexican version was #MiPrimerAcoso, which became a trending topic and had the participation of thousands of women, many of whom experienced their first harassment during childhood at the hands of relatives (Rocha, 2016). This movement strengthened the participation in a feminist demonstration on April 24, 2016, which was summoned by many local collectives around Mexico—with #VivasNosQueremos—to demand security and respect for women, as well as to claim justice for the victims of femicide, rape, and disappearances (Híjar Juárez, 2016).

In the spring of 2017, another hashtag was used to claim for justice and as a way to make visible the systemic violence against women in Mexico and the tendency to revictimize them. #SiMeMatan originated after the body of a young woman, Lesvy, was found in the grounds of the UNAM. The Attorney General's Office of CDMX published on its Twitter account that the victim had been drinking alcohol and using drugs before her death. This caused the indignation of numerous women who began using Twitter with the mentioned hashtag to share details about their lives that could be used to criminalize them in case they became victims (Redacción Animal Político, 2017).

Another relevant example is the #MeToo movement that appeared in Mexico during March 2019, with #MeTooEscritoresMexicanos. The first tweet that originated this movement was published by a user who declared that a known Mexican writer had manipulated, beaten, impregnated, and abandoned more than ten women. After this hashtag became trending topic, the Twitter account @MeTooEscritores was created for users to share their violent experiences with other Mexican writers (Milenio digital, 2019). Later, other accounts appeared in order to expose gender violence on several social and academic fields (Hernández, 2020).

Thus, the use of digital platforms as means for activism to attract attention to social issues and to summon offline movements has been gaining relevance among feminist collectives. In Mexico, the last decade has increasingly seen the use of social media by feminist activists to express their demands and organize public demonstrations.

Femicides and feminist activism in Mexico City and Ciudad Juárez at the turn of the century

The systemic violence against women for their female quality, most of the time perpetrated by men who are in a relational situation of power, is what has been called by feminist theorists as *femicide/feminicide* (Lagarde, 2006). Juárez has been known for being a capital of femicides; however, the violence against women has occurred everywhere in Mexico for a long time.

In CDMX, a metropolis of more than 20 million people, there has been a long tradition of feminist movements since the early 20th century. The ideological bases of these movements have been diverse and evolving, including labor inequalities of working women, gender violence, decriminalization of abortion, support for raped victims, inclusion and recognition of women and of indigenous groups in national politics, and so on (Stephen, 2012). It is in this context that the Fourth Wave feminism arose. It has been proposed that it began in the second decade of the 21st century, arriving in Mexico in 2019 (Galván, 2019). Its characteristic is the use of new digital technologies and the incorporation of youth in social movements (Ballesteros, 2020; Varela, 2020).

Mobilizations began to be more frequent with the use of social media to summon for demonstrations. Initially, the participation of feminist groups was complementary to larger protests or their displays of discontent were represented by a small number of participants. The start of larger mobilizations of women in CDMX happened on April 24, 2016, with the "Violet Spring" movement; thousands of people were summoned on social media with the #24A to demonstrate against gender violence, particularly against femicides (Priego-Broca, 2016). In 2017, these protests continued after the murders of Lesvy and two other women #NiUnaMenos. In 2018, the so-called "Green Tide" of the #26S broke out, characterized by green scarves, a symbol that emerged in Argentina to represent the legalization of abortion (Elige Red, 2017). In 2019, two extremely important demonstrations took place. On August 12th and 16th, with #NoMeCuidanMeViolan,

Mexican women took to the streets to protest against gender-based violence—in this year, the number of murders of women was 9 to 10 per day—as well as for the rape of a female high-school student by the police (Galván, 2019; Redacción Animal Político, 2019). Finally, on March 8, 2020, it was registered the largest participation in a feminist demonstration in CDMX, with 80,000 women. The calling to take to the streets in order to commemorate the International Day of Working Women was joined by a general outrage after the femicide and dismemberment of a woman on February 9th with #NiUnaMás (La Equipa Editorial, 2020; Notimex, 2020).

In contrast, Juárez is a city of about 1.5 million people at the northern border with the United States. It has always attracted a migrant population looking to cross to the neighboring country. Since the 1960s, when Mexico implemented an export-led economic model, the city became a receptor of numerous *maquiladoras*—factories mostly destined to low-cost manufacture and assembly processes. This turned Juárez into an attractive destination for people looking for a job in the country. Thus, it has a high percentage of migrant and floating population that, sometimes, live in precarious conditions.

Another characteristic of *maquiladoras* that has shaped the city is that more than half of the workforce is female (Staudt & Campbell, 2008). This situation has been considered as one of the reasons for the infamous violence against women that has characterized Juárez since the 1990s; since, as women entered the labor force and became breadwinners or began to be economically independent, they were perceived as transgressors of the patriarchal system (Monárrez Fregoso, 2010). Between 1993 and 1999, more than 160 women were raped, mutilated, and murdered in Juárez; this number has been a source of debate, because authorities categorized them as homicides, suicides, or accidents (Lagarde, 2006). Most of these victims were identified in the narratives of local and international press as young poor women working at *maquiladoras,* highlighting that they put themselves in risky situations; thus, implicitly or explicitly, blaming them (Monárrez Fregoso, 2000). Since then, thousands of women—not limited to the media-built stereotype—have been raped, murdered, or disappeared, and more than 90% of cases remain unsolved (M. E. López, 2018).

After decades of impunity and continuous hate and violence against women, civil society activism surged, but not with enough strength to involve wide sectors of population. At the beginning, families and friends of victims led demonstrations claiming justice; soon, diverse human rights and feminist activists—many of them from international groups—joined the activities to raise awareness about violence against women, urging to put the issue on the political agenda (Staudt & Campbell, 2008). However, the "pandemic of femicide in Ciudad Juárez" (M. E. López, 2018, para. 19) has not stopped and feminist activist groups remain painfully ignored by society and authorities, battling against rooted machismo, misogyny, and a generalized violent context.

Development of MOFFyL and Uni Unida

UNAM and UACJ are two public universities in Mexico, but they have very different contexts and history regarding activism. Established in 1973, the UACJ is the major public university in Juárez, having 34,000 students (Universidad Autónoma de Ciudad Juárez, 2019a). Meanwhile, UNAM, founded in 1910, is the largest university in the country, with 360,883 students (Portal de Estadística Universitaria, 2020).

Feminist collectives at UNAM began to appear in the 1980s with the purpose of denouncing misogyny at the university. In the 1990s, various feminists presented the Rector a proposal for the creation of the University Program for Gender Studies, which would promote research on feminist issues and participate in the design of policies on gender equality. The result of this was, in 2004, the project of Institutionalization and Transversalization of the Gender Perspective. In 2005, the addition of Article 2 to the General Statute of UNAM was created establishing that women and men have the same rights, obligations, and prerogatives. In 2014, the network of feminist collectives, Red No Están Solas, began accompanying victims of gender-based violence at the UNAM and denounced the sexual violence of teachers and students. Toward 2016, the Feminist Collective of the Facultad de Ciencias Políticas y Sociales and the Asamblea Feminista de la Facultad de Filosofía y Letras were created and presented a questioning to the Protocol for the Care of Cases of Gender Violence. Finally, in 2017, the MOFFyL emerged (Medina Ramírez, 2020).

The collective MOFFyL was created in order to denounce the ineffectiveness of the UNAM's authorities in addressing gender-based violence, whether physical or verbal, despite the fact that it signed the agreements of the Solidarity Movement for Gender Equality, also called HeForShe, of the UN Women (ONU Mujeres, 2016). Also, they criticized the compliance with the Protocol. From 2002 to 2019, there were at least 16 femicide cases (Michel, 2019); from 2016 to 2019, there were 921 complaints regarding sexual abuse and gender violence (Rincón, 2019). However, several feminist collectives, including MOFFyL, have expressed that those are not the actual number, since the attention to cases of gender violence by the Protocol is insufficient, due to the lack of accompaniment, the minimization of complaints, and the lack of confidence on the part of the students (Ruíz & Pigeonutt, 2019). MOFFyL members also expressed their disagreement with the lack of information regarding Lesvy's case, both by the UNAM's authorities and the Attorney General's Office. They demanded that the authorities did not minimize this murder, calling it "an illegality" instead of addressing it as a femicide. This case caused a discomfort on the feminist collectives and the general community, marking a breaking point that strengthened their political involvement (Ruíz & Pigeonutt, 2019).

In 2018, after International Women's Day, MOFFyL organized *tendederos* in the Facultad de Filosofía y Letras [FFyL], to denounce the internal aggressors, both students and teachers, and they also protested against the ineffectiveness of the Protocol and of the Unit for Attention to Complaints of Gender Violence [UNAD]. During that month, the first feminist strikes were convened at the FFyL. While these movements were taking place, the femicide of a teacher and her daughter, a student, and the disappearance of another student occurred. These cases emphasized the discontent of MOFFyL toward the authorities for their reluctance to provide information to the community, speak to family members, and give them support. Finally, on September 3, while students demonstrated against gender violence in front of the Rectory, a group attacked with cold weapons and Molotov bombs. Feminist collectives, including MOFFyL, denounced the lack of internal security on the university campus and their suspicion that these groups were sponsored by UNAM's authorities (García, 2019).

On November 4, 2019, a student strike began at the FFyL. On that morning, MOFFyL decided to take over the facilities and issued a petition consisting of 11 demands; the more relevant were: the modification of the UNAM's General Statute to regard gender violence as meritorious of expulsion or termination of the work contract; the creation of a Tripartite Commission to attend cases of gender violence, constituted by students, teachers, and workers; the reformulation of the UNAD; and, the reopening and reviewing of complaints rejected by the Faculty General Advocacy. The strike finished on April 14, 2020, when, due to the health contingency caused by COVID-19, the FFyL was delivered even though some points were still under negotiation.

On the other hand, as mentioned before, Juárez is a city where activism has struggled to reach the support of the larger society. Inside the UACJ, the context was not different. Most students have jobs outside the campus and almost 20% of the total student population is older than 25 years old, which makes it difficult for them to get involved in extracurricular activities or groups (Universidad Autónoma de Ciudad Juárez, 2019b). However, in 2019, some episodes of violence against students of the UACJ caused the outrage of some peers and marked the origin of the collective Uni Unida. The first case occurred on February 22, when a male undergraduate student was murdered outside a bar in the city (Ramírez, 2019). On February 24, another male student alleged that some local police officers sexually abused him (Tovar, 2019). These two cases caused a small group of their peers to plan a public demonstration at City Hall to ask for justice. Most of these students had no previous experience in activism, but the few who did participate worked together with local feminist collectives. They made use of WhatsApp groups to coordinate themselves, organized in principle by a female student. A few days later, to promote the support for the cause, they also opened a Facebook page called Uni Unida, which was used to mean "university united" (Uni Unida, n.d.). Only about 50 people responded to the summoning (Aguilera, 2019).

It was the murder of Dana, an 18-year-old female student, the case that finally caused more people inside the UACJ to respond. On Saturday April 6 at 3 a.m., her friends enquired about her whereabouts on the Facebook account of their academic program; they asked for help because she had been missing since the night before (Licenciatura en Literatura-UACJ, 2019). By 9 a.m., it was announced that the police had found the body of the student and local news reported that she had been allegedly murdered by her ex-boyfriend (M. López & Silerio, 2019). That day, students began to organize a rally and a subsequent public manifestation against violence, insecurity, and injustice, through Uni Unida's social media—Facebook and Twitter—with the motto: "Podría ser yo, podrías ser tú" [It could be me, It could be you]. To this calling many other students, with a higher proportion of women, responded, by reacting, commenting, and sharing the posts. This was the birth of Uni Unida as a recognized collective.

On Monday April 8, about a 1000 people responded to the calling of Uni Unida, marched and congregated at the Rectory Building to present to the Rector their petitions: to put pressure on the local authorities in order to support the femicide investigation up to the conviction of Dana's murderer; also, they asked for the suspension of classes for the rest of the week to use the time and university facilities for activities to promote social consciousness regarding the violence in the city, particularly, gender violence (Uni Unida, n.d.). In an unprecedented move, the Rector accepted the petitions (Universidad Autónoma de Ciudad Juárez, 2019b). This week can be considered historical for the UACJ, as all activities were organized completely by students, with the participation of some professors who were invited only to talk about the welfare of the university community.

A month later, another case caused a new mobilization of Uni Unida. A female professor accused four male colleagues of having sexually abused her during a party held outside the university (Coria Rivas, 2019; Gallegos, 2019). The collective reached and helped her during the process of filing a complaint; members also accompanied her to talk to the university authorities to ask for the impeachment of the accused professors. As a result, Uni Unida was consolidated as a mixed collective of UACJ students with a core of feminist activists who, nonetheless, wanted to preserve the principle of inclusion of the general student community. Since then, some members have organized or become members of other activist groups, inside and outside the UACJ, with different ideologies and objectives.

Uni Unida and MOFFyL on social media and the evolution of their digital activism

Uni Unida opened its Facebook page on March 7, 2019, after the first members organized the demonstration at City Hall, regarding the alleged abuse of a student by police officers. Their first entries were reposts of news covering the demonstration and the case, where the reactions were limited to the members. According to those who created Uni Unida, this lack of response by the UACJ's community and public provoked a momentary disappointment among them. Nevertheless, after Dana's murder, they quickly re-organized via WhatsApp and used their Facebook page to expand their presence and summon for the rally and demonstration of April 8. On this occasion, the UACJ's community responded, which can be confirmed by the increased number of reactions, which, in turn, contributed to the participation of about a 1,000 people in the public demonstration. This event marked the positioning of Uni Unida as a relevant collective inside the UACJ. One of the members explained that once they achieved the authorities' consent to organize cultural activities, the creation of other social media accounts was essential to reach more students and promote conscientization. They created a Twitter account—@uni_unida—on April 9 and an Instagram account—uni_unidacolectivo—on April 13th. In all its social media, members began sharing pictures, videos, and chronicles about the activities.

Nevertheless, after analyzing the evolution of the posts and reactions on these accounts, it is evident that Twitter and Instagram were not the main platforms to share information and to call for public summoning. The social media of preference by the members of Uni Unida were WhatsApp, for internal organization, and Facebook, for public communication. As of May 14, 2020, Uni Unida's Facebook Page had 5393 likes and 5512 followers; its Instagram account, 120 followers; and its Twitter account, only 12 followers. These are managed by a few members, while WhatsApp groups are operated by other members, depending on the internal commissions. Thus, Uni Unida's Facebook page, following the collective's principles, has become the gate for students and activists to exchange ideas on the problems they find inside the UACJ and society, locally and globally. According to some of the members, Uni Unida has been contacted and received support by local, national, and international collectives of other universities and feminist groups via their Facebook and Instagram pages, even though they did not initiate this contact, a fact that they enthusiastically emphasized during the interview. As a result of this exchange of virtual intercommunication, they added, Uni Unida also has accompanied other collectives in some demonstrations against discrimination and violence of diverse types.

Analyzing the posts and comments, it is evident that the main topic of common interest for all the community is gender violence and, particularly, the systemic violence against women in the city, which has presented itself in the form of sexual harassment inside the UACJ. As the collective began receiving accusations against some professors through its social media, the approval of the Sexual Harassment Protocol by the University Council became one of its main objectives. The collective is constantly using its social media to share information to help victims of violence. It does *tendederos* online and offline or contact victims to offer them help and guidance. Another important activity, according to the interviewed members, is to observe and denounce people or groups who promote violence, misogyny, and machismo through digital media, such as the case of Imperio Alpha, an online club of mostly local men who use WhatsApp groups and a Facebook account to share *packs* or intimate pictures of local women without their authorization.

At the beginning of March 2020, in preparation for the International Women's Day, Uni Unida promoted on its social media the local demonstrations and organized an open conversation at the UACJ's main library in which some of the members shared their stories on how they became feminists. Although the offline activism stopped on March 17, 2020 because of the COVID-19 pandemic, Uni Unida kept using its social media, mostly its Facebook page. On April 5, it published an online demonstration—in the form of a video—in honor of Dana's 1st death anniversary, demanding local authorities to sentence her murderer to the highest punishment regarding the femicide. This video had almost 3000 views and was shared by dozens of people. On May 7, 2020, in the context of Mother's Day, it published a video to support the mothers of murdered and disappeared women in the city.

The collective also uses its social media to make visible other vulnerabilities. In the context of COVID-19 and the change to online classes, it shared the concern for students who did not have the technological tools or the conditions to follow their classes properly. Thus, it asked UACJ's authorities to have empathy and look for ways to support them. Also, it offered help to women who, in the context of the quarantine, found themselves captives in a domestic violence situation.

On another hand, the MOFFyL collective's Facebook page was created on May 15, 2017, a week after Lesvy's murder. As of May 2020, it had 14,702 followers and 13,161 likes. As mentioned above, its creation was based on gender violence at UNAM and the lack of immediate response by its authorities, as well as the absence of a full compliance to the protocol.

During 2017, the page functioned as a medium of diverse activism targeting the FFyL community. The predominant theme was Lesvy's case, with nine publications showing the discontent regarding the course of the legal process of her murder, with #NiUnaMenos and #JusticiaParaLesvy, and calling students to demonstrations and rallies. The members also created Facebook events to form the Organized Women's Assembly, with # ElMiedoNoSeRompeConMásEncierro. It is also noteworthy to mention the posts dedicated to the disappearances of students and of members of the indigenous community. Finally, it is observable a concordance with the events of the CDMX and the internal mobilizations, due to the posts dedicated to the demonstration on November 25, under #25N and #NosQueremosVivas. Despite the constant activity of the page during this year, the posts had a low response from the community, with an average of ten reactions. The exception was a post denouncing a man harassing students in the parking lot of the FFyL, with 74 reactions.

In 2018, this changed drastically. The explanation is the change in the content of the page, focusing on three main functions: harassment complaints in the FFyL, the active strikes, and the disappearance of Vanessa, a student of the FFyL. Firstly, since January 16, the members began to share information about a harassment complaint by a female student toward a male teacher, with #laUNAMrespaldaacosadores and #fueramachosdelaUNAM. Although in 2017 the MOFFyL page already shared complaints, the number increased from 2 to 20 posts, regarding other professors and even students. Secondly, the aforementioned complaint generated a series of active feminist strikes throughout 2018, starting on March 15. Since the first one, the MOFFyL page declared itself as the only truthful medium of information. It shared the activities during the strikes and the support from other local, national, and international institutions to its movement. Thirdly, regarding Vanessa's disappearance, the page registered a total of 11 posts. Although the reactions to these posts were never more than 50, the relevance of the follow-up is that the disappearance of Vanessa will be one of the main elements in the MOFFyL petition sheet during the 2019–2020 strike.

During the first half of 2019, only three posts were registered. It is also noteworthy to mention that although there was a student strike on September 9, only the calendar of activities was shared. This changed dramatically on November 3, with the taking of the facilities; as it was detailed previously, the proposed 12 hours became a student strike that would last until April 14, 2020. The MOFFyL page recovered its function as the only instance of communication with the student community, and it acquired a new one: sharing the various responses by MOFFyL to the FFyL authorities regarding the negotiations. Also, it was on this page where MOFFyL called the entire community to create the petition list. Later, this was published, along with the broadcasting of the press conference where the authorities were notified. Even though the calls to participate in the creation of the petitions had only a couple of dozen reactions, the post regarding the document and its communication exceeds 200. The posts with the most reactions, around 500, were those where MOFFyL responded and clarified the allegations of fulfilment of the petitions emitted by the authorities.

Although there is a page on Twitter, called Mujeres Organizadas FFyL, created in December 2019, which only has 2362 followers, barely a seventh part of the Facebook page, which shows that, as in the case of Uni Unida, the community's preference lies on the original medium. Finally, it should be noted that the trend of reactions has been decreasing since the delivery of the facilities in April 2020, with double digits per post. The post with more reactions after that, with 211, addressed the issue of harassment in online classes and the fact of sharing a space, even virtually, with the victimizers.

After the analysis of the use of social media by Uni Unida and MOFFyL, it is evident that they are of utter importance for the development and success of contemporary social activism inside universities. After comparing the analysis of both collectives, three trends can be found regarding their activities on social media: both opened their Facebook pages after an act of violence against a member of the community or in campus; the peak of the responses from the community toward these pages occurred when the collectives took charge of the activities in campus; and finally, although they eventually created accounts on other social media, the preference of the community lied on the original source of communication, which was Facebook, since this is the most-used social media among young adults in Mexico (Newsroom, 2019).

Conclusion

Since the early 21st century, digital activism has gained relevance. And, as young generations become conscious of their citizen status and they start to involve themselves in social causes, the convening power of digital media has only increased, and its role becomes indispensable for offline activism. After the analysis of Uni Unida and MOFFyL some points are clear regarding the use of social media in today's feminist activism in Mexico.

Firstly, for young Mexican people, it is one of their main channels of communication and to become visible and approachable to the society. Also, it was evident that for social media to become a platform for offline activism, the collective needs to choose the one of preference among the community from which it looks to gain support. In these cases, although both collectives opened accounts on Facebook, Instagram, and Twitter, Facebook was the main platform of communication with UACJ and UNAM students.

Secondly, the Facebook pages were created originally to concentrate the collective members' different expressions toward gender violence and to communicate the taking place of demonstrations. However, when the student strikes took place, the pages became the main source of ideological and political attitudes among the local community. Nevertheless, regarding MOFFyL and CDMX, it is also important to note that when these student strikes ended, the original function of these pages were restored, a situation that was reinforced by the COVID-19 quarantine. In contrast, the Facebook page of Uni Unida remained as a platform of activism in the context of the quarantine, being used to make online demonstrations.

Thus, contrary to the idea that digital activism is mere *slacktivism*, we have demonstrated that, in fact, it is an essential part of offline activism. As the change in societies become gradually dependent on young people's involvement, it is evident that the future success of activism lies in the smart use of social media to organize, summon, and protest.

References

Adler, R. P., & Goggin, J. (2005). What Do We Mean By "Civic Engagement"? *Journal of Transformative Education*, *3*(3), 236–253. Retrieved from https://doi.org/10.1177/1541344605276792

Aguilera, C. (2019). *Se manifiestan estudiantes de UACJ con marcha para exigir justicia.* Cristian Aguilera Blog. Retrieved from https://cristianaguilera17.blogspot.com/2019/03/se-manifiestan-estudiantes-de-uacj-con.html

Ballesteros, K. (2020). Cuarta ola del movimiento feminista: el hartazgo ante siglos de extrema violencia. *Contralínea*. Retrieved from https://www.contralinea.com.mx/archivo-revista/2020/03/08/cuarta-ola-del-movimiento-feminista-el-hartazgo-ante-siglos-de-extrema-violencia/

Brimacombe, T., Kant, R., Finau, G., Tarai, J., & Titifaune, J. (2018). A New Frontier in Digital Activism: Anexploration of Digital Feminism in Fiji. *Asia & Pacfic Policy Studies*, *5*(3), 508–521. Retrieved from https://doi.org/10.1002/app5.253

Castells, M. (2015). *Networks of Outrage and Hope. Social Movements in the Internet Age*. Polity Press, Cambridge.

Coria Rivas, C. (2019). Profesores habrían drogado a maestra de la UACJ antes de violarla. *Excelsior*. Retrieved from https://www.excelsior.com.mx/nacional/profesores-habrian-drogado-a-maestra-de-la-uacj-antes-de-violarla/1314861

De la Cruz, N. (2011). *Mujeres a la cantina*. La Fábrica de Mitos Urbanos. Retrieved from http://www.fabricademitos.com/mujeres-a-la-cantina/

De-la-Garza-Montemayor, D. J., Peña-Ramos, J. A., & Recuero-López, F. (2019). La participación política online de los jóvenes en México, España y Chile. *Comunicar*, *61*, 83–92. Retrieved from https://doi.org/10.3916/C61-2019-07

Elige Red. (2017). *#28S. Un día de lucha por la justicia social para la mujeres*. Red de Jóvenes Por Los Derechos Sexuales y Reproductivos, A.C. Retrieved from http://www.eligered.org/28s-dia-lucha-la-justicia-social-la-mujeres/

Gallegos, R. (2019). Se adueñaron de mi cuerpo, busco justicia: maestra violentada por profesores universitarios. *La Verdad*. Retrieved from https://laverdadjuarez.com/index.php/2019/08/15/se-aduenaron-de-mi-cuerpo-busco-justicia-maestra-violentada-por-profesores-universitarios/

Galván, M. (2019). 2019, el año en que la 'ola feminista' sacudió a México. *Expansión*. Retrieved from https://politica.expansion.mx/sociedad/2019/12/28/2019-el-ano-en-que-la-ola-feminista-sacudio-a-mexico

García, J. (2019). *¿Qué pasa en la Facultad de Filosofía y Letras? Feminismo en la UNAM, una historia*. DesInformémonos. Retrieved from https://desinformemonos.org/que-pasa-en-la-facultad-de-filosofia-y-letras-feminismo-en-la-unam-una-historia/

Gerbaudo, P. (2012). *Tweets and the Streets: Social Media and Contemporary Activism*. Pluto Press, London.

Hernández, G. (2020). Los rostros del #MeToo en México: del acoso a la indignación. *Aristegui Noticias*. Retrieved from https://aristeguinoticias.com/0803/mexico/los-rostros-del-metoo-en-mexico-del-acoso-a-la-indignacion/

Híjar Juárez, C. (2016). La primavera será violeta el #24A. *CN Cimacnoticias*. Retrieved from https://cimacnoticias.com.mx/noticia/la-primavera-sera-violeta-el-24a/

Kowalska, D. (2017). *The Fourth Wave of American Feminism: Ideas, Activism, Social Media* [University of Warsaw]. Retrieved from https://doi.org/10.13140/RG.2.2.25482.36808

La Equipa Editorial. (2020). #8M: Como nunca antes, una potente marcha de mujeres lanza grito contra el machismo y violencia feminicida. *Animal Político*. Retrieved from https://www.animalpolitico.com/2020/03/mujeres-marcha-8m-cdmx-protesta-machistmo/

Lagarde, M. (2006). Del femicidio al feminicidio. *Desde El Jardín de Freud*, *6*, 216–225.

Licenciatura en Literatura-UACJ. (2019). *Licenciatura en Literatura-UACJ*. Facebook. Retrieved from https://www.facebook.com/literaturauacj94/photos/a.497937303727895/1176001455921473/?type=3&theater

López, M. E. (2018). *Femicide in Ciudad Juárez is enabled by the regulation of gender, justice, and production in Mexico.* Retrieved from https://blogs.lse.ac.uk/latam-caribbean/2018/02/15/femicide-in-ciudad-juarez-is-enabled-by-the-regulation-of-gender-justice-and-production-in-mexico/

López, M., & Silerio, M. (2019). Estudiantes de la Universidad de Ciudad Juárez inician paro para exigir justicia por el asesinato de Dana Lizeth. *Animal Político.* Retrieved from https://www.animalpolitico.com/2019/04/paro-universidad-ciudad-juarez-justicia-asesinato-dana-lizeth/

Medina Ramírez, B. M. (2020). *La universidad de la violencia. Feminismo en la UNAM.* Revista Consideraciones. Retrieved from https://revistaconsideraciones.com/2020/02/13/la-universidad-de-la-violencia-feminismo-en-la-unam/

Michel. (2019). Feminicidios y asesinatos en la UNAM resaltan indiferencia institucional. *Plumas Atómicas.* Retrieved from https://plumasatomicas.com/noticias/feminicidios-y-asesinatos-en-la-unam-resaltan-indiferencia-institucional/

Milenio digital. (2019). *Me Too Escritores Mexicanos: denuncian en Twitter acoso y violencia sexual.* Milenio. Retrieved from https://www.milenio.com/cultura/too-escritores-mexicanos-denuncian-twitter-acoso-violencia-sexual

Monárrez Fregoso, J. E. (2000). La cultura del feminicidio en Ciudad Juárez, 1993-1999. *Frontera Norte, 12*(23), 87–117. http://www.redalyc.org/articulo.oa?id=13602304

Monárrez Fregoso, J. E. (2010). The Victims of Ciudad Juárez Feminicide. Sexually Fetishized Commodities. In R. L. Fregoso & C. Bejarano (Eds.), *Terrorizing Women. Feminicide in the Américas* (pp. 59–69). Duke University Press, North Carolina.

Newsroom. (2019). Social media: technopolitics, fake news, and freedom of speech. *El Universal.* Retrieved from https://www.eluniversal.com.mx/english/social-media-technopolitics-fake-news-and-freedom-speech

Notimex. (2020). Por feminicidio de Ingrid Escamilla, convocan marchas en todo el país. *Horas. El Diario Sin Límite.* Retrieved from https://www.24-horas.mx/2020/02/13/por-feminicidio-de-ingrid-escamilla-convocan-marchas-en-todo-el-pais/

ONU Mujeres. (2016). *La Universidad Nacional Autónoma de México se suma al Movimiento solidario para la igualdad de género, HeForShe de ONU Mujeres, y presenta Protocolo de atención a víctimas de violencia de género.* ONU Mujeres México.

Portal de Estadística Universitaria. (2020). *La UNAM en números.* Portal de Estadística Universitaria, UNAM. Retrieved from http://www.estadistica.unam.mx/numeralia/

Priego-Broca, M. T. (2016). La primavera violeta. Una marcha histórica. *La Silla Rota.* Retrieved from https://lasillarota.com/opinion/columnas/la-primavera-violeta-una-marcha-historica/110666

Ramírez, C. (2019). Rafael era amigable y tenía muchos sueños. *El Heraldo de Juárez.* Retrieved from https://www.elheraldodejuarez.com.mx/local/rafael-era-amigable-y-tenia-muchos-suenos-3107325.html

Redacción Animal Político. (2017). #SiMeMatan, la reacción de mujeres ante criminalización de una joven y que llevó a la PGJ a rectificar. *Animal Político.* Retrieved from https://www.animalpolitico.com/2017/05/simematan-feminicidio-mexico-unam/

Redacción Animal Político. (2019). #NoMeCuidanMeViolan: mujeres protestan en estados contra violencia y feminicidios. *Animal Político.* Retrieved from https://www.animalpolitico.com/2019/08/nomecuidanmeviolan-mujeres-protestan-estados-violencia-feminicidios/

Rincón, S. (2019). En UNAM, 921 denuncias por violencia contra mujeres … y 4 llegan a condena. *La Razón*. Retrieved from https://www.razon.com.mx/mexico/a-sentencia-solo-0-4-de-ataques-en-unam/

Rocha, F. (2016). Mi Primer Acoso. *Regeneración*. Retrieved from https://regeneracion.mx/mi-primer-acoso/

Ruíz, M., & Pigeonutt, V. (2019). UNAM: Del feminicidio al fallido protocolo antiacoso. *Pie de Página*. Retrieved from https://piedepagina.mx/unam-del-feminicidio-al-fallido-protocolo-antiacoso/

Silverstone, D. (2017). *Crónicas de Feministlán*. Darina Silverstone. Retrieved from http://darinasilverstone.blogspot.com/2017/12/cronicas-de-feministlan.html

Staudt, K., & Campbell, H. (2008). The Other Side of the Ciudad Juárez Femicide Story. *ReVista Harvard Review of Latin America, Violence*. Retrieved from https://revista.drclas.harvard.edu/book/other-side-ciudad-juárez-femicide-story

Stephen, L. (2012). Epílogo. In G. Cano, M. K. Vaughan, & J. Olcott (Eds.), *Género, poder y política en el México posrevolucionario* (pp. 375–406). Fondo de Cultura Económica, Mexico.

Suárez Gómez, A. (2016). *#RopaSucia: misoginia y machismo en el medio cultural*. Horizontal. Retrieved from https://horizontal.mx/ropasucia-misoginia-y-machismo-en-el-medio-cultural/

Tovar, H. (2019). Investiga FGE presunto abuso de estudiante de la UACJ. *El Heraldo de Juárez*. Retrieved from https://www.elheraldodejuarez.com.mx/policiaca/investiga-fge-presunto-abuso-de-estudiante-de-la-uacj-3132164.html

Turley, E., & Fisher, J. (2018). Tweeting Back While Shouting Back: Social Media and Feminist Activism. *Feminism & Psychology*, *28*(1), 128–132. Retrieved from https://doi.org/10.1177/0959353517715875

Uni Unida. (n.d.). *Uni Unida*. Facebook. Retrieved from https://www.facebook.com/Uni-Unida-393310361463317/

Universidad Autónoma de Ciudad Juárez. (2019a). Agenda Estadística 2018-2019. In *Universidad Autónoma de Ciudad Juárez*. Retrieved from http://www3.uacj.mx/DGPDI/SPCOA/Documents/estadisticas/ESTADISTICAS-2018-19 AO.pdf

Universidad Autónoma de Ciudad Juárez. (2019b). *Comunicado Oficial*. Universidad Autónoma de Ciudad Juárez. Retrieved from http://www3.uacj.mx/comunicacion/noticias/Paginas/Comunicado-oficial.aspx

Varela, N. (2020). *El tsunami feminista*. Nueva Sociedad. Retrieved from https://nuso.org/articulo/el-tsunami-feminista/

7 Latin American Indigenous media productions

Digital artifacts of contestation

Milton Fernando Gonzalez-Rodriguez

Introduction

As this chapter shows, documentaries, fictional, and animated films become nods of communication for the producing and consuming communities online and offline. Underrepresented communities enter media spaces by creating cultural visual artifacts that reflect their canons of production, and that reach audiences through digital platforms. This chapter explores to which extent visual narratives produced by Indigenous communities collectively, and Indigenous directors independently, become spaces of empowerment using formats mainly controlled by non-Indigenous producers. The self-representational nature of Indigenous cinema has emerged as an answer to visual narratives made by non-Indigenous filmmakers, biased in form and content, informed by hegemonic ideologies, and embedded in media traditions that have rarely given prominence to the issues that matter to disenfranchised social groups. The main premise is that the selected visual narratives operate as reflections of how indigeneity enters two media realms simultaneously: cinema and social media.

Two sets of data have been utilized to make inferences on themes and approaches throughout the Latin American Indigenous media landscape. On one hand, the first object of analysis is a corpus of 30 works produced in nine countries across the region (Argentina, Bolivia, Brazil, Chile, Colombia, Ecuador, Mexico, Peru, and Venezuela), and released between 2000 and 2015. These are visual narratives that stand out for making an impact at a local, national, and regional level, not only through screenings, but also through their presence within digital spaces. The second object of analysis is a corpus composed of 508 comments posted by viewers as reaction to media productions conceived and disseminated by self-identified Indigenous directors/communities.

This paper holds the view that the reaction of both local and international audiences to the films through virtual spaces such as Facebook and YouTube, and the interplay between viewers and filmmakers are examples of Purposeful Digital Interaction. Throughout this chapter, this term is used to refer to the processes by which users of digital platforms gain and exchange knowledge about specific issues (e.g. mining, oil leakages, abuse of power), based on information disseminated by the groups that are directly affected. Reactions of social media users reflect the power of digital and visual communication as a tool to demand change or at least to shed light on issues that demand public attention.

Indigeneity and cultural artifacts are other key concepts used throughout this chapter. All along, indigeneity is understood as the self-defined affiliation communities claim to share based on their experiences of abuse, discrimination, and oblivion, but most importantly, based on a shared cultural heritage rooted in pre-European civilizations, and threatened by cultural standardization (De la Cadena & Starn, 2007; Van Cott, 2000, 2007). The producers of the films addressed in this study consider themselves to be Indigenous due to their affiliation to communities where pre-Columbian culture and heritage play a significant role. As for cultural artifact, the term refers to those outputs/products that attest to the set of values, ideologies, and sensitivities of their producing societies (Jones, 2007). Cultural artifacts can be used to make inferences on their producers, their sensitivities, attitudes, worldviews, and mindset. Central to this study is the realization that these communities create visual cultural artifacts they intend to consume, and share with other Indigenous communities, and eventually non-Indigenous audiences. In this sense, it is possible to refer to them as cultural processes, rather than artifacts, or as cultural artifacts in process.

Indigeneity in visual arts

As other formats of artistic expression, cinematic productions are reflections of cultures wrapped in optical narratives that engage and lure the viewers. Increased visibility of films scripted and directed by self-identified Indigenous filmmakers (Córdova, 2011), confirm that there are differences between the "folklorizing" (Ajxup Pelicó, 2015, p. 41) representations supported by hegemonic structures (e.g. *Madeinusa,* Peru, 2005), and visual narratives conceived by peripheric groups (e.g. *Paktara*, Ecuador, 2008). Production of Indigenous Cinema, commonly identified as Fourth Cinema, challenges and dismantles "the very myths undergirding settler nationhood" (Thornley, 2017, p. 202), by fossilizing preconceived ideas about hierarchy and otherness. In varying ways and to varying extents, Indigenous media makers fight against the tradition of producing images that spectacularize or exotify underrepresented ethnic communities (Zamorano Villarreal, 2014). In the process, these visual productions challenge approaches, assumptions and portrayals presented in more traditional and conventional cinematic spaces (Schiwy, 2009). As a rule, Indigenous communities are presented as subaltern, peripheric, and static social groups across Latin American cinema (Gonzalez Rodriguez, 2019; Mateus Mora, 2012; Podalsky, 2011; Soares & Limberto, 2012). In general, the most distributed and screened productions from the region approach indigeneity through fiction. The range of representations is broad, but not until recently has there been an attempt on behalf of non-Indigenous filmmakers to present the figure of the Indigenous beyond the paradigm of a one-sided, distant *Other*.

In line with long-established paradigms, Indigenous characters are portrayed as static figures (e.g. *El abrazo de la serpiente*, Colombia, 2015; *Taínos: La última tribú*, Puerto Rico, 2005), or members of societies dependent on help from external agents (e.g. *El facilitador*, Ecuador, 2013; *El verano de los peces voladores*, Chile 2013; *Feriado*, Ecuador, 2014). In several visual narratives produced by non-Indigenous filmmakers, female figures are exotified (e.g. *Madeinusa,* Peru, 2005; *El niño pez*, Argentina/Paraguay, 2009; *La teta asustada*, Peru, 2009; *Ixcanul* Guatemala, 2015), or portrayed as peripheral characters (e.g. *La Ciénaga*, Argentina 2001; *Nosilatiaj. La belleza*, Argentina, 2012). Thematically, indigeneity-oriented films focus on native communities with limited land rights (e.g. *A terra dos homens vermelhos*, Italy/Brazil 2008), "strange" cultures (*Caramuru*, Brazil, 2001), low social status (*¿Quién mató a la llamita blanca?*, Bolivia, 2007), and perceived isolation (e.g. *Los viajes del viento*, Colombia/Germany/The Netherlands, 2009). At the other end of the spectrum, there have been attempts to represent them as communities with full agency (e.g. *Corazón del Tiempo*, Mexico 2008; *El violin*, 2005, Mexico), strongly connected to nature (e.g. *Yvy Maraêy: Tierra sin mal*, Bolivia, 2013), open to outsiders (e.g. *Defensores de la vida*, 2015, Costa Rica), resilient in spite of difficult social conditions (e.g. *Distancia*, Guatemala, 2011; *El destino*, Argentina, 2006), and perfectly capable of living and thriving in rural and urban areas (e.g. *Roma*, Mexico, 2018; *Siguiendo las estrellas*, Panama, 2010; *Vaho*, Mexico, 2009; *Zona Sur*, Bolivia, 2009).

These attempts to recalibrate some of the canons of representation of ethnic minorities are nevertheless steered by processes of production tightly linked to economic structures and commercial interests; often aligned with trends and criteria determined by film festivals and international networks of distribution. Contrastingly, as the subsequent review of themes found in Indigenous Cinema reveals, a sense of purpose at a communicational level is the main drive behind the creation of self-representational productions.

Taxonomy of themes in Indigenous cinema

By applying Visual Data and Stratified Content Analysis to the corpus of 30 documentaries, short and long fictional narratives, and animated films, it was possible to identify eight common themes Indigenous filmmakers address in their productions: injustice, gender, normality, rites and traditions, mysticism, history, and Indigenous-non-Indigenous relations. Under the topic of injustice, Indigenous filmmakers express their concerns about the inequality in the treatment of their communities, compared to the treatment received by non-Indigenous citizens, especially in terms of land rights and natural resources. This category aligns with observations on how communities, for instance in Bolivia, make use of cameras to educate, inform, and mobilize audiences on topics "made invisible by conventional channels" (Archibald, 2011, p. 173).

In films addressing the topic of injustice, mining projects and oil extraction are presented as the most menacing obstacles faced by the Indigenous communities living in rural areas; particularly in isolated zones. Director Matías Estévez explores in *Hidrofractura: El agua, el aire, la tierra ... la muerte* (Argentina, 2012), for instance, the tensions around the extraction of gas and oil in fragile ecosystems, such as the one in Neuquén. This documentary illustrates the concerns of the Mapudungun communities, and their attempts to denounce the environmental consequences of these profit-driven enterprises. A focal point is that the Argentine government tries at any cost to silence activists and hide leaks and accidents from reaching media outlets. Along the same line, in *Puma chirikuna* (Ecuador, 2012), filmmakers Eriberto Gualinga, Mariano Machain, and David Whitbourn chronicle the legal actions undertaken by the Sarayuku peoples against Lucio Gutierrez's government for allowing oil extraction without previous consent. This Ecuadorean documentary from 2012 explores the value governments attach to oil revenues as opposed to a clean planet.

In varying ways, Indigenous Cinema becomes a platform to denounce projects that threaten the livelihood of fragile communities. Compellingly, visual narratives denounce mining projects (e.g. *¡Y siguen llegando por el oro!*, Colombia, 2012), dubious oil extraction concessions (e.g. *Mari Mari*, Chile, 2011), abuse of power (e.g. *Razón de estado*, Chile, 2009), and human rights violations (e.g. *Justicia sin palabras*, Mexico, 2011). Sergio Julián Caballero in *Por la tierra vivimos* presents the ways in which four communities in Oaxaca respond to the Zaniza mining project plans. Produced in 2012, this Mexican documentary which received attention from all corners of the globe explores the reality of communities built on the biggest iron reserves in Latin America; but also, the hypocrisy behind the hegemonic forces and the connections between national authorities and multinationals.

The second category is gender, and in specific, the exploration of the daily lives of Indigenous women within communities embedded in century-old traditions and stratifications. While many of the selected films pay special attention to the notion of freedom, other focal points include social recognition of LGBTQ Indigenous communities (e.g. *Atempa, sueños a orillas del río*, Mexico, 2013), and the role of women within positions of power (e.g. *Paktara*, Ecuador, 2008). Freedom is central in *Atempa, sueños a orillas del río*. The widely screened documentary explores the story of Tino, a Zapotec boy in his teens who dreams of being crowned as a queen of the Muxe and to celebrate his 15 years of age *quinceañera* style. Despite many obstacles, he manages to leave his troublesome past behind and succeed in his endeavor. For the outside viewer, the story stands out for being one of the few productions that address gender identity issues within Indigenous communities. Due to the collective approach of Indigenous cinema, the film can be considered a pedagogical tool to explore the lack of sexual diversity and tolerance within ethnic minorities. The attention the film received from non-Indigenous audiences influenced its impact within the producing community. Although gender plays a significant role in films produced by non-Indigenous filmmakers, in most cases, they do not address the inequalities between women, men, and third-gender individuals within the social groups they seek to portray.

In *El día de las comadres*, director Wanda López Trelles invites audiences to witness how every year, the day before carnival, Coya women gather to celebrate Women's Day. The Argentine documentary from 2013 explores how Indigenous women seek an opportunity to express their desires, liberate themselves, and free their minds in order to start a new cycle of life. This sense of emancipation is also present in Bolivian *Cholitas con fútbol de altura*. Directed by Franklin Gutierrez Zarate, this short documentary from 2014 revolves around Candelaria and Angélica, the founders of the first Aymara football tournament called Achica Arriba. The widely screened documentary tactically debunks preconceived notions about sports, femininity, and traditional roles. In terms of gender, the contestation aspect of Indigenous Cinema lies in its authority to address unbalances from an insider's standpoint.

The third category identified in the corpus of films, normality, consists of productions that approach issues such as divorce, cooking practices, and work life. Since self-representational films are spaces to reclaim identities (Karakartal, 2006), a significant aspect to them is the portrayal of Indigenous groups as individuals leading "normal" lives (e.g. *Dulce convivencia*, Mexico, 2004; *Cuando te vuelva a ver*, Ecuador, 2008; *Ella*, Ecuador, 2011). The focal point in these stories is to present personal accounts and first-hand experiences of belonging to an ethnic minority through a reflection about daily practices. In the widely acclaimed *Dulce convivencia,* director Filoteo Gómez Martínez gives a glimpse into the daily life of people in Quetzaltepec Mixe from two perspectives. On one hand, it shows how they make *panela*; and on the other hand, how they react to the camera while they are being filmed. Images of people cutting cane, grinding it, and transforming it into a product intend to show the sensitivities linked to food practices. Similar to *Cuando te vuelva a ver* by Humberto Morales, and *Ella,* directed by Frida Muenala, the film defends the notion that daily practices, such as preparing food and working in the land lie at the core of their identity. These are also narratives that focus on the contrivances of marital life, without essentializing Indigenous couples as different from non-Indigenous ones.

The fourth category identified in the corpus is the theme of pre-Columbian cosmologies and cultural heritage. *Kotkuphi* (Brazil, 2012), *Q'uma chuyma* (Bolivia, 2013), and *Minkakuy* (Peru, 2014), are examples of productions that focus on rituals and ceremonies as means to document intimate aspects of Indigenous epistemologies. Self-representational cinema challenges conventional cinematic paradigms by presenting embodiments and expressions of cultural legacy from a first-hand perspective (e.g. *Chiqui Pichay—Wayrachirina*, Ecuador, 2012). In *Kotkuphi*, for instance, director Israel Maxakali gives an account of the series of activities needed to complete the *yamiyxop* rite successfully; a ritual surrounding *yamiy* (spirit of mandioca). This Brazilian documentary from 2012 seeks to show the importance of harvesting, cooking, and singing, as essential tasks that lead to the completion of this important ceremony. Along this line, in *La limpia*, Angélica Alomoto aims to illustrate vividly a ritual known as *chiqui pichay* (*purging*), a ritual that aims at freeing spaces from oppressing forces.

Visual narratives told from the perspective of the performers also include *Apaylla* (Ecuador, 2011) and *Minkakuy* (Peru, 2014). Directed by Diego Cabascango, *Apaylla* focuses on how a young man's new flute reintroduces this instrument into the life of an elderly person. As for *Minkakuy*, the documentary serves as a space to reflect on the old tradition of *minka*—collective work—and how solidarity plays a central role in keeping a community together. Director Fredy Alfredo Canchari Quispo focuses on a grandmother who shares her views on the importance of cooperation over economic resources. Along the same line, Blanca Zapanai exposes in *Q'uma chuyma*, the life an *amauta* (sage) who explains how his community operates, the different traditions they have, and how these are crucial elements of Aymara epistemology. Works portraying tradition from a reflective point of view are attempts to register and disseminate producing communities' "autoverdad" (self-truth) (Karakartal, 2006, p. 13). This applies in particular to films that explore the ways in which Indigenous communities understand the notion of mysticism.

The fifth category identified in the corpus is made up of stories that suggest there is a strong link between native communities and unearthly forces, specifically those supernatural figures that embody Mother Nature (e.g. *Pewma jadkulu*, Chile, 2000). These are mainly visual narratives that revolve around Indigenous cosmologies and the ways in which native communities understand their place in the world. *Ayni, un viaje al futuro* (Bolivia, 2013), for instance, explores the position of native communities from a long-term, futuristic perspective; a rarity in films that address the topic of indigeneity. Directed by Omar Huanca Hermoso, *Ayni* depicts a future where humans have exhausted water resources and cities have become unbearable places to live. In a compelling way, these images are contrasted with the visuals of a rural Indigenous community that has known how to preserve the precious liquid.

The sixth and seventh categories include historical accounts and visual narratives that offer in-depth accounts of the interaction between Indigenous and non-Indigenous societies. On one hand, documentaries such as *Jiisa Wece: Raíz del Conocimiento* (Colombia, 2010), *Inacayal* (Argentina, 2011), *Wachikua: Nuestra Historia* (Colombia, 2014), and *Varayuqkuna* (Peru, 2015), seek to explain the importance of memory for fragile communities that have faced abuse for centuries. A commonality in these productions is a desire to shed light on the truth behind historical events that the "official story" frames from a different viewpoint. Presenting the community's perspective is the main drive of Myriam Angueria and Guillermo Glass in *Incayal,* a documentary that illustrates how and why Argentine authorities portray Indigenous leader Modesto Incayal, even posthumously, as subversive and uncooperative. Through the voices of his descendants, the story sheds light on his mysterious death in 1994. Due to the controversial aspect of the account, it is logical that it emerges from a space of self-representation. Historic films stand out also for a nostalgic approach to pre-Columbian heritage of the communities involved. Epieyu Aranaga, for example, chronicles the history of the Wayuu community throughout the course of six centuries in *Wachikua: Nuestra Historia.* Along the same line, Fredy Alfredo Canchari Quispe, in *Varayuqkuna*, interviews a group of elders about the time when being Indigenous and serving the community were a matter of pride.

The last category consists of stories that seek to illustrate the coexistence of individuals not necessarily sharing similar worldviews, sensitivities, or attitudes. *Jukua'ipamajatü wayuu*, produced by Mauricio Escobar, for instance, introduces audiences into the daily life of the Office of Social Affairs in Zulia State. Indigenous citizens come to the office seeking solutions for their unsettled problems with other members of their communities, but also with non-Indigenous residents of Zulia. The Venezuelan film from 2012 succeeds in showing that there are animosities within groups, often considered overtly homogenous, but also that coexistence requires the acknowledgement of differences, without using them to create hierarchies. Along the same line, *Malki,* directed by Ecuadorian director Narciso Conejo, portrays the friendship between two boys with different ethnic backgrounds. The story bears earmarks of new formats of Indigenous cinema where non-Indigenous figures are also included, not necessarily as catalyzers, but as elements that complement the multicultural reality of the region. Self-representational cinematic productions operate as repositories of heritage and memory, but also as spaces where images are used to reframe collective identities, and innovative ways of appreciating and displaying culture (García, 2006). More importantly, as discussed in the subsequent section, Indigenous Cinema has become a vehicle to purposely communicate, interact, and convey information about the reality of the producing communities (Purposeful Digital Interaction). Reactions of audiences to these visual productions on digital platforms are evidence of their compelling capacity to reach viewers beyond their primary target audiences.

Taxonomy of entries in digital spaces

To determine the ways in which the selected films have created spaces of communicational interaction with audiences, 508 entries in digital spaces have been analyzed. These are comments posted by viewers of the films, and which serve to verify how Indigenous communities across Latin America deploy visual productions in the context of communication. The study of digital data available on platforms such as YouTube and Facebook allows us to make inferences about the ways in which these images are understood, consumed, and received by both Indigenous, and non-Indigenous audiences. Digital spaces create platforms for the exchange of ideas, opinions, and views, but also to enter into a dialogue with others through exchanges that retain their socio-cultural value (Cantijoch, Gibson, & Ward, 2014).

Although it is questionable whether some of the entries are authored by viewers who identify with a group to which they do not necessarily belong—Indigenous or non-Indigenous—the central idea is that Indigenous cinema manages to transmit specific messages, draw attention to a particular story, underline elements of the cultural and social reality of underrepresented communities, and contest images created by non-Indigenous filmmakers. In this sense, the background of the authors of the entries seems irrelevant, although in many cases, it is clear by the context when it is the case (e.g. *estoy tan orgulloso de ser wayuu/I am so proud of being Wayuu*). As Table 7.1 illustrates, there are three main types of posts, subdivided in 13 categories

Table 7.1 Taxonomy of entries by viewers in digital platforms (Facebook and YouTube) ($N = 508$)

Topic of the comment	*Number of comments expressing solidarity with Indigenous communities about issues presented in the films*	*Number of comments disregarding the issues addressed in the films*	*Number of comments expressing antagonistic attitudes about issues presented in the films*
Acknowledgment	123		
Advice about filmmaking		3	
Advice about political approach	19		
Advice about positionality			3
Empathic identification	19		
Interest in Indigenous cultures	30		
Negative views on Indigenous communities			11
Negative views on the film		4	5
Outrage about government policies	98		
Sense of pride	78		
Sense of self-pride	69		
Shame on behalf of a non-Indigenous majority	25		
Tourist interest	2	19	
	463	26	19

according to the topic of each entry. In total, 463 comments express solidarity with Indigenous communities about issues presented in the films, 26 entries disregard the issues shown in the visual narratives, and 19 express antagonistic attitudes toward the producing communities.

The taxonomy of entries confirms that the selected films have generated mainly a sense of acknowledgment among the viewers. For many, these are the first images they see of communities in their actual places of residence, as opposed to staged scenarios, commonly found in films produced by non-Indigenous directors. With 78 entries, the sense of (national) pride is noticeable in comments posted by viewers of all generational groups. This is especially the case when films touch upon the struggle of communities to protect their territories, water resources, and traditions. In like manner, a sense of self-pride is perceivable in the entries posted by members of the communities living in urban spaces, or away from the places they call home. For these viewers, these films have become repositories of memory and culture, but also points of reference and platforms to interact digitally with their communities from a distance.

Since the films are primarily directed to members of the producing communities or other Indigenous groups, there are plenty of examples of spectators who feel proud of their ancestry (e.g. *los indígenas somos únicos/we, the Indigenous people, are unique*). It becomes clear through the posts written by members of Indigenous groups other than the producing ones, that these films are cultural artifacts in process that serve as vehicles for exchange of experiences, knowledge, and contestation in the face of abuse, oblivion, and underrepresentation. A valid observation is that supportive comments are the most popular entries in spaces where these films are advertised, shown, or mentioned (e.g. digital newspapers). In fact, a large number of viewers express their anger and frustration about the role of authorities in protecting these communities and the areas where they live. Mining, oil extraction, and privatization of land are the topics that cause most indignation among the authors of the posts. For many Facebook and YouTube users, the films have become spaces of awareness about the inequalities endured by ethnic minorities, especially those living in rural spaces. Their comments confirm observations (Arreaza, 2010) about the importance of training Indigenous filmmakers, who can eventually document their stories and make them widely available; preferably, according to the users of digital platforms, beyond their communities.

The posts where viewers express interests in Indigenous cultures, and a desire to deepen their knowledge about these minorities are in line with attestations that Indigenous cinema has the capacity of creating awareness and a sense of appreciation that more formal strategies have not achieved. Another type of interest perceivable in the entries is related to the landscapes and distant geographies used as background to the stories. Many express their admiration for these "lugares mágicos" (mystical places) where some of the communities live. Although some of these comments are enhanced with a certain level of exotification, they are mostly entwined with admiration for places that have remained (relatively) unchanged, when compared to urban spaces or more highly frequented parts of the continent. Surprisingly, messages charged with a sense of empathic identification are less common than one might assume, considering the topics discussed in the films. A possible explanation is that the productions denote a sense of agency and empowerment. At various levels, the visual productions are proof that Indigenous communities are collectively struggling for their survival, but also that they lead normal lives, that they are aware of their traditions and that they apparently have a keen sense of identity.

Other categorization includes advice in terms of political approaches, filmmaking, and worldviews. Some of the posts include tips on how to operate the cameras, use of color (e.g. *las escenas son muy oscuras/the scenes are too dark*), or advice about places where the films can be downloaded to increase their dissemination. In terms of positionality and points of view, a few comments suggest that the films could have shown the mainstream side of the story, to allow valid comparisons. At last, only a few negative comments are made on the Indigenous communities producing the films. Some of them are directed to Indigenous communities in general (e.g. *indios perezosos/lazy Indians*), whereas others are about the lack of cooperation in terms of privatization of resources. The most prominent aspect of the posts is that they highlight the attention the films have received, denote that the concerns have been voiced and heard, and show that the productions have reached places far beyond where the Indigenous communities have been able to reach.

Indigenous cinema and purposeful digital interaction

The deployment of codes of aesthetics, at least at a basic level, is assumed to turn a storyline into an experience. This is what ultimately draws audiences into the movie theatres, or as is often the case of Indigenous communities, to screenings organized by the community and to digital platforms where the films are uploaded. An analysis of films touching upon Indigenous communities, therefore, needs to identify the strategies used in the creation and dissemination of the works. To answer the question of how Latin American Indigenous communities deploy films and documentaries in the context of communication, it is essential to understand that the filmmaker–audience binary plays a role in how indigeneity is portrayed. Films produced by Indigenous communities seek to become platforms where themes such as injustice, gender inequalities, the daily lives of ethnic minorities, rites and traditions, historical accounts from an insider's perspective, mysticism, and the relations between Indigenous and non-Indigenous communities are favored. They seek to present stories that have not been heard before, draw attention to topics that are ignored, and more importantly, they attempt to create their own visual narratives.

In the case of Indigenous Cinema, it can be argued that it contributes to the development of producing communities because it allows them to create platforms where they can raise awareness among themselves, among other Indigenous communities in similar situations, and among mainstream audiences who are rarely acquainted with issues that hegemonic channels of dissemination are reluctant to favor. Moreover, the creation of film is the creation of a repository of memory and evidence that strengthen a position vis-à-vis dominant force. After reviewing 508 entries on digital spaces, it becomes clear that the films have a power of dissemination that goes beyond their original target audiences (the producing communities). As Figure 7.1 illustrates, these same entries serve as evidence of Purposeful Digital Interaction in the sense that audiences gained knowledge about key issues (e.g. mining, oil leakages, abuse of power) from the perspective of the groups that are directly affected.

The documentaries, fictional, and animated films work as nods of communication from two standpoints. On one hand, as visual narratives that are digitally available and that allow us to make inferences about their producers, ideologies, and, most importantly, the messages they intend to convey. On the other hand, they generate and elicit sensitivities in the form of digital reactions that prove the messages have been delivered. This is after all the goal of communication. An important aspect to consider is that Indigenous films are mostly conceived as parts of "a *process*, not a product" (Archibald, 2011, p. 173).

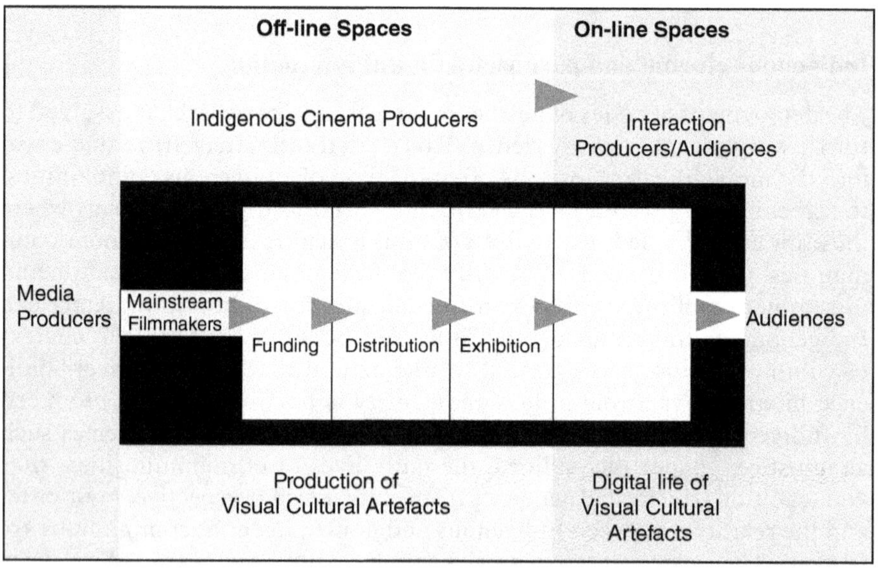

Figure 7.1 Indigenous cinema as an example of purposeful digital interaction.

Conclusion

The main findings of this study are that Indigenous cinema creates films that thematically differ from the visual narratives produced by directors that do not belong to the community they seek to portray, and that the films have an impact beyond the target group. Indigenous films are artifacts of contestation, but at the same time, processes by which these underrepresented and misrepresented communities decide to express themselves, voice their concerns, correct misleading preconceptions, create media spaces for overlooked issues, and choose their own way of telling their stories. These films are also produced collectively, both in terms of content, form, and production. This explains the fact that justice is the most salient theme Indigenous communities wish to address in their works. Out of thirty productions, eight choose to denounce the discrimination, abuse, and inequality ethnic minorities face across the region. The six films that touch upon gender-related issues have as a commonality the portrayal of empowered women. These are stories that convey the notion that being Indigenous and female can be a challenge, but that women are able to overcome adversity and set themselves free. The human side of these communities is a central element in most films, but also the rites, traditions, history, and mystic elements that are part of pre-Columbian heritage. As confirmed in the analysis of digital entries, the films that have the most impact on audiences are the stories that denounce the obstacles Indigenous groups face to protect themselves, their lands, and to safeguard fragile ecosystems.

The relationship between the themes chosen by the Indigenous filmmakers and the reactions of audiences leads us to conclude that their message has resonated among spectators, that their voice has been heard, and that cinema has provided a sense of agency for these often-silenced communities. These reflections also lead to new questions about the future of self-representational cinema. Since filmmaking is becoming a wide-spread practice among Indigenous groups (Schiwy, 2009), perhaps it is possible to imagine a proliferation of online and offline spaces where these visual productions are formally screened. In terms of dissemination, due to the power and accessibility of the Internet, there are few limits to the outreach of visual narratives made by native communities. In terms of format, bearing in mind that Indigenous Cinema is constantly evolving, it is worth asking to which extent Indigenous media producers might be willing to expand the spectrum of topics they address in their narratives. Ultimately, as this review has shown, documentaries, fictional narratives, and animated films are examples of processes that operate as nods of communication and media spaces that propel progress. To gain a deeper knowledge of the processes behind the production of self-representational films, future research might focus on the ways in which Indigenous communities experience their participation in the films. In like manner, eventual studies could assess the role these films play as part of the cultural memory of societies for whom digital repositories are relatively new. Future studies might also include interviews with filmmakers and audiences that explore their views on communication as part of processes of empowerment and agency.

References

Ajxup Pelicó, V. (2015). Contexto social, político y económico de la dinámica guatemalteca actual. *Revista Análisis de la Realiad Nacional, 69*(4), 38–44.

Alomoto C. A. (Producer & Director) (2012). *Chiqui Pichay—Wayrachirina* (La Limpia). [Documentary]. Ecuador.

Angueira, M. (Producer & Director) (2011). *Inacayal* [Motion Picture]. Argentina: INCAA.

Archibald, P. (2011). *Imagining Modernity in the Andes*. Lanham, MD: Bucknell University Press.

Arreaza, E. (2010). Representación del indígena en el cine venezolano de ficción. *Fermentum, 20*(57), 130–150.

Brevis, G. (Producer & Director) (2009). *Aniceto. Razón de estado*. [Documentary]. Chile.

Caballero, S. J. (Producer & Director) (2011). *Justicia sin palabra* (Mute justice). [Short Film]. Mexico: Ojo de Agua Comunication.

Caballero, T. E (Producer & Director) (2013). *Atempa* (Sueños a orilla del rio). [Documentary].Mexico: Infraterra productions.

Canchari, Q. A. (Producer & Director) (2014). *Minkakuy* (Collective work). [Documentary]. Peru.

Canchari, Q. A. (Producer & Director) (2015). *Varayuqkuna* (Ancestral Authority). [Documentary]. Peru.

Cantijoch, M., Gibson, R., & Ward, S. (2014). *Analysing Social Media Data and Web Networks*. London: Palgrave Macmillan.

Colectivo Cineminga (Producer & Director) (2010). *Jiisa Weçe (Roots of Knowledge)*. [Documentary]. Colombia: Cineminga.

Córdova, A. (2011). Estéticas enraizadas: Aproximaciones al video indígena en América Latina. *Comunicación y Medios, 24*, 81–107.

De la Cadena, M., & Starn, O. (2007). *Indigenous Experience Today*. Oxford: Berg.

Epieyu, A. (Producer & Director) (2014). *Wachikua: Nuestra Historia* [Documentary]. Colombia.

Escobar, M. (Producer) & Uriana L. (Director) (2012). *Jukua'ipamajatü wayuu* (Asuntos Indigenas). [Documentary]. Venezuela.

Escuela de comunicación propia Putumayo (Producer & Director) (2012). *Ga'tëya sziaya co'ca, kudumani kat jainui huai, dachi druade embera bedea banduvada ñucata allpa yacuta micham, atun llagta putumayo alpa iakup rimai* (Palabras de Agua). [Documentary]. Colombia.

Espinoza, M. (Producer & Director) (2011). *Mari Mari*. [Short Film].Chile: Complot Estudio Creativo.

Estévez, M. (Producer & Director) (2013). *Hidrofractura: El agua, el aire, la tierra ... la muerte*. [Documentary]. Argentina: TVC Neuquén SOTERMUN-Spain: Unión Sindical Obrera (USO).

García, H. J. (Producer & Director) (2000). *Pewma jadkulu* (El conflicto en el sueño Mapuche). [Documentary]. Chile.

García, J. J. (2006). Video: comunidad y vida/vidéo, communauté et vie. *Cinémas d'Amérique Latine*, *1*, 23–29.

Garcia, J. J. (Producer) & Cabllero, S. J. (Director) (2012). *Por la tierra vivimos* (We live for the land). [Short Film]. Mexico.

Gil, N. S. (Producer & Director) (2012). *Zhamayama: Nuestra música.* [Documentary]. Colombia.

Ginsburg, F. (1995). Mediating Culture: Indigenous Media, Ethnographic Film, and the Production of Identity. In L. Devereaux & R. Hillman (Eds.), *Fields of Vision: Essays in Film Studies, Visual Anthropology, and Photography* (pp. 256–261). Berkeley, CA: University of California Press.

Gómez, M. F. (Producer & Director) (2004). *Dulce convivencia* (Sweet gathering). [Documentary]. Mexico.

Gonzalez Rodriguez, M. F. (2019). *Histrionic Indigeneity* (Doctoral dissertation). University of Amsterdam.

Gualinga, E. (Producer & Director) (2012). Puma chirikuna (Los descendientes del Jaguar). [Documentary]. Ecuador.

Gutierrez, Z. F. (Producer & Director) (2014). *Cholitas con fútbol de altura.* [Documentary]. Bolivia: CEFREC- Telesur D.R.

Hearne, J. (2012). *Native Recognition: Indigenous Cinema and the Western.* Albany, NY: State University of New York Press.

Himpele, J. D. (2008). *Circuits of Culture: Media, Politics, and Indigenous Identity in the Andes* (Vol. 20). Minneapolis, MN: University of Minnesota Press.

Huanca, H. O. (Producer & Director) (2013). *Ayni, un viaje al futuro.* [Documentary]. Bolivia.

Jones, A. (2007). *Memory and Material Culture.* Cambridge University Press.

Kamikia, K., Suya K., Suya W., and Suya K. (Producers & Directors) (2012). *Txejkho Kham Mby (*Warsome Women). [Documentary]. Brazil.

Karakartal, E. (2006). Réinventer un cinéma comme espace de libération et de réappropriation de soi: Récit de l'expérience de l'Atelier Tokapu à Villa El Salvador (Pérou). *Cinémas d'Amérique Latine*, *14*, 3–22.

López, T. W. (Producer & Director) (2013). *El día de las com*adres [Short Film]. Argentina: Itín Productions.

Mateus Mora, A. (2012). *L'Indien: images et conflits.* Paris: L'Harmattan.

Maxakali, I. (Producer & Director) (2012). *Kotkuphi.* [Documentary]. Brazil: Pajé Films. Morales, H. (Producer & Director) (2008). *Cuando te vuelva a ver.* [Short Film]. Ecuador.

Muenala, A. (Producer) & Cabascango D. (Director) (2011). *Apaylla.* [Short Film]. Ecuador.

Muenala, F. (Producer & Director) (2011). *Ella.* [Short Film]. Ecuador.

Muenala, W. (Producer) & Conejo N. (Director) (2008). *Malki.* [Documentary]. Ecuador.

Nahuelpan, H. (2015). Los desafíos de un diálogo epistémico intercultural: pueblo mapuche, conocimientos y universidad. In X. Leyva et al. (Ed.), *Prácticas otras de conocimiento(s): Entre crisis, entre guerras* (pp.159–180). San Cristóbal de las Casas: Editorial Retos.

Plascencia, C. G., & Monteforte, G. (2006). El cine y video en los pueblos indígenas: acciones y reflexiones. *Cinémas d'Amérique Latine*, *1*, 30–34.

Podalsky, L. (2011). *The Politics of Affect and Emotion in Contemporary Latin American Cinema: Argentina, Brazil, Cuba, and Mexico*. New York: Palgrave.

Schiwy, F. (2009). *Indianizing Film: Decolonization, the Andes, and the Question of Technology*. New Brunswick, NJ: Rutgers UP.

Secué, H. (Producer & Director) (2012). *Y siguen llegando por el oro!*. [Documentary]. Colombia: ACIN.

Soares, R., & Limberto, A. (2012). Caras audiovisualmente pintadas: visibilidades e representações em torno da questão indígena. *Rumores*, *6*(12), 39–62.

Thornley, D. (2017). ImagineNATIVE Film + Media Arts Festival: Collaborative Criticism through Curatorship. In S. Tascón & T. Wils (Eds.), *Activist Film Festivals: Towards a Political Subject* (pp. 199–213). Bristol, UK: Intellect.

Van Cott, D. L. (2000). *The Friendly Liquidation of the Past: The Politics of Diversity in Latin America*. Pittsburgh, PA: University of Pittsburgh.

Van Cott, D. L. (2007). Latin America's Indigenous Peoples. *Journal of Democracy*, *18*(4), 127–142.

Wehrheim, M. (2012). Indigenous Cinema. In I. Queipo Maurer (Ed.), *Socio-critical Aspects in Latin American Cinema(s)* (pp. 387–389). Frankfurt: Peter Lang.

Yallico, P., & Gómez, R. (Producers & Directors) (2008). *Paktara* (Cuidado). [Short Film]. Ecuador.

Zamorano Villarreal, G. (2014). Crafting Contemporary Indigeneity through Audiovisual Media in Bolivia. In H. Gilbert & C. Gleghorn (Eds.), *Recasting Commodity and Spectacle in the Indigenous Americas* (pp. 77–95). London: School of Advanced Study, University of London.

Zapana, B. (Producer & Director) (2013). *Q'uma chuyma* (Clean Heart). [Documentary]. Bolivia: CEFREC-CAIB.

8 Digital media in citizen participation and collective action for spatial justice

Laura Pinzón Cardona

Introduction

The supposed omnipresence of Information and Communication Technologies (ICT) raises questions of potential transformation in the relationship between citizens and their governments, as suggested in the aims of this book. This chapter explores that relationship, looking at the case of Manizales, Colombia, and more specifically, between local government and collective actions contesting urban planning practices. Thus, the following sections explore two equally important questions. Firstly, how do governmental initiatives around citizen participation and digital innovation relate to the everyday life of social organizations seeking a more democratic way of planning the city? Furthermore, what are the roles and implications of digital and non-digital media in collective action toward spatial justice?

Manizales is a medium-sized city in the Colombian Andes. Like in many other countries in Latin America, government programs in Manizales seem to be responding to national and international expectations to innovate. They are doing so in the uses of technology, not only for urban infrastructures, but also in public management and citizen participation. The city has been recognized by national institutions like the ICT Ministry and by international standards (Luna, 2015) as one of the leading municipalities in the country, in terms of efforts around digital engagement and social progress. Given this context, Manizales provided a fitting example to illustrate the local level of urban struggles. To do so we examined the everyday life of citizens who clamored for more inclusive ways to construct the urban in a city that portrays itself as participatory and innovative. Moreover, to understand the use and potential innovation of digital media in social movements in a Latin American city, the initial focus needs to be placed on the most popular platforms of social media. Therefore, those that can penetrate the everyday routines of the lowest-income sections. These are typically the places where participation, seeking to affect city transformation, is needed the most.

This chapter starts with a short description of critical elements of Manizales' context for a better understanding of the analysis and conclusions. The next section briefly explores the methodology that formed the basis for this chapter.[1] Following this, two sections address the two questions as discussed in the introduction. This is followed by an analysis around power imbalance in innovation and participation, and the importance of digital and non-digital media in collective action to reflect on broader urban studies of this kind. Finally, conclusions offer key points and reflections from the development of the research.

Manizales

For a great part of the last century, Manizales was a major center for coffee and other agricultural production in Colombia (See figure 8.1). Today, the city is also known nationally and internationally because of its cultural industry, and it is becoming increasingly recognized as a tourist destination (See table 8.1). Additionally, there are fifteen higher education institutions in Manizales, including three important public universities. It receives thousands of students from cities near and far, and by 2017, it was reported that there were over 46,931 university students in the city. (MCV, 2018). In comparison

Figure 8.1 Manizales, Colombia.

Table 8.1 Manizales, Colombia. 2019

Population	400,154 by 2018 (Projection by DANE, 2019)
Year of foundation	1849
Economy	Coffee, higher education, agriculture, technology services, tourism, cultural industry
Unemployment rate	13.6% by February 2019 (CIE-Manizales, 2019)
Poverty rate	13.8% by February 2017 (Ibid.)
Informality rate	40.0% by February 2019 (ibid.)

to other Colombian cities, Manizales was recognized as one of the most desirable cities to live in according to El Tiempo (2015). Living in Manizales was reputedly less expensive than in bigger cities such as Bogota or Medellin, where transportation, education, and housing prices tend to be higher.

The city's governance model for the last 30 years could be described as technocratic, one that deals with city management based on a top-down business model (Acebedo, 2014; Carrion & Erazo, 2016). In this context, Manizales also presents a model of urban entrepreneurialism (Harvey, 1989), where the city's government is shaped by and serves private interest over the needs of its citizenry. It is also one where welfare and wealth distribution goals rest on the facilitation of economic development for local businesses.

Methodology

The research on which this chapter is based was conducted between 2016 and 2019. There was a year of digital ethnography (Kozinets, 2015), and five months of participant observation in the city, including interviews and perception exercises. Digital ethnography, or Netnography, involved following key actors and urban collectives on social media, particularly Facebook and Twitter, while producing notes and a record of the experience. Moreover, researchers became members of four group chats on WhatsApp and helped coordinate a Facebook page related to the sub-cases of study (see below). The ethnographic exercise was mostly developed with social leaders and supporters of the collectives who participated in the research. In addition, the interviews gained insights from the point of view of the local government, third sector, and academia.

The research looked into three socio-territorial movements in Manizales, as sub-cases of study exploring complementary trends of digital and non-digital media in the relations between discontent citizen collectives and local government. The movements studied shared a common general disagreement with decision-making processes in the city, and they were born out of local conflicts where citizens fought for social, spatial, and environmental justice. Due to the limited length of this chapter, it will not elaborate on the particularities of each sub-case. Instead, it will draw attention to the crucial findings from the group of participants as a whole, which is particularly relevant as most of the collectives and individuals participating in the research were involved with two or all three sub-cases. Thus, this chapter explores Manizales as a case study, framed by these socio-spatial conflicts and between 2017 and 2018 as the time when the fieldwork took place.

Despite the former annotation, it is important to get a brief context from each of the sub-cases, for a better understanding of the following sections. The first sub-case was a socio-territorial movement acting as a form of resistance against an unfinished macro-project for urban renovation near the city center, in the San Jose commune. The project had run for over 10 years, was poorly implemented, affecting over 5000 families. It left many homeless while they waited for the payment or the promised new units. Citizen groups in San Jose appealed for recognition as victims and compensation for the affected families. They also called for a reformulation of the project, in an inclusive and socially responsible manner. The second socio-territorial movement was a convergence of collectives, NGOs, individuals, and academics in opposition to a change of land use from green buffer to urban expansion, and the related permits for a housing project in the boundaries of a natural reservoir outside Manizales. The reservoir Rio Blanco supplies the city with 30% of its drinkable water and it is recognized nationally for its biodiversity. The convergence "*Todos somos Rio Blanco*" condemned the change of land use and the allocation of building permits for the housing project as dubious and unconstitutional. They advocated for a new environmental assessment, legal action to be taken by the city against the project developer, reparations for the ecological damage, all while arguing for more participation in decision-making about land management in the city. The third sub-case was a continuous conversation about the Right to the City and the different meanings that civic collectives gave this concept in their own struggles. It started as a weekly series of conversations in the Plaza de Mercado Popular. Leaders from some of the collectives soon defined the need for more spaces of encounter and exchanges among civic groups in Manizales. Bearing in mind this need, we co-designed a workshop in commemoration of the 50th anniversary of the Right to the City, following an international social media call, from the Global Platform for the Right to the City. The initial conversations naturally grew into a movement, becoming a space where collectives kept meeting regularly.

Perceptions from the field

The many conversations and interviews carried out during the fieldwork exhibited a significant heterogeneity of views, opinions, roles in relation to digital innovation, participation, and collective action in the city. With the aim of translating such variety in a brief manner, Table 8.2 gathers some of the most pertinent positions that are often contradictory or complementary to each other. Perceptions are grouped into three columns representing the source of the various participants. The first column lists the common perceptions from participants working in governmental institutions such as the Planning Office, the Secretary for ICT and Competitiveness, the

Table 8.2 Perceptions from the field

Topics	*Municipal officers*	*Participants from socio-territorial movements*	*Supporters of participation*
Digital innovation	• Manizales was leading citizen participation, employing multiple channels of digital and traditional media. • Manizales was recognized nationally for their use of social media (Facebook and Instagram, WhatsApp and Twitter) despite not having the budget for a specialized team. • Innovation programs in the Secretary of ICT and Competitiveness were aimed at local business development and education.	• Digital innovation did not reach marginal communities. Large parts of the city had no access to the internet on a regular basis. • Technology investment in the city was based on private interests. • Some citizens lacked skills to integrate digital and social media into their everyday life. • Younger participants perceived "digital innovation" as the development of their own capacities to create and share content in diverse platforms (i.e. self-taught video editing for YouTube, or using Canvas to design posters and invitations).	• There was interest from the city in digital innovation, but efforts were focused only on elites. • Despite the development model of "Manizales as a city of knowledge and technology," the most visible outcomes were motivated by private interests and the benefit of external investment. One outcome was a complex of call centers, and the second outcome was the National research Centre for Bio-informatics and Computational Biology (BIOS), which is arguably the most important initiative of science and technology in the country, but has no connection to social problems in Manizales. • Rankings showing Manizales at the top of social progress and innovation were based on manipulated data. Grounded research challenging the city's reputation was usually silenced.

(*Continued*)

Table 8.2 Perceptions from the field (*Continued*)

Topics	*Municipal officers*	*Participants from socio-territorial movements*	*Supporters of participation*
Citizen participation	• The Plan for Territorial Management (*POT—Plan de Ordenamiento Territorial*) as well as the creation of the Women's Secretary were two examples given of good practices in participatory processes. • By law, there were several instances of participation during the POT design. However, the Planning Secretary decided when and whom to invite. • Manizales received national recognition for their participatory mechanisms in the creation of the Women's Secretary. They asked people several questions via multiple channels including social media, telephone, SMS, and face-to-face surveys. The municipality defined the mission and programs of the new secretary based on people's opinions.	• Citizen participation was perceived as institutional events with topics and mechanaisms already defined. Such events tended to be only informative. • Institutions tended to misuse citizen participation in search of political recognition to manipulate people's opinions in support of prefabricated decisions. • Exploring participation took them to the realization that social interests from the government and the community are completely different, being the reason why participation (as understood by the government) cannot be enough. • Some expressed more trust and interest toward participatory mechanisms related to political control; these are legal tools established by the National Constitution. Since citizens initiate the production of such spaces, governmental representatives often assumed a defensive or evasive response, complicating the chances for a constructive debate.	• Municipal initiatives are short, restrictive for the majority, but also permissive to a few privileged, according to their interests and the private interests of strategic allies. The municipality is not interested in citizen participation that is not under their control. • Lack of awareness about formal participatory mechanisms of political control, particularly among younger leaders. • Participation without enough information to argue against the power structures was a weak form of participation.

Collective action	• Some referred to collective action as activism (with a negative connotation of destructive opposition). • For some, citizen collectives had the capacity to propose solutions. Collective action however, was not seen as citizen participation without a prior invitation from an institutional initiative.	• Frustration with the status quo led citizens to work on alternatives that moved beyond protesting into assuming a political role by proposing other possible solutions. • In Colombia, the possibility of transformation must go hand-in-hand with social pressure. • There is a need for training and education so collective action can intervene directly in decision-making. • Citizen's collectives need to work together. One of the causes of disconnect and mistrust is due to corruption at very local levels (i.e. political favors in Community Action Committee).	• Some saw Manizales society as conformist and apathetic to contest government, as a result of decades of boosterism and cultural expectations for high sense of belonging. • Collective action in the last decade brought the topic of city planning as a new matter of public debate. • Organized collectives were generally reactive but willing to offer proposals and collaboration. • Citizen organizations, when weak, had been the usual targets for politicians in electoral campaigns (i.e. buying votes, political favors). • Issues around environment, heritage, diversity, public space, and spatial justice were among the most common motivators for collective action.

Municipal Press Office, and the Online Government Office. The middle column lists perceptions of participants who belong to one or several of the socio-territorial movements. Finally, the third column includes the perceptions gathered from a group of varied participants from academia, private, and third sector. I term this group "supporters," since they have collaborated on several joint projects, despite not necessarily being members, leaders, or activists in the social movements.

Relations of governmental initiatives and the everyday of collective action

This section deals with the question of how governmental initiatives around citizen participation and digital media uses relate to the everyday of social organizations that seek more inclusive ways of planning the city of Manizales. In order to identify such relations, it is important to recognize the initiatives from Manizales municipality around innovation and participation, while examining the possibilities and limitations in improving the environment of local democracy and citizen engagement.

As mentioned earlier in this chapter, Manizales was gaining recognition for their practice of citizen participation using multiple channels, and due to their presence and activity on social media platforms such as Facebook, Twitter, and WhatsApp. The sixteen secretaries in the city government, the City Council, Mayor's Office, Press Office, Municipal Comptroller Office, and Ombudsman Office had official accounts on Facebook and Twitter, and the directors of such offices are in daily communication through various WhatsApp groups. According to one interviewee from the Press Office, some offices were more active than others on social media, and some struggled to add content or interact through their accounts on a daily basis. Furthermore, the ten people in the Press Office, who in practice were mainly responsible for social media uses, were mostly overworked. From my interviews, it became apparent there was an assumption among the municipal officers that having more digital channels would immediately increase and improve communication with more citizens. This approach however neglected the existing issues of accessibility and digital illiteracy within marginal sections of the population. It also appeared to give the impression that opinions and interactions that took place on those platforms were representative of the majority of the population, which resulted in a poor understanding of the ways in which platforms like Facebook govern the communication of organic content (not paid or promoted),[2] independent of the organization type.

Going back to the city initiatives, since 2000 Manizales incorporated the city model of "Manizales, a center for knowledge" in urban policies and development plans. Each following government slightly changed the name of the model, but in principle, it remained the same. Manizales wanted to use its many universities and students as a competitive asset to become a national center for innovation. However, the city model produced few tangible results which improved the quality of life of its citizens, particularly for students and professionals who graduated from local universities. Two of the most visible, and criticized, projects were the creation of a top-level research center for bioinformatics and computational biology, called BIOS, whose principal clients and associates were big national and international companies and research centers from local and regional universities. The second project (also mentioned in Table 8.2) was perhaps more controversial. It was the creation of policies and benefits for the establishment of a complex of call centers in the city. Despite the promises of economic development and regional connectivity associated with this project, people had a common complaint about the low quality of the contracts versus the excessive demands of the job. Some participants also claimed this project had nothing to do with Manizales as a center of knowledge, and that it was primarily a result of private interests and political favors.

> [T]hey proudly said; "this is the city of call-centers," and I found that offensive! It is maquila! They [people working there] were teenagers doing shifts from 10pm to 6am and then heading to class. Now, the moment these companies find somewhere cheaper to set a call-center in a different place [...] they would close the "sheds," unplug everything and off they go. What does it leave for Manizales? Nothing at all! It does not leave knowledge; it does not leave infrastructure."
>
> (Participant, academic)

Going back to the question for this section, what was found in Manizales was a relationship of limited interests. In other words, efforts from the local government, around citizen participation and digital innovation were in place to follow national standards and regulations. However, the biggest investments from the city around participation and innovation seemed disconnected from the most visible problems that were emphasized by urban contestation. Thus, what seemed to be the source of pride in the municipality for their recognition around good practices for citizen engagement, appeared to have no meaningful impact in the everyday life of civic groups who were fighting against spatial injustices, and for more opportunities to participate in planning decisions. Participants from socio-territorial movements in Manizales asserted that the presence of the Municipality on social media was not changing the dynamics of their communication. They reported that government representatives were careful not to engage in discussing sensitive topics on Facebook or Twitter; sometimes they got superficial answers from the Mayor or municipal officers, at other times their questions were not addressed at all.

Drawing from conversations with city government representatives, it seemed that there were more than one possible reason contributing to the poor relationship between governmental initiatives and collective action in

Manizales. It would be simplistic to attribute this issue only to the lack of political will, particularly in a government who insisted that they were doing their best to improve citizen engagement. Nevertheless, the participants felt no connection, and indeed none was found, between political interests in the city and directing technological innovation toward transforming the local landscape of democracy, especially around collaboration between civic movements and institutions. Therefore, the deficiency of political will in this sense was indeed a key reason behind the problem.

Another possible explanation lies in the various interpretations about citizen participation in Manizales. For the local government, the meaning of participation seemed to imply a controlled and temporary exercise initiated by the Municipality; a role traditionally noted in the literature as a main limitation in citizen participation (Arnstein, 1969; Korn & Voida, 2015). This understanding cannot possibly recognize citizen-initiated actions as participatory, thus all other initiatives outside governmental interest, including those recognized as legal forms of participation for political control, fall into categories of political opposition and activism. These last two aspects could naturally relate to collective action; however, in the Colombian context these terms generally carry a negative connotation, which in turn seems to justify the inability of governments to include the difference into their programs. The way the government of Manizales dealt with participation showed no possible room for dissent toward a collective construction of the city.

There is another possible cause, which is simultaneously a consequence, of the limited interest from the government in digital innovation and citizen participation. It is about the narrow role given to social media and digital technology; a role that primarily digitalizes old procedures for the sake of efficiency and liability (Foth, Brynskov, & Ojala, 2015). Despite finding people in government with the interest to explore and expand the possibilities that digital media can allow, the obstacles in practical terms came to be a deficiency of institutional capacity and resources, versus the expectations of results according to national standards. Manizales government, due to its size, was granted only a small team of journalists to manage communication and press, a group that was also in charge of everything related to social media. From what was observed, such officers were as active and resourceful as their roles expected them to be, but their work on multiple social media platforms was limited to an amplification of old systems for petitions, claims, and complaints. Without doubt, this was seen by many as an improvement in the communication; however, it could not transform citizen participation on its own.

Digital media in collective action

When exploring the roles of digital (and non-digital) media in collective action toward spatial justice in Manizales, it was important to begin with defining the most popular media found in the field (presented in Figure 8.2).

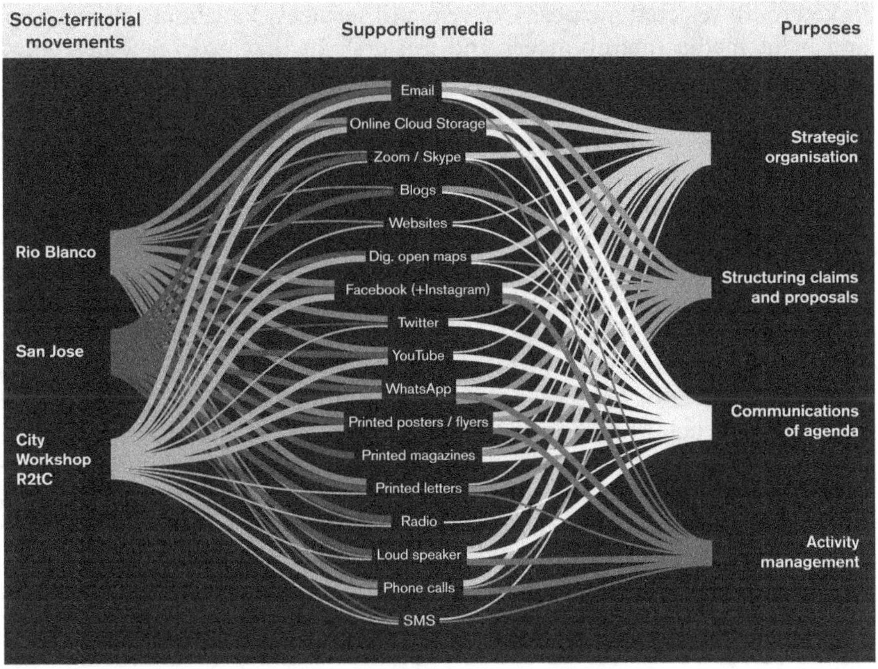

Figure 8.2 Fluvial diagram of media uses and purposes in relation to collective action for spatial justice in Manizales. (Author.)

Simultaneously, the reasons behind favorite media platforms in connection with specific purposes were established through interviews and conversations. For example, leaders from San Jose used Facebook to connect with larger audiences in and out of the city, while recognizing that this platform was not ideal for communicating with people inside of their neighborhoods. This situation seemed to be related to major issues of accessibility and digital illiteracy in the area. In contrast, the most efficient methods to transmit a message quickly to the whole community included printing posters for strategic spaces such as parks, churches, or bakeries, and walking the streets making loudspeaker (or megaphone) announcements.

The diagram in Image 2 shows connections found in the data between types and uses of media and the crucial activities of collective action grouped into four purposes. The lines on the left show the different types of media used by the three socio-territorial movements studied in Manizales, and lines on the right show the purposes in connection to such uses. Thicker lines represent a stronger presence of connections in everyday life.[3]

Following the connections with the elements in the media column, in Image 2, there are a few distinctive features to highlight. The media channels that were frequently used by all the socio-territorial movements, and linked to all selected purposes, were email services, Facebook, WhatsApp, and print media (mainly flyers and posters). In that order, media linked to online cloud storage (i.e. Google Drive or Dropbox), printed letters, video-conference services such as Skype or ZOOM, and loudspeaker, were also frequently used by the participants, although not necessarily for all purposes. To some surprise, the use of Twitter and blogs, while important to some participants in their routines, were not described as deeply relevant for collective action in general. Similarly, websites seemed to be at risk of extinction. One possible explanation might be the prominence that Facebook has gained as the dominant space for updated information and news according to the collectives studied. This in turn makes the maintenance of a website an unnecessary and time-consuming effort.

In the connections between uses of media and purposes for collective action, it is crucial to understand that factors of time, economy, culture, political events, and even individual choices can create very different readings, even in the same case study. Preferences among generational groups can also change the way of interpreting what the most relevant media is for a particular purpose. For example, older participants from the collectives tended to prefer calling someone on the phone before reaching out to them through Facebook or WhatsApp. On the other side, younger leaders would leave a phone call as the last resource for reaching a person. Additionally, behaviors and good practices of different media were perceived in varied manners among groups and individuals, showing noticeable differences between younger and older participants. Older participants involved in social movements were usually more organized and structured during meetings in comparison to younger leaders, yet this last group tended to be more disciplined in online group conversations on WhatsApp and Facebook Messenger. Some older participants would use these scenarios to share content unrelated to the purpose of the groups, obstructing the flow of online conversations more frequently than younger participants did. However provocative these observations are, it is important to clarify that this topic would require a whole research project to explain the nature of the differences and complementarity. Furthermore, findings in this matter are simply a reflection of our perceptions in studying Manizales during a specific period.

Being aware of, and balancing, the particularities and common habits of the participants around using various media allowed us to conclude the following as the key roles of digital and non-digital media in collective action toward spatial justice in Manizales.

Connecting and visualizing citizen initiatives

Connectivity and the amplification of communication are characteristics of digital media frequently mentioned in studies and literature (Castells, 2009; Foth et al., 2015; Sassen, 2015; Shirky, 2009). Despite this being obvious, it was important to test the extent to which these attributes were potentially transforming collective action. Early in the fieldwork, we realized that a common ongoing project from several collectives was to map and understand the networks of civic organizations in Manizales. This endeavor was born out of a concern about the general disconnection of citizen movements, that were formed around various interests but in essence were reflecting discontent with the status quo. In search for strengthening collective action and structures for social pressure, members of these groups felt it was important to understand backgrounds, fields of interest, political stances, and types of actions from civic organization, independent of their scale. Social media and digital tools allowed the exercises of mapping and thematic networking to be developed in prompt and efficient ways by several people simultaneously (i.e. sharing an open document online as a work-in-progress data base, or co-managing an open map in Google Maps or Open Street Map). Additionally, collectives defined a range of groups with similar interests, and these became target contacts who could share and repost each other's content on Facebook, Instagram, WhatsApp, and Twitter. Thus, this not only increased the connectivity but also contributed to amplifying relevant information to wider networks. Intentions of inclusion and collaboration found limitations innate to social relationships. It seemed that personal discrepancies, the fear of competition for scarce resources, and differences in political stances were the principal obstacles in networking efforts.

Reaching out to promissory allies

Social media facilitates exchanges with individuals and organizations beyond geographical boundaries, a well-known attribute of digital communications that did not come as a surprise in the case of Manizales. However, through this research we gained insight into the ways in which such connections could become strategic in a socio-territorial movement's agenda, particularly in the cases of Rio Blanco and San Jose. Rio Blanco was a movement that evolved quickly, gaining supporters in various sections of society in the city. In about a year, they managed to take concerns about the Rio Blanco reservoir outside Manizales to various political and academic scenarios. Arguably, two of the most crucial events were their participation in an international forum about the natural environment in Bogota,[4] and the continuous exchange of communications that they had with the Regional and the National Attorneys. During the international forum, members of the Rio Blanco movement presented their case and used the chance to make their struggle visible to potential allies, some of whom could influence local authorities in Manizales. Additionally, they contacted recognized public figures (among them, Carlos Vives, a Grammy—award—winning artist and Nairo Quintana, a recognized gold-medal winner racing cyclist) to share information about Rio Blanco with them and to pose for photographs and videos with flyers of the movement. Furthermore, the support from the Regional and the National Attorneys manifested in communications commanding a formal response from the city government about citizens' demands, that asked planning authorities to cancel building permits of the housing project next to the reservoir. The argument taken up by this paper is not to suggest that such influential contacts were only possible because of digital and social media, instead we acknowledge that personal contacts and the participation of academia played a key role. However, the frequency and quality of audio-visual content created by amateur members, and shared on social media, were crucial for this very local movement that quickly became visible not only in the society in Manizales, but also outside the region, going beyond merely transmitting a message to gain attention for the alliance in an overloaded information sphere.

Adding a layer in the search for legitimacy

In comparison to the previous roles presented, this one surfaced unexpectedly from the analysis of the case. It seems that having more tools to access information and create content play a role in the pursuit for legitimacy in collective action. The integration of digital media into daily routines allows not only for the visualization of locally curated content to support citizens' demands, but to also reach scientific and technical information to support their petitions or proposals. This, in turn, can empower civic groups to defend their demands with more confidence during public debates with authorities. However, the extent to which this role is influencing social movements in positive or negative ways needs to be studied locally, considering existing relationships of power around decision-making in the city. In the case of the socio-territorial movements in Manizales, the research showed high levels of commitment from the groups to back local claims with policies, regulations, socio-economic surveys, and academic and technical studies, mostly facilitated by the relationship with local students and academics. Despite these notable efforts, in two interviews with municipal officers, and one with a representative from the third sector, interviewees perceived processes of contestation in the city as generally weak and argued that an informed type of participation could strengthen it. It seemed that highlighting a social or spatial injustice was not enough to start a serious conversation with authorities in Manizales. Now that "everybody" had the tools to do more, citizens were indeed expected to achieve more for their demands to increase levels of legitimacy. Thus, one wonders whether having more access to information is empowering social movements or diminishing the importance of citizen claim as the basis for contestation.

The quality of the material produced and gathered in support of the socio-territorial movements in Manizales was an effort applauded by nationally and internationally prominent figures advocating for citizens' rights. Some of whom became crucial allies to put pressure on the local government, as explained in the earlier section.

"Knocking down technology from its pedestal"

While efforts around digital innovation from the municipality were described by numerous participants during fieldwork as intended for privileged sections of society such as academia, local industry, and external investment, we found a few (but promising) cases of young independent collectives encouraged to "knock down technology from its pedestal," as one participant described the objective of her collective. What they meant was to place digital technology closer to people's needs and according to their capabilities. In other words, they worked with people in marginalized communities, sharing with them how to use audio-visual techniques, which seemed high-tech and complex to many, as a simple and affordable way to support social movements. Some of their projects included tools such as video-mapping and digital interactive installations. While doing workshops using these tools, a common obstacle appeared to be that the level of digital literacy and access to digital devices was poorer than what they expected in low-income groups. Limitations of this nature made it clear to us, in agreement with some of the participants' views, that the critical need of digital innovation projects today, ideally from the government but also effectively from independent collectives, is to aim at and develop digital literacy in marginalized communities. Only in this way, can new technologies transcend the media hype and become a resource in closing informational and justice gaps in the city.

Concluding remarks

The first question explored in this chapter outlined the links between governmental initiatives, around participation and digital innovation, and the everyday life of collective action in Manizales. We name the findings as a relationship of "limited interest," where efforts from local government responded to private interests and the competitive pressure to excel using digital and social media, without going much beyond a mere digitalization of traditional services of petitions, claims and complaints, and broadcasting.

Furthermore, the big problem around local democracy, digital innovation, and the just development of the city have not been addressed by urban policies or the allocation of resources. While local governments in Latin America take refuge in the assumption that digital and social media use can improve our cities, and the relationship between government and citizens, in effect the conflict between power and interest, remains unresolved. Clay Shirky (2012), who studies the interrelations of the Internet technologies and the shape of societies today, has a claim that the case of Manizales helps to illustrate. Shirky states that people with the power to experiment and innovate in citizen participation are not interested in doing so, and those who are interested and experimenting, within their own limitations, have no legislative power to produce sustained change (Ibid.). Moreover, if we explore that conflict between power and interest at higher levels where the Internet and popular platforms of social media get shaped, we would find that the results respond to the needs of corporations and governments (MacKinnon, 2012), which may, or may not, be interested in opening technology to support a meaningful transformation in democratic processes. The question about the possibilities for citizen initiatives to impact spaces where the Internet is structured was outside the scope of the research here. However, it is not a matter far from urban studies; rather it is closely related to the future of socio-territorial movements in the city. Drawing from this research, we believe that academia and independent creative collectives play a crucial role in collective action. However, academics interested in innovating participation can partake more significantly by challenging structures with lawmaking power in the city, particularly in places where innovation efforts are reduced to merely the benefit of elites.

The second question in the chapter addressed the roles that digital media played in collective action promoting spatial justice in Manizales. There, we found that digital media acted in the capacity of enhancing the mapping and visualizing of collective action in the city, gaining attention and support from strategic allies, and placing technology closer to the needs of marginal communities. Additionally, we urged critical examination of the impacts that digital media could potentially have in the pursuit of legitimacy. For years, authors like McCullough (2005) and more recently Sassen (2015), and Horelli et al. (2015), have highlighted the social responsibilities of digital media in the construction of the city. Drawing from their work, there is a common call to contemplate the potential impacts of digital technologies as either improvement or detriment of inclusive processes of space-making. In other words, digital media that is accessible and approachable even by the poorest communities can potentially lead to positive innovative transformations, where technology finds its place closer to people's needs, responding to local particular conditions, as McCullough (2005) highlighted. On the other hand, the promotion of digital media as protagonist in the relations between citizens and government, in a city where vast numbers have limited or no access to digital interactivity in their everyday, is an endeavor that can certainly broaden the gap between those traditionally included and excluded.

When it comes to examining possible implications of digital media uses for collective action, in relation to matters of spatial justice and the Right to the City, the findings suggest new dynamics at play in the protocols and strategies of communication between socio-territorial movements, partners, and governmental institutions. We consider urban contestation in Manizales an exercise of transgressive citizenship (Earle, 2017) instead of one of complete insurgency. This means that collective action recognizes and uses some governmental structures as a legitimate means to support their agendas (i.e. law for citizen participation, or tools for political control), while also acting in open disagreement with local government programs, and developing alternative proposals in parallel to supply local needs (i.e. appropriation of voids in the city to develop community gardening projects). Such practices, however strategic or situational, translate in the uses of digital media, in addition to non-digital. According to Gladwell and Shirky, people contesting the city use the Internet "to play by different rules than incumbents" (2011: 154). Social media, defined as spaces for deliberation, are not bound (yet) to governmental protocols of participation. This allows collective action to appropriate these spaces as much as the platform design admits them to, allowing them to promote their projects.

This chapter attempted to challenge suppositions of correlation between digitalization, innovation, and democracy, through an angle of inquiry exploring the everyday of collective action at the margins of formal urban processes in the city. Only in this way can questions of equitable access to technology and innovation, digital illiteracy, and strategic and transgressive uses of media be explored beyond the perceptions portrayed by the city government.

Finally, this is an invitation to academics and professionals interested in participatory processes and the uses of digital media to move beyond the hype of technology, recognizing that the digital is only a part of the question, or a part of the solution, which requires critical exploration in trends of communication and social organization. Studying from the "ground-up" would advise us about power imbalances, illusions, and obstacles in local democracy and innovation, while reflecting the significance of existing socio-political relationships, local history, and culture.

Notes

1. The methodology and the sections presented here were part of the author's doctoral research.
2. By their current regulations, none of their content in Facebook could be "promoted," in other words, the Municipality could not pay Facebook to increase the visibility and impact of their content. This meant that only a section of the Municipality's followers would see their activity on their news feed.
3. The data supporting the analysis presented in Image 2 was of a qualitative nature, and the connections and line intensities were the result of an interpretations of the data collected.
4. Pacto Mundial por el Medio Ambiente. Bogota, 2018. Organized by the General National Attorney, Bogota's Chamber of Commerce, Center for Sustainable Investment of Columbia University and the Sustainable Development Solutions Network.

References

Acebedo, L. F. (2014). Del derecho a la ciudad a la justicia especial. Indignación y Resistencia contra los macro-proyectos urbanos como negación de la función social del urbanismo. *V Congreso Internacional Derecho y Sociedad. Por un pensamiento latinoamericano*. Universidad de Manizales, Colombia.

Arnstein, S. R. (1969). A Ladder of Citizen Participation. *Journal of the American Institute of Planners*, *35*(4), 216–224.

Carrion, F., & Erazo, J. (2016). *El derecho a la ciudad en América Latina: Visiones desde la política*. Universidad Nacional Autónoma de México. International Development Research Centre IDRC. CLACSO

Castells, M. (2009). *Communication Power*. Oxford: OUP Oxford.

CIE-Manizales. (2019). *Indicadores Manizales*. Centro de Información y Estadística—CIE. Alcaldía de Manizales. Retrieved from http://cie-sigalcmzl.opendata.arcgis.com/

DANE. (2019). *Dirección Nacional de Estadística*, Presidencia de la Republica—Colombia. Retrieved from https://www.dane.gov.co/

Earle, L. (2017). *Transgressive Citizenship and the Struggle for Social Justice. Studies of the Americas*. Palgrave Macmillan London, UK.

El Tiempo. (2015). Manizales, la mejor ciudad para vivir en Colombia. *El Tiempo news*. Retrieved from http://www.eltiempo.com/bogota/manizales-mejor-ciudad-colombia-encuesta-red-de-ciudades-como-vamos/16446764

Foth, M., Brynskov, M., & Ojala, T. (2015). *Citizen's Right to the Digital City: Urban Interfaces, Activism, and Placemaking*. Springer, Singapore.

Gladwell, M., & Shirky, C. (2011). From Innovation to Revolution: Do Social Media Make Protests Possible?, *Foreign Affairs*, *90*(2), 153–154.

Harvey, D. (1989). From Managerialism to Entrepreneurialism: The Transformation in Urban Governance in Late Capitalism. *Geografiska Annaler: Series B, Human Geography*, *71*(1), 3–17.

Horelli, L., Saad-Sulonen, J., Wallin, S., & Botero, A. (2015). When Self-Organization Intersects with Urban Planning: Two Cases from Helsinki, *Planning Practice & Research*, *30*(3), 286–302.

Korn, M., & Voida, A. (2015). Creating friction: infrastructuring civic engagement in everyday life, *Proceedings of The Fifth Decennial Aarhus Conference on Critical Alternatives*. Aarhus University Press, Aarhus, Denmark.

Kozinets, Robert V. (2015). *Netnography*: redefined (Second edition). Los Angeles: SAGE

Luna, D. (2015). *Manizales y Caldas: modelo nacional en tecnología*. Colombian Ministry of ICT. Retrieved from http://www.mintic.gov.co/portal/604/w3-article-12756.html

MacKinnon, R. (2012). *Consent of the Networked: The Worldwide Struggle for Internet Freedom*. New York: Basic. Print.

McCullough, M. (2005). *Digital Ground: Architecture, Pervasive Computing, and Environmental Knowing*. Cambridge, MA: MIT.

MCV. (2018). *Como vamos en educación superior*. (Annual report) Manizales Como Vamos. Retrieved from http://manizalescomovamos.org/como-vamos-en-educacion-superior/

Sassen, S. (2015). Urbanizing Technology. (Epilogue). *Citizen's Right to the Digital City: Urban Interfaces, Activism, and Placemaking*. Springer, Singapore.

Shirky, C. (2009). *Here Comes Everybody: How Change Happens When People Come Together*. Penguin UK, New York.

Shirky, C. (2012). *How the Internet will (one day) transform government*. TED Global conference. Retrieved from https://www.ted.com/talks/clay_shirky_how_the_internet_will_one_day_transform_government

9 Social media and political polarization in Latin America

Analyzing online discussions during the 2018 presidential campaign in Colombia[1]

Jean-Marie Chenou, Daniel Cabarcas Velandia and Maria Nicoll Sepulveda Marin

Introduction

In October 2019, *El Tiempo*, the national newspaper with the highest circulation in Colombia, published an interview with a psychology professor titled "Social networks are destroying democracy" (Neira, 2019). The interview illustrates the tone which dominates the debate on the role of social media in the current crisis of democracy, a debate which is taking place in Colombia as well as in most regions of the world. In the wake of the 2016 presidential election in the US and of the Brexit referendum, social media was accused of undermining democracy and favoring the rise of populism. This line of argument was further used in Latin America in different contexts, such as the rejection of the peace agreement by plebiscite in Colombia in 2016, or the election of Jair Bolsonaro in Brazil in 2018.

Interestingly, social networks were hailed as "tyranny's new nightmare" (Rutten, 2009) only a decade ago. They were described as the main tool used by the opposition during the Arab Spring, which was even dubbed the "Twitter revolution" by some analysts (for a critique, see Mejias, 2011).

Against this background, it is necessary to avoid technological determinism in the analysis of the ambivalent relationship between social media and democracy. While social media indubitably participates in the extension and deepening of the worldwide crisis of liberal democracy, they cannot be singled out as the main explanation. Without ignoring the importance of algorithms, it is important to highlight the role of user agency in shaping online communications (Seargeant & Tagg, 2019).

This chapter explores the case of Colombian youth as social media users in the context of the 2018 Presidential elections. It investigates the relationship between social media and polarization through a user-centered analysis of the creation and reproduction of filter bubbles and echo chambers. This chapter describes how Colombian students participated in WhatsApp groups and chose the information they wanted to consume on social media in the context of the presidential election. It argues that Colombian students are aware of the biases that might affect information on social media, but voluntarily exercise their ability to select information and to choose the political discourses that best fit their own political views.

Based on the observation of WhatsApp groups during the campaign and on an exploratory survey of university students, the chapter identifies elements of online political polarization that seem to stem more from the political context in the country than from the effects of algorithmic curation. This allows us to draw some conclusions on the ethical implications of online communication in highly polarized political contexts.

The remainder of the chapter is organized as follows. First, we discuss the notion of filter bubbles and highlight the role of users, especially among the youth. Second, we outline the political context of the 2018 presidential election in Colombia and the role of social media in the campaign. Third, we describe the results of the observation of three WhatsApp groups during the campaign. Fourth, we present the results of the preliminary survey on information selection. Finally, we discuss the findings and explore the ethical concerns raised by online polarization.

Filter bubbles and online polarization: The agency of users

While notions such as filter bubbles and echo chambers are useful in order to analyze the role of algorithms in curating online information, current political debates tend to adopt a deterministic stance on technology and underestimate the agency of users, especially among educated youth.

Filter bubbles, echo chambers, and online polarization

The digital transformation affects the way in which we access information. Traditional models of newspapers, radio, and TV news are competing with—and increasingly replaced by—online sources of information. According to a 2018 Pew Research Center Survey, about two-thirds of US adults get their news at least occasionally on social media (Pew Research Center, 2018). While access remains an issue in Latin America, mobile social media penetration rates in the region are among the highest in the world. It amounts to 61% in South America and 59% in Central America, figures that are similar to those of Northern Europe and North America (We are social, 2019). Moreover, the time spent per day on social media in the region is well above the world's mean (over 3 hours per day in countries such as Brazil, Colombia, Argentina, and Mexico compared to a worldwide mean of 2:16) (We are social, 2019).

Against this background, analysts have started to investigate the consequences of the digital transformation over the last decade, not only on our news consumption patterns, but also on the general public debate that shape democratic politics. Two elements of the transformation are of utmost importance. First, user-generated content circulates along with information produced by professional journalists and traditional news outlets. Second, social media companies use algorithms to curate the flows of information. Algorithms select information, organize it, and present it in a user-friendly fashion aimed at increasing the attractiveness of the platform.

Eli Pariser (2011) describes how algorithmic curation creates invisible and custom filters that trap users in a virtual bubble. For example, Google's PageRank algorithm draws from 57 indicators such as the place of connection, or the topics searched, to discover "who you are and what kind of pages you like." As a result, a Google query shows different results depending on the personal experience of the user. The same phenomenon happens on social media such as Facebook and Instagram. Filter bubbles are likely to affect particularly the most active populations on social media such as the youth (Youth Observatory, 2017).

While the academic debate on filter bubbles remains focused on the Global North, and especially on the United States following the 2016 presidential election, the phenomenon has also been studied in Latin America (Rodríguez Cano, 2018; Rossi, 2018). Algorithmic curation in the region also leads to information that is more concentrated and to the formation of filter bubbles.

On a similar note, researchers have evidenced a tendency of social media to amplify and reinforce users' pre-existing beliefs through the creation of echo chambers. The circulation of information within relatively closed networks (such as a followers' network on Twitter) might lead to the repetition of some news and to the attenuation of others, based on the ideological orientation of the network of users. Studies have shown the emergence of high levels of homophily within networks of followers on Twitter (Colleoni et al., 2014) and the consequent polarization of online debates (Barberá et al., 2015).

The agency of users and the critique of technological determinism

Based on the findings of the research on filter bubbles and echo chambers, many commenters have adopted a perspective inspired by technological determinism. In this view, the current crisis of liberal democracy, as evidenced by the global retreat of democracy over the last few years (The Economist, 2019), is caused by the polarization of political positions and the emergence of populist candidates on social media (for a discussion, see Groshek and Koc-Michalska, 2017). Moreover, early studies on filter bubbles and echo chambers focused on the United States and its two-party political system, which introduces a bias toward the identification of polarization (Borgesius et al., 2016). They also tended to minimize the high diversity of information sources (Dubois & Blank, 2018).

This chapter adopts a more nuanced perspective by focusing on the agency of users. Recent research on filter bubbles and echo chambers on social media have tended to minimize the role of algorithm and to stress the importance of the political context and the psycho-political biases of users (Spohr, 2017). Faced with pluralist perspectives, people choose information that reinforces their existing preferences. Therefore, filter bubbles and echo chambers are not only the product of algorithms created by internet and social media companies. A series of factors related to the political and institutional context, as well as those particular to each person, come together and give way to the presence of these phenomena.

In order to study the consumption of news from social media by Colombian youth, we argue that it is necessary to describe the already highly polarized political context, to acknowledge the competence of young and educated users, and to stress their ability to select from multiple information sources. Based on the assumption that social media both increases exposure to ideologically distant news material, and at the same time reinforce polarization (Flaxman et al., 2016), we adopt a user-centric perspective in order to understand the creation and reproduction of filter bubbles and echo chambers beyond algorithmic curation.

The Colombian political context and the role of social media in the 2018 campaign

In a highly polarized context, ideological cohesion is often achieved through denigration of opponents. In this context, social media plays a key role.

Political polarization since the plebiscite

As mentioned earlier, the two-party system favors a clear polarization along the ideological spectrum. This polarization can be reproduced and reinforced by the circulation of information on social media. However, in the Colombian case, the historical two-party system was replaced by a multi-party system in the 1990s and early 2000s (Caicedo, 2008; Pizarro Leongómez, 2002). Therefore, while the 2014 presidential election was presented as polarized in the media, research suggests that individuals failed to perceive major differences among the positions of presidential candidates (Plata Caviedes, 2017). This limited polarization among respondents to large-scale surveys must be contrasted with an increasing online polarization illustrated by behavior in Facebook groups that prefigured the "*Uribistas vs. Antiuribistas*" polarization (Acosta V., 2012).

The 2016 plebiscite on the peace agreement between the government and the FARC guerrilla marked a strong polarization of Colombian politics. The close victory of the "no" reflected a division between followers of the former president and main opponent to the peace agreement Álvaro Uribe (the *Uribistas*) and the rest of the voters (Rodríguez-Raga, 2017).

In this context, the 2018 presidential election took place in a highly polarized context. Apart from the different program of the six candidates, an overarching issue was the division between supporters and opponents to the peace process. The two candidates that qualified for the second round were the left-wing candidate Gustavo Petro, who supported the peace process, and Iván Duque, the right-wing candidate supported by former President Uribe and representative of the opposition to the peace process. The use of social media by the two candidates evidenced the polarization with hostile political communication aimed at "demonizing" the other candidate (Prada Espinel & Romero Rodríguez, 2019). The third candidate in the first round was Sergio Fajardo, a centrist and supporter of the peace process. His role as a possible kingmaker made his campaign relevant throughout the two rounds.

The role of social media in Colombian politics

According to many observers, the innovative use of social media in political campaigns became salient during the 2010 presidential election (Richard, 2011; Semana, 2010). Antanas Mockus, a centrist candidate, created an unexpected "green wave" by targeting young voters through internet and social media (especially Facebook, YouTube, and Twitter). The candidate rose from a 3% voting intention in February 2010 to a leading 38% in the polls in April (Richard, 2011). While the "green wave" diminished in the final weeks of the campaign and Mockus was finally eliminated in the first round of the election with less than 22% of the votes, his innovative use of social media became a reference in Colombian politics (Rincón, 2011).

Eight years later, presidential candidates were aware of the importance of social media in political campaigns and of their potential to attract young voters in particular. However, the use of social media had evolved, both on the side of the politicians and their communication teams and on the side of the audience. As we have seen, the online debate became more polarized as parties understood the strength of more radical messages, and even used trolling and fake news as part of the campaign toolkit. Online campaigning was no longer the innovative experiment of the educated few. It became a massive communication tool. The success of the Trump or the Brexit campaigns paved the way for more polarized campaigning (Groshek & Koc-Michalska, 2017).

The audience also evolved between the early days of campaigning 2.0 in Colombia and the 2018 presidential election. For example, the research presented in this chapter originally set out to analyze Facebook feeds. However, exploratory interviews showed that Facebook was used less as a social media to share user-generated content than as an alternative World Wide Web, where students visited Facebook pages of mainstream media. Another evolution was the increased "media competence" of young and educated internet users (Geschke et al., 2019). The students that we interviewed were aware of the potential manipulation of content shared on social media. Finally, students interested in one or the other candidate usually joined closed groups on WhatsApp.

Researching user practices in online communications

The first step of the research involved a series of semi-structured exploratory interviews with students in order to obtain information on their social media practices. These interviews helped determine the most often used social media platform and to adapt the methodology to the local context. For example, WhatsApp was cited as a more relevant social media platform than Facebook. The interviews with students were complemented with interviews with a limited number of social media experts and "fact checkers" in order to outline the practices of online campaigning.

The second element of the methodology was an observation of WhatsApp groups. The case study focused on analyzing the conversations and viral social media "chains" sent in groups for the three most important presidential candidates to the 2018 elections in Colombia: Iván Duque, Sergio Fajardo, and Gustavo Petro. The content of these groups was collected during the last two months of the campaign. It is important to highlight that the link to these groups was available through the official Facebook pages of the candidates, illustrating the close relationship between open and closed social media. By expressing interest in their political agenda, people who "liked" these pages were invited to be part of WhatsApp groups, to become aware of the events and debates within each campaign. A content analysis was performed on the material collected during the two months.

The third component consisted of a survey that reached a sample of 50 students across 4 universities in Bogotá. The survey was divided into three exercises. For each, respondents had to choose their preferred article among a group of four. The first group of articles was selected from *Semana* magazine, to evaluate the behavior of the participant when facing a wide variety of topics and relatively low bias. The second exercise consisted of several articles related to politics, with a low bias; this group of articles intended to focus on the relevance of the source (in this case, the news platform). Finally, the third group consisted of several articles that intentionally showed significant bias regarding the presidential elections and was intended to focus on evaluating the importance of the participants' political stance and ideology on content selection. A last section tried to characterize the participants' behavior in general within digital environments (use of social media, political activism, and perception on the existence of filter bubbles, among others).

WhatsApp groups: Closed communication spaces as echo chambers

WhatsApp has become one of the key channels through which political debates take place in Latin America. The first reason is the widespread use of WhatsApp in the region, which is the most used social messenger application in the region (We are social, 2019). Another reason could be the lesser degree of exposure. While public figures generate debates and take strong positions publicly on Twitter, everyday users of social media tend to construct political positioning in more friendly and closed environments. The strategy in terms of political campaigning seems to be the creation of a closed echo chamber in order to foment subsequent diffusion in open networks. As part of the Facebook ecosystem, WhatsApp is both a messaging application and a social media. Its closed nature differs from Facebook, Twitter, or Instagram. However, the group communication that WhatsApp allows is clearly used as a more selective social media.

According Saboia (2016), WhatsApp is within reach of all people who have a cell phone, allowing a wide range of population categories to access information. These elements influence the time that people devote to this social network and the rapid dispersion of information. Instant messaging application had a transcendental role in these presidential elections, since a rapprochement between the candidate and the masses is produced. Similarly, campaigns post-chain content and memes to unite, mobilize and polarize citizens.

Firstly, we found multiple common points in the use of WhatsApp between different groups, such as the heavy reliance on sending images and videos. Iván Duque's group, entitled "*Con Uribe-Iván Duque Centro Democrático*," evidenced the use of images discrediting the other candidates, multiple threads of information in support of Álvaro Uribe and little content on the candidate Iván Duque. Likewise, the information disseminated mainly highlighted the achievements of the presidency of Álvaro Uribe, the main promoter of Duque's campaign.

> Uribe gave a new hope to Colombia, a state that was failing; and taught us to dream of freedom and democracy. He is the only president who fulfilled his duty with the constitution to defend the integrity of the State and the Territory of the State. (With Uribe-Ivan Duque, 2018).

It is clear how, through these threads, future voters were invited to rely on the experience of former President Uribe to guide their decision to vote for the candidate they supported. However, as we have seen, ex-President Uribe is the main polarizing figure. By focusing on him rather than on the candidate, Duque's campaign framed the election as a choice between *Uribistas* and *Anti-Uribistas* and fomented a clear line of division within the electorate.

Secondly, fake news had a privileged role in influencing the thinking of people who do not take the time to verify its veracity. Fake news content was found in such groups as "*Con Uribe-Ivan Duque: Centro Democrático*," where messages were sent within a community to have impact and also to be diffused outside the community. Likewise, this group was characterized by religious threads, in which it was stated that with the help of God, Ivan Duque would win.

In comparison to this group, Gustavo Petro's groups entitled "*Uniandinos con Petro, Docentes con Petro, Trends Oficiales Petro*," evidenced a diffusion of information more related to issues of campaign organization and support events. Similarly, a flow of survey results was observed, and the content of candidate Gustavo Petro's campaign and calendar was emailed to people who joined these groups. Unlike the first group mentioned above, no threads were found discrediting other candidates directly. The constant diffusion of optimistic polls can also be understood as the creation of an echo chamber to mobilize core voters and to foment bottom-up campaigning beyond the closed groups.

Thirdly, the last group entitled: "*Colombia Andes Coalition*," has particularities with respect to the two previous ones. First, all the members of the group are not only ideologically close, but also work as volunteers in the candidacy. Similarly, by joining the group, or following the candidate Sergio Fajardo on other social networks such as Facebook, the option was given for people to have the private number of Sergio Fajardo. By saving it, everyone was sent a welcome message and a video presenting all the proposals of the candidate and opening a space to answer questions regarding the proposals. Therefore, this group was configured more like a WhatsApp campaign group than as an echo chamber. However, as illustrated by Figure 9.1, meme material was also shared within the group.

Figure 9.1 Anti-polarization stance by the Fajardo campaign.

Source: WhatsApp group "Colombia Andes Coalition", 2018

Based on the results presented, and analyzing the discourse and content of the threads, the groups selected for this research were different, since Iván Duque's group was a support group, while Sergio Fajardo's and Gustavo Petro's groups were constituted as campaign groups. In all groups, the flow of information corresponded to direct speech in favor of a presidential candidate, alluding to his political career and achievements, as justification to guide the voting decision of Colombians. The repetition of information corresponds to the artificial creation of an echo chamber to promote a candidate rather than to an attempt to polarize and promote biased information. On the other hand, there is also evidence, though limited in scope, of the use of populist discourse and fake news, in which voters are motivated to vote, not with figures and arguments, but with their feelings regarding the presidential candidates and their supporters, as in the case of Álvaro Uribe and Iván Duque. Finally, it is clear how the use of social networks and private messaging contribute to the rapid dispersion of information during presidential campaigns.

Information selection beyond algorithmic curation

While echo chambers were created through WhatsApp groups, users experienced filter bubbles in open social media during the campaign as well. Thus, we conducted a survey to characterize respondents in terms of their habits and conduct on social media and online news platforms and to understand whether their behavior is influenced by existing filter bubbles or rather create these bubbles by informed selection.

Respondents were asked whether they considered themselves active regarding political discussion on a scale ranging from 1 to 5 (Table 9.1). Out of the 44 responses, the mean for this answer was 3.11, which shows that students are not particularly active or inactive politically. This statement is consistent with the expected randomness of the sample. Most respondents agree to a greater or lesser extent that the most important criteria when selecting which content to access is content itself (i.e. expected information that an article contains) and if it is of interest for them. Respondents also stated that graphic display of content is slightly more decisive than source, but both are relevant for decision-making.

Exercise 1—magazine

The survey was divided into three exercises to test the different selection criteria described by Flaxman et al. (2016). The first proposed a wide variety of topics and relatively low bias. The second exercise consisted of several sources with low bias. Finally, the third group consisted of several articles that intended to show significant bias to evaluate the importance of the participant's political stance and ideology on content selection.

Table 9.1 Respondents' attitudes on social media

Statement	*Mean*	*Statistically significant*
I consider that, when choosing which articles to read, which newspapers to buy, what TV shows to watch, etc., the most important thing is its content, that is, what is it about and if this is of interest to me.	4.18	Yes 90% Confidence Interval: 3.92–4.45
The origin of the content is relevant to determine my choice.	3.45	Yes 90% Confidence Interval: 3.20–3.70
My attitude toward available content varies depending on its origin. For instance, if an article is published in a magazine I do not like, I will probably read with caution or skepticism.	3.65	Yes 90% Confidence Interval: 3.37–3.95
When any piece of content evidences positions that are contrary or incompatible with mine, I am willing to consider its arguments with an open mind and up to discussion.	4.11	Yes 90% Confidence Interval: 3.94–4.29
Graphic display of content is decisive in my choice.	3.56	Yes 90% Confidence Interval: 3.24–3.89
I search for variety in content. This is, I usually try to stay informed about a variety of topics regarding different areas of knowledge.	3.95	Yes 90% Confidence Interval: 3.70–4.21
I usually hold on to my arguments and positions even when I know about some valid arguments that contradict mine.	2.47	Yes 90% Confidence Interval: 2.19–2.77
When an article or other type of content shows positions regarding any topic which are contrary or incompatible with mine, I look for the weak spots of the arguments and use them as a counterargument that supports mine.	3.77	Yes 90% Confidence Interval: 3.49–3.96

Source: Elaboration by the authors.

As expected, respondents gave little importance to article bias, context and author in this first exercise. The option to select the author was not included as the main reason of choice but was included when respondents were asked to list in order of relevance the factors that may had had an impact on this choice. In addition, it must be noted that significant variance is found for all factors, which is consistent across all three exercises, as the box plots show (Figures 9.2, 9.3, and 9.4).

Twenty-seven per cent of students responded that title or appearance was their main reason of choice, while 73% of respondents selected content as

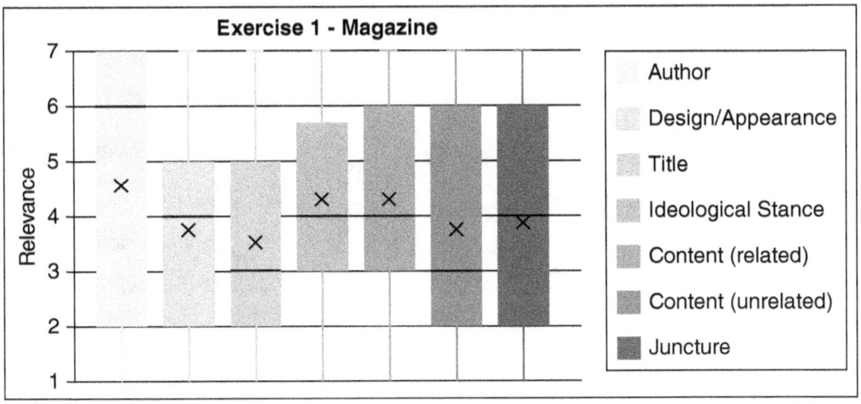

Figure 9.2 Relevance of different factors of choice of magazine articles.

Source: Elaboration by the authors

their primary reason (Figure 9.5). The fact that content is related to the students' undergraduate program or area of knowledge seems to not be as important as expected. In fact, when applying statistical tests, neither appearance, title nor related content were found to be statistically different from the middle value of the scale, which implies that the relevance of each factor varies widely among individuals (Figure 9.5). Still, the exercise offers reasonable statistical inference to sustain content plays a major role in the students' content selection compared to title phrasing and article appearance.

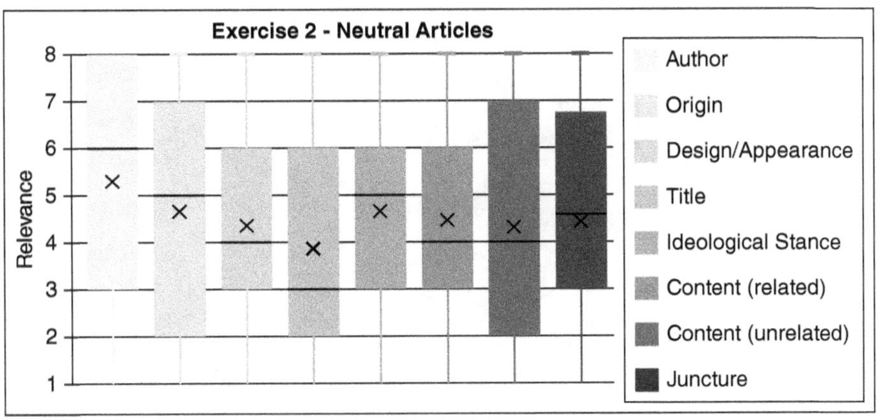

Figure 9.3 Relevance of different factors of choice of neutral articles.

Source: Elaboration by the authors

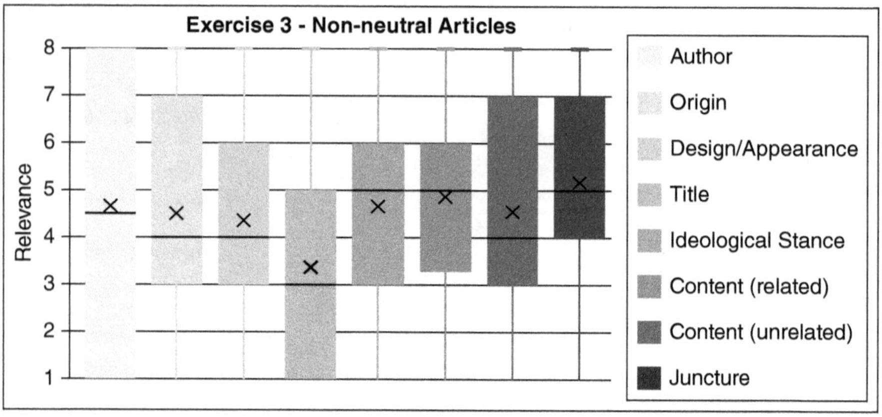

Figure 9.4 Relevance of different factors of choice of non-neutral articles.

Source: Elaboration by the authors

Exercise 2—neutral articles

For the second exercise, respondents were able to choose between four different articles. The four articles discuss an overview of the presidential elections and its content is similar. Thus, this second scenario attempted to control for the content variables precisely by inducing little variance in

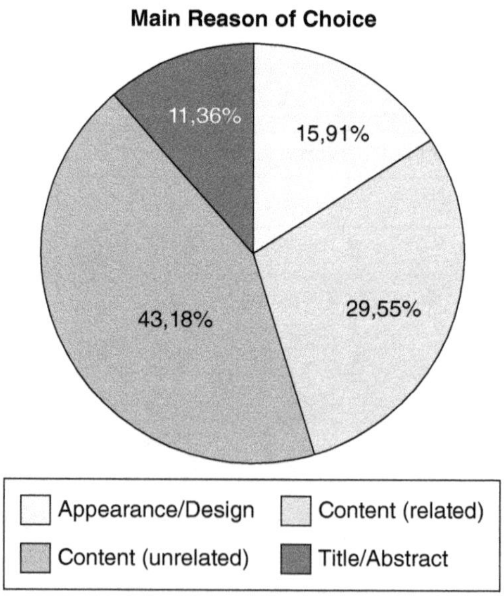

Figure 9.5 Main reason of choice of magazine articles.

Source: Elaboration by the authors

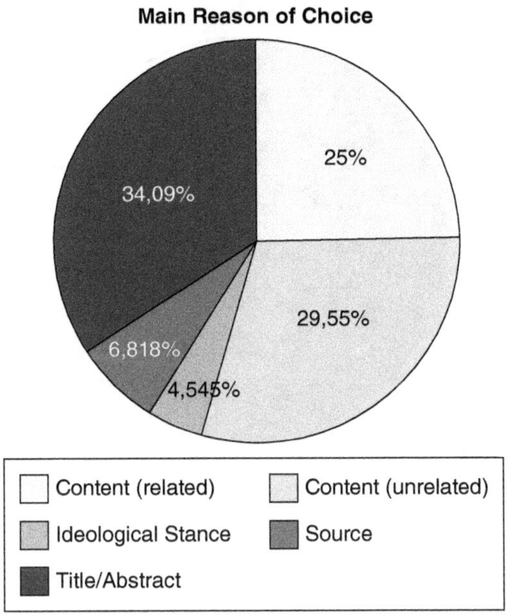

Figure 9.6 Main reason of choice of neutral articles.

Source: Elaboration by the authors

these factors. Regardless of relative homogeneity, content was still the main reason of choice for about 55% of respondents (Figure 9.6). The articles chosen for this exercise also differed from those chosen for the first exercise in the sense that source varied, and each was taken from a different online news platform. Likewise, this set of articles explicitly stated the author of each text. A fair 35% of students claimed the title phrasing to be their main reason of choice (Figure 9.6), and the statistics extracted from the box plots also suggest that author and origin/source are statically significant factors that affect the respondents' decision when content variation is relegated to the background (Figure 9.3).

Exercise 3—non-neutral articles

The set of articles selected for this exercise were taken from several sources and their content showed markedly biased positions in favor of or against one or more presidential candidates. The content of the article, unlike the previous exercises, became a less important factor of selection. Instead, title and bias gained relevance as determinants of the respondents' choice (Figure 9.7). It must be noted as well that content related to the students area of knowledge is selected much less as the main reason compared to the previous exercises, and this reduction is also important compared

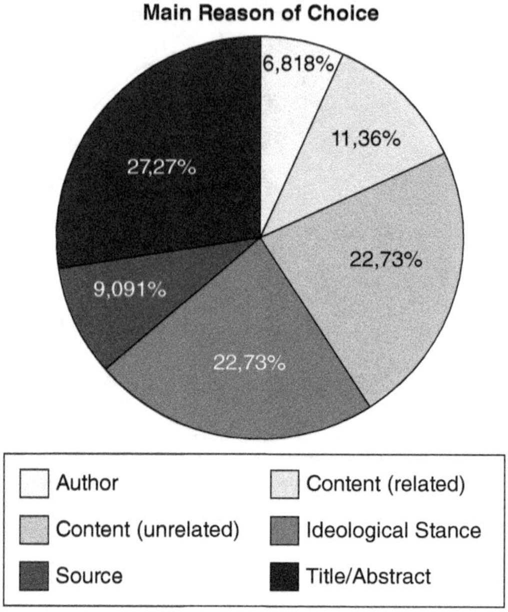

Figure 9.7 Main reason of choice of non-neutral articles.

Source: Elaboration by the authors

to the reduction of unrelated content as a main reason from the second to the third exercise. The box plots suggest context, ideological bias, and source are the most relevant factors explaining the students' article selection when they are presented with conflicted biases (Figure 9.4). Statistical tests applied on the data used for the box plots support this last statement as well.

Most participants, about 80%, stated that they never or rarely like and/or share posts that do not concur with their points of view. Instead, 50% of respondents usually or often like and/share posts that concur with their points of view. This is consistent with Liao and Fu's (2013) findings regarding selective exposure. The first two exercises suggest content may be the most relevant factor among the one that were considered, followed by author and source, which imply a rather rational decision on which content to access. Yet, the third exercise, as it introduces bias, suggests ideological stances are also a relevant factor. The methodology used to carry out the survey may not be sufficient to conclude whether filter bubbles are truly amplified due to external information filters, such as algorithms. However, it does seem to supply evidence that supports Liao and Fu's (2013) findings that selective-exposure may exist even in the absence of these external information filters so common to the digital era, stressing the relevance of user agency in the creation and reproduction of filter bubbles.

Discussion and conclusions

This chapter explores two characteristics of political campaigning in the digital era in Latin America: the creation of echo chambers and that of filter bubbles. In both cases, it stresses the importance of user agency. This allows us to discuss the role of the audience in the creation and reproduction of these phenomena. It also hints toward the responsibility of users and the influence of the political and institutional context rather than on the disruptive consequences of technological change. Finally, this exploratory study points out some elements that would require further research.

The first finding of the chapter is the importance of WhatsApp groups during political campaigns in creating echo chambers, where a limited number of convinced followers receive positive information, potentially viral content, and even elements of language about the candidate. These echo chambers emerge from public social media like Facebook, but they are created by forming smaller communities using closed social media. The objective is to provide material to small-scale influencers that is then diffused through open and closed social media, not directly by the campaign team or the party but rather by active supporters. Echo chambers in this case are not only the result of the effect of small circles of like-minded people on social media but a voluntary decision to create small communities around a candidate. Most of the content collected during this research was support material. This does not mean that fake news and hate speech were not used during the campaign, but WhatsApp support groups of the candidates studied did not directly diffuse them to students.

The second finding is related to the agency of social media users in the emergence and reproduction of filter bubbles. While filter bubbles may be partly created by algorithmic curation of information, they are also the result of information selection by users. In the case of students in the context of the 2018 Colombian presidential election, information was selected based on different reasons including ideological bias. Students tended to intentionally reproduce the polarization of Colombian politics when facing a choice. This result is consistent with recent studies of filter bubbles. Social media increased the exposure to a variety of information sources. Algorithms might privilege certain types of information that is consistent with the users' views, but they are also trained by users' practices. Media-competent users are aware of the bias and use bias as a selection criterion in their consumption of information.

Social media has the potential to spread fake news and hate speech. At the time of this writing, social media companies are reluctant to set democratic standards on their platforms. This situation raises the issue of ethics in the use of social media. One of the solutions, as illustrated by the findings of this chapter, is a more ethical use of social media by media-competent users. However, this does not solve the problem of the broader context of the crisis of liberal democracy and the role of social media in the crisis. While this chapter focused on university students in the capital city of Colombia, it does not address the digital divide that exists within countries in terms of access and (social) media literacy. This issue is particularly relevant in Latin America, in a political context of crisis of liberal democracy and a return of authoritarianism.

Technological solutions to the emergence of filter bubbles are rooted in liberal and deliberative conceptualization of democracies and target the very population that is already aware of the possible biases. As a result, they miss fundamental aspects of the current crisis of democracy (Bozdag & van den Hoven, 2015). Drawing upon agonistic and contestatory conceptualizations of democracy, Bozdag and van den Hoven highlight several elements that might improve ethical standards on social media beyond self-regulation of users. Efforts should foment the visibility of minorities and other marginalized groups and promote politically relevant issues that are marginalized by algorithms (e.g. neutral information on voting procedures). Experts and activists should design platforms for effective contestation (which is part of a broader and more inclusive definition of democracy). Regulation should allow relevant information to be notified to users even if the information is not commercially relevant for platforms, and make sure that the design of the platforms allows for a reflection on opposing viewpoints. Finally, platforms should inform users of algorithmic curation and ensure the possibility of information selection by users beyond dominant viewpoints. These elements could inform debates on the regulation of social media in the region.

The preliminary findings outlined in this chapter question the idea that social media is destroying democracies. On the contrary, it shows that social media is an important tool in the context of political campaigns to actively involve young voters and to include social media users in political campaigns. Polarization is not an effect of algorithms. It is a fundamental feature of democracy that is reproduced by user practices on social media. Thus, the cause of the current crisis of liberal democracy is structural and not technological.

Note

1. The chapter is the result of the work by the Technology, Power, and Globalization stream of the Semillero en Estudios Globales at the Universidad de los Andes, Bogotá. The authors would like to thank the participants of the Semillero for their inputs.

References

Acosta V., G. L. (2012). Gestión de pasiones y polarización en las redes sociales. Un análisis del aplicativo Grupos en Facebook. *Discurso & Sociedad*. Retrieved from http://repository.udem.edu.co/handle/11407/3389

Barberá, P., Jost, J. T., Nagler, J., Tucker, J. A., & Bonneau, R. (2015). Tweeting from left to right: Is online political communication more than an echo chamber? *Psychological Science*, *26*(10), 1531–1542. https://doi.org/10.1177/0956797615594620

Borgesius, F. J. Z., Trilling, D., Möller, J., Bodó, B., Vreese, C. H. de, & Helberger, N. (2016). Should we worry about filter bubbles? *Internet Policy Review*. Retrieved from https://policyreview.info/articles/analysis/should-we-worry-about-filter-bubbles

Bozdag, E., and van den Hoven, J. (2015). Breaking the filter bubble: democracy and design. *Ethics and Information Technology*, *17*(4), 249–265.

Caicedo O., J. A. (2008). Democracia, nación y sociedad: La crisis y decadencia del bipartidismo en Colombia. *Latinoamérica. Revista de Estudios Latinoamericanos*, (46), 9–39 vol. 2008/1.

Colleoni, E., Rozza, A., & Arvidsson, A. (2014). Echo chamber or public sphere? Predicting political orientation and measuring political homophily in Twitter using Big Data. *Journal of Communication*, *64*(2), 317–332. https://doi.org/10.1111/jcom.12084

Dubois, E., & Blank, G. (2018). The echo chamber is overstated: The moderating effect of political interest and diverse media. *Information, Communication & Society*, *21*(5), 729–745. https://doi.org/10.1080/1369118X.2018.1428656

Flaxman, S., Goel, S., & Rao, J. M. (2016). Filter bubbles, echo chambers, and online news consumption. *Public Opinion Quarterly*, *80*(S1), 298–320. https://doi.org/10.1093/poq/nfw006

Geschke, D., Lorenz, J., & Holtz, P. (2019). The triple-filter bubble: Using agent-based modelling to test a meta-theoretical framework for the emergence of filter bubbles and echo chambers. *British Journal of Social Psychology*, *58*(1), 129–149. https://doi.org/10.1111/bjso.12286

Groshek, J., & Koc-Michalska, K. (2017). Helping populism win? Social media use, filter bubbles, and support for populist presidential candidates in the 2016 US election campaign. *Information, Communication & Society*, *20*(9), 1389–1407. https://doi.org/10.1080/1369118X.2017.1329334

Liao, Q. V., & Fu, W. T. (2013, April). Beyond the filter bubble: interactive effects of perceived threat and topic involvement on selective exposure to information. In Proceedings of the SIGCHI conference on human factors in computing systems (pp. 2359-2368).

Mejias, U. (2011). The Twitter revolution must die. *International Journal of Learning and Media*, *2*(4), 3–5. https://doi.org/10.1162/ijlm_a_00060

Message from the WhatsApp group "Con Uribe-Iván Duque Centro Democrático", April 2018.

Neira, A. (2019). "Las redes sociales están destruyendo la democracia." Interview with Belén del Rocío Moreno Cardozo. (2019, October 10). Retrieved from https://www.eltiempo.com/politica/partidos-politicos/asi-funcionan-los-asesinatos-ahora-en-las-redes-sociales-421518?fbclid=IwAR2aZyGotLcrD23F38zSCgrlQfWIU-vCV9kWISoi_TKXLfBbR1rQeEGKOd9E

Pariser, E. (2011). *The Filter Bubble: What The Internet Is Hiding From You*. Penguin London, UK.

Pew Research Center (2018). News Use Across Social Media Platforms 2018. September 2018. Retrieved from https://www.journalism.org/2018/09/10/news-use-across-social-media-platforms-2018/

Pizarro Leongómez, E. (2002, January). *La Atomización Partidista en Colombia: El Fenómeno de las Micro-empresas Electorales*. Kellogg Institute For International Studies Working Paper #292. Retrieved from https://kellogg.nd.edu/documents/1585

Plata Caviedes, J. C. (2017). ¿Polarización? Posiciones ideológicas durante la campaña presidencial colombiana en 2014. *Colombia Internacional*. No 87. Retrieved from https://revistas.uniandes.edu.co/doi/abs/10.7440/colombiaint87.2016.08

Prada Espinel, O. A., & Romero Rodríguez, L. M. (2019). Polarización y demonización en la campaña presidencial de Colombia de 2018: Análisis del comportamiento comunicacional en Twitter de Gustavo Petro e Iván Duque. *Revista Humanidades: Revista de la Escuela de Estudios Generales*, *9*(1) (January–June), 14.

Richard, E. (2011). Storytelling, narrativas de campaña. Campañas electorales para la presidencia en Colombia, 2010. *OPERA*. 11, 11 (2011, November), 129–145.

Rincón, O. (2011). Mucho ciberactivismo... pocos votos: Antanas Mockus y el Partido Verde colombiano. *Nueva sociedad*, (235), 74–89.

Rodríguez Cano, C. A. (2018). Los usuarios en su laberinto: Burbujas de filtros, cámaras de eco y mediación algorítmica en la opinión pública en línea. *Virtualis*, *8*(16), 57–76.

Rodríguez-Raga, J. C. (2017). Colombia: País del año 2016. *Revista de Ciencia Política (Santiago)*, *37*(2), 335–368. https://doi.org/10.4067/s0718-090x2017000200335

Rossi, A. (2018). ¿Burbujas de filtro? Hacia una fenomenología algorítmica. *InMediaciones de la Comunicación*, *13*(1), 263–281. https://doi.org/10.18861/ic.2018.13.1.2836

Rutten, T. (2009, June 24). Tyranny's new nightmare: Twitter. *Los Angeles Times*. Retrieved from http://articles.latimes.com/2009/jun/24/opinion/oe-rutten24

Saboia, F. (2016). The Rise of WhatsApp in Brazil Is About More than Just Messaging. *Harvard Business Review*. (2016, April 15). Retrieved from https://hbr.org/2016/04/the-rise-of-whattsapp-in-brazil-is-about-more-than-just-messaging

Seargeant, P., & Tagg, C. (2019). Social media and the future of open debate: A user-oriented approach to Facebook's filter bubble conundrum. *Discourse, Context & Media*, *27*, 41–48. https://doi.org/10.1016/j.dcm.2018.03.005

Semana (2010). Redes sociales, la novedad de la campaña. Retrieved from http://www.semana.com/politica/articulo/redes-sociales-novedad-campana/116619-3

Spohr, D. (2017). Fake news and ideological polarization: Filter bubbles and selective exposure on social media. *Business Information Review*, *34*(3), 150–160. https://doi.org/10.1177/0266382117722446

The Economist (2019). The retreat of global democracy stopped in 2018. (2019, January 8). *The Economist*. Retrieved from https://www.economist.com/graphic-detail/2019/01/08/the-retreat-of-global-democracy-stopped-in-2018

We are social (2019). Global Digital Report 2019. Retrieved from https://wearesocial.com/global-digital-report-2019

Youth Observatory (2017). Analyses of a Connected Youth: Internet Governance. Retrieved from https://es.scribd.com/document/394217256/Analysis-of-a-Connected-Youth-Internet-Governance

Part III

Journalism and media integrity in the age of post-truth

10 Digital native media in Central America: Reshaping the online news sphere

Ramón Salaverría and Silvia-María Corzo

Natives re-colonizing Central America

On April 25, 1998, a digital news media outlet called El Faro (www.elfaro.net) was founded. This fact would have been nothing in particular if it were not for two additional—and quite surprising—details: the type of medium and the place where it was founded. El Faro was launched as a digital native medium, with exclusive presence on the Internet, something extremely exceptional for a publication founded in the 1990s. This exceptionality was even greater due to a second detail: it appeared in El Salvador, a small Central American country, with limited development of digital communications and telecommunications in general.

At a time when, even for the most consolidated media brands, it was challenging to bet on the Internet as a publishing platform, in the most unexpected place, with hardly any potential audience to reach, a group of journalists allied to found something as unusual as a digital native medium. Against all odds, the project has turned out to be much more than an ephemeral lunacy. After more than 20 years, El Faro has become one of the hallmarks of independent journalism not only in El Salvador, but in Latin America as a whole (Harlow & Salaverría, 2016; Molina Tamacas, 2016).

El Faro sets a milestone in the development of Latin American digital journalism. It has shown that a small news medium, created by a group of journalists with hardly any resources, can be consolidated in the long term, practicing independent journalism far from the commercial model of traditional corporations of journalism. In a country like El Salvador, where journalism has been traditionally controlled by family communication companies, El Faro is a radically different alternative. It brings a model of cooperativism-based journalism, where the journalists are workers and owners at the same time, and which has been sustained, especially during its first years, thanks to the support of international foundations that promote freedom and economic development. With this economic support, El Faro has promoted a type of journalism that focuses on quality; news investigations published in this media were granted the 2016 the Gabriel García Márquez Journalism Award and in 2019 the King of Spain International

Journalism Award, the two most important Spanish language journalism awards (FNPI, 2016). Apart from these awards, El Faro has become a relevant news actor within its country and throughout Central America; for example, in 2010 it was chosen by the WikiLeaks organization to exclusively deliver cables over El Salvador, Honduras, and part of Guatemala. It is, in short, a medium that is contributing to setting up a new online news sphere in the Central American region.

Although El Faro claims on its website that it is the "first Latin American digital newspaper," it is not the first digital publication in Latin America, or even in Central America. The first newspaper in the continent with an Internet edition was Jornal do Brasil, whose first issue on the web appeared on May 28, 1995 (Barbosa, 2016), almost three years before El Faro. Likewise, other digital-born media projects preceded El Faro in places no less unexpected than El Salvador. In 1995, Notifax, a digital newsletter with news summaries, was founded in Nicaragua. It remains active a quarter of a century later, although today it is published from Mexico, and happens to be the first digital native media in Latin America (Salaverría, 2016). Without leaving Nicaragua, there were other digital native news media founded at an equally early date: the now extinct Ciberdiario de Nicaragua (www.ciberdiario.com.ni), for example, was founded in 1996 (Solórzano Canales, 2016; Zuniga Gutiérrez & Hopmann, 2013). Although also extinct, another pioneering digital native media in the Caribbean was the Dominican Electronic Journal, DEDOM, founded on March 20, 1996 in the Dominican Republic (Ortiz, 2016). In total, before the turn of the century some dozens of digital native titles appeared in the Latin American media market. However, the real boom came after the year 2000 and, more specifically, from 2010 onwards (Solórzano Canales, 2016; Molina Tamacas, 2016; Arce Sanabria & Morales Zúñiga, 2016; Alas, 2016; Perdomo de Zelaya, 2016; Hernández Aguirre, 2016).

This phenomenon is located in Central America, a region comprised of seven countries. Within them there inhabited about 49 million people in 2017, according to the World Bank, spread over a territory of just over half a million square kilometers: Guatemala (16.9 million; 108.888 km^2), Honduras (9.3 million; 112.492 km^2), El Salvador (6.4 million; 21.041 km^2), Nicaragua (6.2 million; 129.999 km^2), Costa Rica (4.9 million; 51.100 km^2), Panama (4.1 million; 75.517 km^2), and Belize (0.4 million; 22.966 km^2). The first six countries have a common official language, Spanish, which coexists with hundreds of indigenous languages and dialects. In Belize, meanwhile, English is the official language, although Creole, Spanish, and several Mayan languages are also spoken. Marked by economic inequality, these countries have small-upper classes, growing middle classes, and a majority of people in poverty. This fragmented social and cultural space has seen, since the late 1990s, the birth of a hardly measurable amount of media on the Internet, much of it digital native. No research has counted or analyzed all this digital media yet; due to this lack of previous studies, for this chapter (leaving Belize aside) we have based our research on a sample of 88 digital native media located across these six Spanish-speaking countries, whose characteristics are detailed below. In any case, one gets an approximate idea of the vast quantitative dimensions reached by the digital native media phenomenon in this region.

In this regard, Central America is no exception within Latin America. A similar expansion has occurred in other countries such as Brazil, Argentina, Colombia, Mexico, Peru, Ecuador, Chile, and Venezuela, to name just the largest and most populous. The truth is that, at the beginning of the third decade of the 21st century, all Latin American countries have digital native media in their news markets, some of them with notable journalistic influence (Salaverría, 2020; Rodríguez-Hidalgo et al., 2020).

The emergence of hundreds of digital native media is contributing to the transformation of the profile of journalism throughout Latin America and, especially, in Central America. For the time being, their impact is limited but clearly noticeable. The Open Society Foundations, a global grant-making network founded by business magnate George Soros, has described the region's digital native media as "an emerging third sector [that] has proved fragile and limited in reach, but is potentially a significant vehicle for public interest news" (Ávila & Gutiérrez Valdizán, 2013, p. 7).

Indeed, since the beginning of the 21st century, Central American journalism has witnessed a decline in traditional media, especially the print media, in line with what had been happening in Western countries for years before. Although traditional press, radio, and mainly television news brands continue to attract the majority of the audience and enjoy the highest levels of recognition, it is no less true that over the last quarter of the century there has been a consolidation of a fourth journalistic actor, digital media, with increasing levels of political and social influence. In several countries of Central America, burdened by a long-lasting social inequality and even by a deficit of freedoms, Internet media and especially the digital natives have become influential public actors, publishing uncomfortable information for governments and for big economic corporations.

In Nicaragua, for example, Confidencial (confidencial.com.ni) has been a target of pressure and threats by forces bound to the Sandinista government of Daniel Ortega. In December 2018, the newsroom of this digital native medium was occupied by the police, which confiscated journalists' computers and numerous documents. Subsequently, the 2019 General Assembly of the Inter-American Press Society placed Nicaragua, along with Venezuela, Mexico, and Cuba, as one of the four countries in Latin America where "physical attacks against journalists exercising their function are becoming more common, from the confiscation of equipment and press material, until unjustified arrests" (SIP, 2019).

Although they have not suffered such direct pressures, Guatemala's digital native media also stands out for their journalistic boldness. There, Plaza Pública (www.plazapublica.com.gt) has become a benchmark of investigative journalism. In 2013 the Open Society Foundations described it as a medium dedicated to producing "more investigative reports than any other newspaper in Guatemala." Some of the native digital media of this country, especially Soy502 (www.soy502.com) and Nómada (www.nomada.gt), have also been noted for their important role in the journalistic revelations that led to the resignation and detention President Otto Pérez Molina in 2015, for various cases of corruption (Knight Center, 2015).

Sometimes, Central American digital native media aims at more basic objectives. When the problem is to inform a society with barely any access to communication technologies and with very limited media literacy, the main goal is not to make the most innovative and up-to-date journalism. In those cases, the real challenge is to reach the citizenship. There are many examples of this primary vocation. In her study on alternative journalism in El Salvador, Summer Harlow, assistant professor of journalism at University of Houston and specialized in Latin American media landscapes, explores the case of Voces (voces.org.sv), a modest digital native newspaper. Harlow explains that the journalists of this news medium, who she interviewed, state that they aim to democratize communication and facilitate access to news, seeking "creative ways to include in society and politics those who do not have access" (Harlow, 2017, p. 119). On the other hand, there is media that seeks to go beyond the mere access to information by citizens, and whose purposes include the construction of a state under the rule of law. That is the case of Soy502 in Guatemala, as it can be read in their "about us" page:

> We dream of a country where the rule of law prevails, where there is equality in front of the law and universal access to justice. We want to see the country prosper, based on solid republican and democratic institutions. We believe in responsibility and accountability. We consider our duty to work for Guatemala to become an inclusive country, without hunger, where we can all aspire to a dignified life and a future with well-being. [Authors' translation]

The native digital media of Central America constitutes, in short, an increasingly diverse set of journalistic publications. Many show a strong ideological alignment, often oriented toward leftist positions, but there are also those who prefer to be distinguished by their commitment to innovative formats. It is noticeable, in this regard, the interest shown by several native media outlets in data journalism (Durán, 2010) and multimedia storytelling. Although many of the digital native media outlets continue on the path of traditional journalism, some of them are committed to long-form journalism and innovative ways of presenting information. It should be noted, however, that this commitment to multimedia storytelling and data journalism is not exclusive to digital native media. Some legacy media outlets in the region have distinguished themselves for the excellence of their data journalism, especially La Nación newspaper of Costa Rica (see www.nacion.com/data/).

Central American landscape of digital native media

There are no complete records that list how many Internet media outlets are published in Central America, and of them how many are digital native, as of 2019. At most, there are some incomplete directories of these media outlets. In fact, in recent times, there are hardly any academic studies on the profile of journalism in this region (Rockwell & Janus, 2010; Harlow, 2017).

The two most complete sources are a couple of databases compiled by SembraMedia (www.sembramedia.org), a non-profit organization based in the United States dedicated to the promotion of digital media in Latin America, and the Observatorio de Nuevos Medios (New Media Observatory; www.nuevosmedios.es), an Ibero-American directory of digital news media developed by a team of Spanish scholars in 2015. As of this writing, in October of 2019, the SembraMedia database was cataloging 95 native journalistic projects in the six Spanish-speaking countries of Central America, while the Observatorio de Nuevos Medios counted 71 websites in the same territory, with the breakdown by countries indicated in Table 10.1.

By our own count, according to the conditions of our research methodology, there are 102 digital native media outlets in the region. However, only 88 of them remained active, i.e. they had been updated at least once in the three months prior to our coding. This is one of the reasons that explains the slight discrepancy of our sample data regarding the SembraMedia directories and the Observatorio de Nuevos Medios. The other reason is that, in these two directories, some of the journalistic websites listed are not exactly news media, but neighboring projects such as personal blogs or activism websites. In general, for the selection of media and its subsequent coding, we applied the methodology used in a similar study in 2018, in which nearly 3000 digital media outlets were counted and analyzed in Spain (Salaverría et al., 2018).

First, the number of platforms that were being used by each of the 88 news media outlets was recorded. We found that, despite being digital native media, a quarter of them (23 [26.1%]) had extended their presence to other

Table 10.1 Number of active digital native media in Central America (October 2019)

	SembraMedia	*Observatorio de Nuevos Medios*	*Authors' sample*
Costa Rica	24	19	19
El Salvador	13	12	11
Guatemala	22	9	21
Honduras	10	9	16
Nicaragua	17	8	14
Panama	9	14	7
Total	**95**	**71**	**88**

Sources: SembraMedia, Observatorio de Nuevos Medios, and authors.

platforms, such as print editions, television, radio, or mobile applications. That is, they first appeared on the web and later expanded their brands to other platforms. Costa Rica was the Central American country with the largest number of cross-platform native media (9). It was followed by El Salvador (4) and Guatemala (4), Honduras (3), Nicaragua (2), and Panama (1). The significant use of traditional platforms in addition to the web (printed press, radio, television, and mobile applications) is indicative of the will of these media outlets to connect with their audiences. It should not be forgotten that these countries suffer from low levels of access to the Internet, so that the use of more traditional platforms makes it possible for them to connect with audiences that are difficult to reach through digital media.

Almost three quarters (73.9%; 65) of the native media of our sample had a presence only on the web. Nineteen and one-thirds percent (17) were present on two platforms, 6.8% (6) on three platforms, and there was no medium published simultaneously on four or five platforms. The most common multiplatform modality of native web publications occurred with television (13 media outlets), followed by radio (8), newspapers or printed magazines (7), and mobile applications (3). However, it has to be clarified what the Central American digital native media outlets understand by television: in many cases, it is not a conventional television, delivered through cable or satellite, but a section of their websites, where they gather video reports or summaries of news, uploaded onto video platforms such as YouTube.

The subjects covered by the digital native media were also studied. First, general news publications—those covering simultaneously topics such as politics, economy, culture, sports, and so on—were listed. Secondly, we examined those whose focus was on a specialized topic, either because they called themselves "specialized" media or because we deemed them as such according to our own analysis.

The same amount of media dedicated to general news (44) and specialized information (44) was counted. Despite the balance between the two modalities, there were differences by country. Native media dedicated to general issues were the majority in Panama (5 media out of 7 [71.4%]), Honduras (10/16 [62.5%]), El Salvador (7/12 [58.3%]), and Nicaragua (8/14 [57.1%]); the presence of general media was somewhat smaller in Costa Rica (9/19 [47.4%]) and, above all, in Guatemala (5/21 [23.8%]). Obviously, the figures for specialized information media in each of those six countries were exactly inverse.

In relation to the subject typology of Central American digital native media, an interesting fact stands out: most specialized media align with alternative journalism (Atton & Hamilton, 2008; Harlow, 2017), which covers topics often disregarded by mainstream media. Indeed, publications focusing on political and social issues abound, as well as on the claim of civil rights. Specifically, the most common subjects among Central American specialized media were, in this order, politics (16 of 44 specialized media [36.4%]), culture (12/44 [27.3%]), human rights (7/44 [16%]), sports (2/44

[4.5%]), leisure and entertainment (2/44 [4.5%]), environment (2/44 [4.5%]), feminism (2/44 [4.5%]), and transparency (1/44 [2.3%]). The notable presence of political and social content is an indication that many journalists in Central America have taken advantage of the ease of publication and low cost of digital native media to publish distinct topics to those published by the legacy media. Also, in countries with authoritarian regimes, digital native media have given a platform for independent and critical journalism against the government.

Another relevant aspect when studying the characteristics of native news media in the Central American region is their geographical scope. By their nature, every digital medium has a potentially global reach, but the truth is that each medium is aimed at a specific target audience. Our study distinguishes four categories: (1) hyperlocal media, that is, online publications targeted at specific communities within a city, such as neighborhoods; (2) local media, aimed at areas smaller than the countries, including states, provinces, cities, and villages; (3) national media, whose coverage is of interest to an entire country; and (4) global media, targeted to an international audience. In our sample, 84.1% (74) of Central American digital native media had a national reach. The following category corresponded to the media outlets with global reach, which represented 10.2% (9). Clearly behind were the local media, with just 5.7% (5). No medium of hyperlocal coverage was identified.

It is quite understandable that the digital native media aiming at a national audience are the vast majority. Due to the small population of these six countries, Central American digital native media cannot address smaller target audiences, they would hardly survive. These countries range between 16.9 million inhabitants in Guatemala and 4.1 million in Panama, far less than the borderline countries of Mexico (126.2 million) at North and Colombia (49.6 million) at South. The solution of Central America media is seeking larger audiences outside their national boundaries, aiming at the population who moved to other countries. According to data from the Migration Policy Institute (MPI), in 2017 the number of immigrants settled from Central American countries in the United States exceeded 3.5 million (O'Connor et al., 2019). Although the United States is the main target of Central American emigration, there are hundreds of thousands of migrants displaced in other countries of the world (Bayona-i-Carrasco et al., 2018). Given this high level of emigration, many digital media outlets, both native and non-native, target a good part of their content to the migrant diaspora.

Another conditioning factor in the profile of the published news content is the age of the media outlets. Usually, the longer a life a digital medium reaches, the greater the diversity of content it develops. In this sense, it is noted that digital native media is a very young phenomenon in Central America: almost half of those media outlets analyzed in our study were born after 2013, that is, were six years old or less (see Figure 10.1).

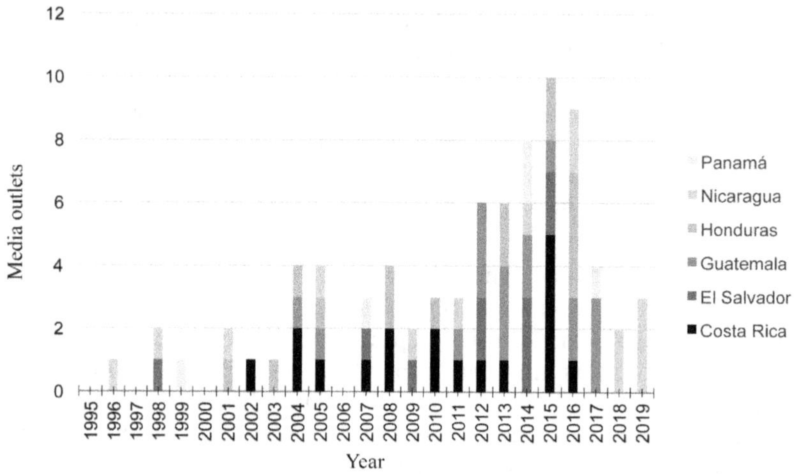

Figure 10.1 Year of launch of digital native media in Central America (1995–2019).

In 2019, most digital news outlets, native and non-native, still struggled to find a sustainable business model. Twenty-five years after the appearance of the first web media outlet, this is a persistent challenge in digital journalism worldwide (Salaverría, 2019). This is also the case, of course, in Central America.

To face this economic challenge, the Central American digital native media outlets show an increasing diversity of funding sources (Tejedor et al., 2020). In the sample studied, in addition to advertising and subscriptions, some media outlets resorted to alternative means such as advertorials (Goodlad et al., 1997), general sponsorships, sponsored or branded content (Sabate et al., 2014), marketing campaigns in social media, crowdfunding (Belleflamme et al., 2014), and merchandising, among others. Forty and nine-tenths percent (36) of the media analyzed showed a single source of funding: advertising. On the other hand, 42.1% (37) were being financed by two or more avenues of income. The two most financially diversified media outlets in our sample were combining four or up to five different financing paths. However, in some cases the financial aspect seemed to be secondary: in 17% (15) of the publications studied, there were apparently no financing sources or, at least, they could not be identified.

Although advertising is the most pervasive source of income, other forms are also explored by the digital native media (see Table 10.2). Some publications show quite sophisticated marketing strategies, so they advertise their services through integrated commercial packages or media kits, also known as press kits. A remarkable case is the one of Niú (niu.com.ni), a publication dedicated to cultural and technological news in Nicaragua: when performing our study, Niú was offering to advertisers a media kit with demographic data of its audience that included the geographical location from which users were accessing the portal, the most read news, the advertising

Table 10.2 Income sources of digital native media of Central America, by country (N = 88)

Country	Adverti-sing	Sponsored content/ advertorials	Paid subscription	Public sponsorship	Private sponsorship	Donations/ crowd-funding	Other sources
Costa Rica	13	6	1	0	0	3	8
El Salvador	8	1	0	2	2	1	5
Guatemala	7	4	0	2	6	1	9
Honduras	11	4	0	0	0	1	4
Nicaragua	8	4	0	2	1	4	4
Panama	6	2	0	0	0	0	2
Total	53	21	1	6	9	10	32

Sources: Authors.

formats available and the spaces where brands could advertise their products. Another example is La Voz de Guanacaste (www.vozdeguanacaste.com), from Costa Rica: besides its advertising space, it had a whole section devoted to explaining its advertising options, as well as an online store. It was also offering the services of a laboratory made up of professionals in graphic design, photography, video production, marketing, and communication. In Guatemala, Nómada had divided its commercial area into three: advertising and digital products, academic and recreational events, and a content agency that was offering design, video and political analysis services. 4to Mono (www.4tomono.com) is a Nicaraguan digital native publication which business model, at the time of performing this analysis, was based on web and newsletter advertising; it had also a media kit in which it portrayed the profile of its users.

Sponsored content publishing, as well as the sponsorship of the media as a whole, by public or private organizations—often foundations,—are the third main financing method for the media analyzed. In Nicaragua, Boletín Ecológico (boletinecologico.org) did not offer advertising spaces but was publishing advertorials, accepting donations and allowing its users to publish news and reports. Soy502 in Guatemala was also offering, through a media kit, different formats of sponsored content, not only to publish on the website but also in a weekly printed magazine and in its social media profiles. In Nicaragua, Confidencial was using a mixed strategy: together with the free digital native medium, it was publishing a printed magazine weekly by means of a paid subscription (quarterly, semi-annual and annual). All in all, a remarkable diversity in the sources of income could be detected.

Conclusion: Toward a new media sphere in Central America

Have digital native media already transformed the journalistic landscape of Central America? It may be too bold to say such a thing as of yet. In the six Spanish-speaking countries of the isthmus, the most influential and far-reaching journalistic brands remain unquestionably in the hands of the legacy media. The hegemony of the most important media corporations—Grupo La Nación in Costa Rica, Casa Editora Prensa Libre in Guatemala, the publishing group of La Prensa Gráfica in El Salvador, and others alike,—owners of the leading newspapers and some of the television networks with the largest audience rates, remain the core of journalism and media-related business in those countries. Despite the limitations of journalism in the region, these legacy media have the best technological resources, the most extensive and experienced teams, the largest economic funds, and the most well-known brands. Their leadership is, in short, absolute. However, something is changing.

As it has happened in other regions of the world, a new wave of digital media is breaking through and regenerating journalism in Central America (Harlow & Salaverría et al., 2019). Although their impact is still limited, digital native media is bringing journalism back to basics. For these media outlets, the profitability is not so much an objective as a condition, but one that allows them to fulfill their main purpose: to exercise an independent and often openly critical journalism, without depending on the pressures of the political powers or the advertisers. This decision positions these media outlets as outsiders frequently, exerting a counterweight in front of the for-profit journalism practiced by the more traditional media. Many of the Central American native digital media devote special interest to news subjects that have been traditionally outcast or forgotten by for-profit media. They proudly defend social causes like civil rights, the environment, and social freedoms in general. This critical position often makes them uncomfortable for governments and some economic powers. They publish news and provide points of view that are not easy to find in non-native media. In the most extreme cases, some digital native media have become the subject of even harassment and intimidation campaigns, such as the one against Confidential in Nicaragua in 2018.

Meanwhile, Central American digital native media suffers a deep economic weakness. It is true that almost no media in the region, digital or otherwise, enjoys a buoyant economic situation. However, in the case of digital native media this situation is particularly difficult. In a context in which advertising revenues decline, these media are forced to diversify their sources of income. To gather the necessary funds, in many cases they request collaboration of their users, who they invite to become not only subscribers, but also members, donors, or even partners. This is an interesting phenomenon, insofar it converts the public into a community, forming bonds that go beyond the commercial relationships that prevail in the legacy media (Arrese & Kaufmann, 2016). Also remarkable is the support that some of these digital native media receive from international foundations for economic development. This support is another indication that these digital media outlets play a role in the region that goes beyond that of legacy media. Native digital media receives financial support precisely for practicing independent and alternative journalism, which contributes to diversifying the media market in the countries of the region.

In any case, the phenomenon of digital native media in Central America is still in progress. These publications show high levels of mortality: our initial sample of 102 media outlets had to be cut to 88, because the rest had ceased their activity after a (very) short life. Nobody knows if digital native media will be capable of adapting to the rapid changes that the journalism profession is undergoing. Perhaps the mere fact of being digital natives will put them in a better position to adapt to the upcoming challenges. In any case, the resilience of these publications in the emerging media ecosystem will rely on their adaptability to technological changes as well as the social and economic transformations in these countries.

In short, we must not magnify the real impact of these media outlets in their respective journalistic markets, and in the region as a whole. But the truth is that this impact exists and extends to all countries, without exception. Time will tell if these alternative publications, with their strengths and weaknesses, will pave the way for a new journalism in Central America.

References

Alas, R.: Guatemala. In: R. Salaverría (ed.) *Ciberperiodismo en Iberoamérica*, 211–223. Fundación Telefónica & Editorial Ariel, Madrid (2016).

Arce Sanabria, I.M., & Morales Zúñiga, L.: Costa Rica. In: R. Salaverría (ed.) *Ciberperiodismo en Iberoamérica*, 97–111. Fundación Telefónica & Editorial Ariel, Madrid (2016).

Arrese, Á., & Kaufmann, J.: Legacy and Native News Brands Online: Do They Show Different News Consumption Patterns?. *International Journal on Media Management*. 18(2), 75–97 (2016).

Atton, C., & Hamilton, J.F.: *Alternative Journalism*. Sage, New York (2008).

Ávila, R., & Gutiérrez Valdizán, A.: *Mapping Digital Media: Guatemala*. Open Society Foundation, London (2013).

Barbosa, S.: Brazil. In: R. Salaverría (ed.) *Ciberperiodismo en Iberoamérica*, 37–59. Fundación Telefónica & Editorial Ariel, Madrid (2016).

Bayona, J., Pujadas, I., & Tàpies, R.A.: Europa como nuevo destino de las migraciones latinoamericanas y caribeñas. *Biblio3W. Revista Bibliográfica de Geografía y Ciencias Sociales*. XXIII (1242) (2018).

Belleflamme, P., Lambert, T., & Schwienbacher, A.: Crowdfunding: Tapping the Right Crowd. *Journal of Business Venturing*. 29(5), 585–609 (2014).

Durán, J.R.: Honduras: el periodismo de investigación da sus primeros pasos (Ensayos). *Chasqui Revista Latinoamericana de Comunicación*. 109, 78–81 (2010).

FNPI. Estos son los ganadores del Premio Gabo 2016. Retrieved from https://premioggm.org/2016/09/estos-son-los-ganadores-del-premio-gabo-2016/

Goodlad, N., Eadie, D.R., Kinnin, H., & Raymond, M.: Advertorial: Creative Solution or Last Resort?. *International Journal of Advertising*. 16(2), 73–84 (1997).

Harlow, S.: *Liberation Technology in El Salvador: Re-appropriating Social Media Among Alternative Media Projects*. Springer International Publishing, Cham (2017).

Harlow, S., & Salaverría, R.: Regenerating Journalism: Exploring the "Alternativeness" and "Digital-ness" of Online-native Media in Latin America. *Digital Journalism*. 4(8), 1001–1019 (2016).

Hernández Aguirre, E.: Panamá. In: R. Salaverría (ed.) Ciberperiodismo en Iberoamérica, 273–286. Fundación Telefónica & Editorial Ariel, Madrid (2016).

Knight Center for Journalism in the Americas (2015): Journalism played a central role in the fall and arrest of the president of Guatemala. Retrieved from https://utw10693.utweb.utexas.edu/en/blog/00-16284-journalism-played-central-role-fall-and-arrest-president-guatemala

Molina Tamacas, C.: El Salvador. In: R. Salaverría (ed.) *Ciberperiodismo en Iberoamérica*, 145–167. Fundación Telefónica & Editorial Ariel, Madrid (2016).

O'Connor, A., Batalova, J., & Bolter, J.: MPI: Central American Immigrants in the United States. Migration Policy Institute (August 15, 2019). Retrieved from https://www.migrationpolicy.org/article/central-american-immigrants-united-states

Ortiz, I.M.: República Dominicana. In: R. Salaverría (ed.) *Ciberperiodismo en Iberoamérica*, 361–383. Fundación Telefónica & Editorial Ariel, Madrid (2016).

Perdomo de Zelaya, R.: Honduras. In: R. Salaverría (ed.) *Ciberperiodismo en Iberoamérica*, 225–239. Fundación Telefónica & Editorial Ariel, Madrid (2016).

Rockwell, R., & Janus, N.: *Media power in Central America*. University of Illinois Press, Chicago (2010).

Rodríguez-Hidalgo, C., Rivera-Rogel, D., & Romero-Rodríguez, L.M.: Information Quality in Latin American Digital Native Media: Analysis Based on Structured Dimensions and Indicators. *Media and Communication*. 8(2), 135–145 (2020).

Sabate, F., Berbegal-Mirabent, J., Cañabate, A., & Lebherz, P.R.: Factors Influencing Popularity of Branded Content in Facebook Fan Pages. *European Management Journal*, 32(6), 1001–1011 (2014).

Salaverría, R. (ed.): *Ciberperiodismo en Iberoamérica*. Fundación Telefónica & Editorial Ariel, Madrid (2016).

Salaverría, R.: Digital Journalism: 25 Years of Research. Review article. *El Profesional de la Información*. 28(1), e280101 (2019).

Salaverría, R.: Exploring Digital Native News Media. *Media and Communication*. 8(2), 1–4 (2020).

Salaverría, R., Martínez-Costa, M.P., & Breiner, J.: Map of Digital News Media in Spain in 2018: Quantitative Analysis. *Revista Latina de Comunicación Social*. 73, 1034–1053 (2018).

Salaverría, R., Sádaba, C., Breiner, J.G., & Warner, J.C.: A brave new digital journalism in Latin America. In: M. Túñez-López et al. (eds.) *Communication: Innovation & Quality*, 229–247. Springer International Publishing, Cham (2019).

SIP (Sociedad Interamericana de Prensa): Conclusiones de la 75 Asamblea General de la SIP October 7th, 2019. Retrieved from https://www.sipiapa.org/notas/1213492-conclusiones-la-75-asamblea-general-la-sip

Solórzano Canales, R.: Nicaragua. In: R. Salaverría (ed.) *Ciberperiodismo en Iberoamérica*, 255–272. Fundación Telefónica & Editorial Ariel, Madrid (2016).

Tejedor, S., Ventín, A., Cervi, L., Pulido, C., & Tusa, F.: Native Media and Business Models: Comparative Study of 14 Successful Experiences in Latin America. *Media and Communication*. 8(2), 146–158 (2020).

Zuniga Gutiérrez, L., & Hopmann, C.: *Mapping Digital Media*: Nicaragua. Open Society Foundation, London (2013).

11 Disinformation and news consumption in a polarized society

An analysis of the case of Venezuela[1]

Javier Serrano-Puche, Carmen Beatriz Fernández and Jordi Rodríguez Virgili

Introduction and theoretical framework

Up until a few years ago, disinformation used to be synonymous with "lack of information," ascribable to citizens' low interest in public affairs. However, since 2016 and especially as a result of the U.S. electoral campaign (Allcott & Gentzkow, 2017) and Brexit (Bastos & Mercea, 2019), disinformation also becomes a spoken about factor, above all referring to the deliberate efforts of certain agents to misinform with lies and half-truths, intoxicating and even saturating the citizen, in what have been called "disinformation operations." Much of the success of these false news lies in their virality, that is, in their ability to be shared by Internet users throughout different social networks and instant messaging applications.

From a broader perspective, disinformation is a modality within what has been called "problematic information" (Jack, 2017), which includes various types of information that are inaccurate, misleading, improperly attributed, or totally fabricated. Although it is true that these contents are not novel—their existence goes back to the origins of modern journalism with the yellow press (Campbell, 2001) and to the use of propaganda in the World Wars (Lasswell, 1927), the existing communicational characteristics in the digital age do promote new ways for problematic information to be created, circulated, and received by users, increasing its potential effects (Freelon & Wells, 2020). In the words of Boczkowski (2017): "fake news [have] been around for as long as real news. But a differentiating element of the contemporary moment is the existence of an information infrastructure with a scale, scope, and horizontality in information flows unprecedented in history" (p. 4).

This information infrastructure is related to aspects of a technological, but also political, social, and economic nature, giving rise to a "disinformation order" (Bennett & Livingston, 2018). This is manifested through the public sphere in many countries, which has suffered a disruption due to growing challenges that confront "the democratic centering principles of (a) authoritative information, (b) emanating from social and political institutions that (c) engage trusting and credulous publics" (Bennett & Livingstone, 2018, pp. 126–127). For this reason, according to authors such as Chadwick (2019), this drift has to be framed in a broader crisis of public communication. A sign of this crisis is the decline in confidence in political institutions as well as the media, which traditionally has the role of ensuring the proper functioning of these institutions. Again, the configuration of the digital ecosystem accentuates both the financial and identity problems of journalistic media.

In a context marked by the overabundance of information and by the power that platforms hold over the production and distribution of content (Nieborg & Poell, 2018; Nielsen & Ganter, 2018), the media outlets must compete for users' time and attention, against many other players also seeking to monetize from it. Among these, other companies that operate without the demands of impartiality, rigor, and professionalism required for serious journalistic endeavors, since they base their editorial model on offering partisan information that feeds the growing "affective polarization" of citizens (Iyengar & Westwood, 2015; Tucker et al., 2018). These partisan media take advantage of phenomena such as selective exposure, in which the consumer tries to avoid any type of cognitive dissonance (Walter et al., 2019). Thus, the breakage in institutional authority and processes of political representation, combined with the rise of alternative information channels that try to exploit ideological niches in a "clickbait economy" (Munger, 2020), gives rise to a great variety of problematic information flows.

In order to understand the contemporary information ecosystem, we must pay attention to several elements (Wardle, 2017): the different types of content that are created and disseminated, the motivations of those who create those contents, the ways in which these are disseminated and, finally, the ways in which people consume news in actuality.

Firstly, regarding the types of content that fall under the paradigm of "problematic information," the term "fake news" has reached the most popularity (to the extent that it was chosen as the 'word of the year' by the Oxford Dictionary in 2017). However, there are numerous researchers (Freelon & Wells, 2020; High Level Expert Group on Fake News and Disinformation, 2018; Wardle & Derakhshan, 2017) who advocate for using more appropriate concepts to describe the complex phenomenon of disinformation in all its variants. In addition, it is a biased term and has been used as a political weapon, being often used by politicians to pressure journalistic companies whose news coverage is critical of them (Khaldarova & Pantti, 2016; van der Linden, Panagopoulos, & Roozenbeek, 2020). Therefore, it is preferable to opt for the concept of disinformation, understood as "all forms of false, inaccurate, or misleading information designed, presented and promoted to intentionally cause public harm or for profit" (HLEG, 2018, p. 5).

Secondly, this definition for disinformation, employed by the High-Level Expert Group on Fake News and Disinformation designated by the European Commission, includes a second parameter that aids us in cataloguing the ensemble of misinformative genres: the motivation of whoever creates the content. Indeed, the intention to cause harm or to seek profit is a vector that allows malicious disinformation and deliberately polarized content to be distinguished from other modalities where online content is not truthful, such as satirical news or journalistic pieces that turn out to be imprecise due to misinformation or lack of professionalism, even if there is no motivation for causing intentional deception or confusion. Considering Molina et al. (2019), aspects such as the content itself (factuality, lexical, and syntactic features, presented evidence), the sources consulted, and the identity and intentions of the issuing agent and other structural elements (such as URL, the transparency of the website that broadcasts it or the metadata), allow the establishment of a taxonomy of false content modalities that contrast with the "real news." The modalities might vary, going from manufactured news to disguised advertising, passing through parodic news or information from hyperpartisan sources.

Thirdly, attention must be paid to how disinformation is disseminated in the digital environment, starting with the idea that traditional and new media actors coexist in the "hybrid media system" (Chadwick, 2013), which operate on overlapping and competing media logics, presenting different levels of potential reach, epistemological authority, and manipulative skills. Along with this, the act of "sharing" has become a dominant pattern in digital consumption habits (John, 2016). The preeminence of the act of sharing, together with the logic of prosumption (according to which each user can be both a producer and a consumer of content), causes a multiplication of agents broadcasting to potential recipients within the digital space. Thus, in the contemporary information cycle, multiple actors are involved, both in the creation phase and in the dissemination of content.

For this reason, following Giglietto et al. (2019), it is convenient to challenge previous perspectives and not only focus on the potential creators of disinformation, instead broadening the focus and analyzing the propagators—intentional or not—of said disinformation. In this sense, for Valenzuela et al. (2019) political commitment is an important consequence of the use of social networks for information and it becomes a decisive factor when it comes to sharing false news. According to Giglieto et al. (2019), the distribution of these contents takes the form of "cascades of false information" (635), where:

- The intention of, what they call, the "injector" does not determine the future evolution of the false information cycle (and thus, what started as a parody or journalistic error might be amplified for manipulative purposes).
- The information advances in a process where different actors, according to criteria related to the source, the narrated facts, and the context, evaluate the veracity of the content (or lack of thereof).
- The social consensus around the veracity of the information, even when it has been subjected to fact checking, will hardly be unanimous, given the "confirmation biases" and tribalism (Nickerson, 1998; Sunstein, 2017) that underlie informational consumption habits of broad social groups.

After briefly reviewing the types of content that are created and disseminated, the motivations of those who create those contents, and the ways in which they are disseminated, it is necessary to address the last dimension on the ways in which people consume news. Exposure to news by citizens is conditioned by the action of various factors, among which are the overabundance of information from different channels, constant connectivity, the economy of attention, the multiplicity of screens and their simultaneous use, and the socialization of information consumption (Serrano-Puche, 2017). These factors, in the aforementioned hybrid media system, cause the "cross-mediality" between online and offline platforms, as one of the keys to news consumption. This cross-mediality, considering that social networks represent the main channel of dissemination of hoaxes (Paniagua, Seoane, & Magallón-Rosa, 2020; Resende et al., 2019; Salaverría et al., 2020), increases the potential consequences of disinformation. Indeed, in the consumption of digital news, there is often a phenomenon called incidental exposure to information, which occurs when the person who accesses the Internet with motivations such as entertainment or sociability, meets the news without looking for it directly (Serrano-Puche, Fernández & Rodríguez-Virgili, 2018). News consumption thus becomes a by-product of online activities. It ceases to be an independent activity and forms part of a continuous connection to the online environment, in such a way that news are not sought per se, but still reach the user mixed with other social and entertainment content, therefore making news devoid of context and hierarchy.

Considering the above aspects, new examinations on disinformation and the relationship between information use and trust in media content seems to be pertinent (Kalogeropoulos, Suiter, & Eisenegger, 2019). Numerous previous investigations highlight variables such as group membership, partisanship or membership in a certain party, which affect the credibility attributed to the media (Gronke & Cook, 2007; Lee & Shin, 2014; Oyedeji, 2007; Paniagua et al., 2020). In the following section we examine the relationship between the media ecosystem, disinformation, and social polarization, using Venezuela as a case study.

Media in Venezuela: A review of recent history

The development of a "communication hegemony" was declared as an explicit objective of the Chávez government in 2007 in the Nation's medium-term plan. Starting with a first tweet in April 2010, Chávez became an enthusiastic promoter of the network, motivating his physical followers to also become digital followers. Two months earlier, he had warned: "The Internet is a combat trench that is already bringing a current of conspiracy" (Primera, 2014). With the birth of his Twitter account, Chávez also aspired to conquer cyberspace. With this notion of Twitter as "combat trench," "Twitter battalions" quickly began to assemble. There is evidence that in Venezuela, the later called "troll farms," which would become so famous in the post-electoral analyzes of the 2016 North American race, started very early. The trend in Venezuela would have started around 2011 (Fernández, 2018a), in company of other countries in the subregion where there is also evidence of early appearances, such as Brazil in 2010 or Ecuador in 2014 (Bradshaw & Howard, 2017).

This information oligopoly came accompanied with exercises of "problematic information" of a different nature. However, this total communication hegemony was not consummated during the Chávez government but during the presidency of Nicolás Maduro. Starting with the highly disputed presidential election of April of 2013, with a virtual tie between the two political blocks in the country, one of these blocks was silenced in the traditional media, due to the new editorial direction acquired by the media network. A new communicational architecture was consolidated during the second semester of 2013 (Fernández, 2018b). Between the years of 1974 and 2004, the Venezuelan State had counted on a public television channel: Venezolana de Televisión. From that sole official television signal, the amount of State-run public television channels grew up to six. By 2013, the Venezuelan government operated three national radio circuits and more than 250 community radio stations. To this were added three newspapers financed with public funds, as well as several private media outlets whose editorial lines echoed the official ones. All this would configure the "Mixed-Authoritarian" communication landscape (Cañizales & Matos-Smith, 2015), which forces the content and editorial line, but allows for the presence of the private sector. The Maduro government combined the aggressive occupation of some media outlets with the acquisition of others. In several cases, the government facilitated access to preferential currency exchange for pro-government business sectors to acquire communication channels. Since Maduro's rise to power in 2013 until October of 2018, 115 media outlets (including 25 newspapers) felt forced to close in Venezuela (Ramírez-Alvarado, 2020).

Despite the hegemony over the media, the Maduro government failed to seize the audience. A television audience report by pollster Nielsen, released in August 2013, showed that almost half of the national audience was concentrated on five private television stations, while the five national public television stations holding just 8% of the audience (Nielsen, 2013). As a paradigmatic example, after the government refused to renew the signal concession for Venezuela's leading channel, RCTV in 2007, the public state-backed channel that replaced it, TVES, saw its audience decrease significantly: from 46% to less than 2% of the national audience (Fernández, 2018b).

The failed effort to conquer their own audiences resulted in the indiscriminate use of "cadenas," government-forced overtakes of radio and television networks for short periods of time. President Chávez spoke on "cadenas" of national radio and television networks for more than one hundred hours a year. His disciple and successor, Nicolás Maduro would follow with an even more intense rhythm, averaging half an hour of forced content daily (Monitoreo Ciudadano, 2020). With the increase of "cadenas" in radio and

TV channels, the country's cable operators found a very important incentive in selling paid channels. The cable television industry flourished to the point that nowadays two-thirds of urban households in Venezuela have access to subscription television, free from governmental "cadenas." In this new communicational architecture, the penetration of cable television increased 11 points in 2013, from 55.75% to more than two-thirds of the country, 66.86% equivalent to 1,390,608 households (Fernández, 2018b).

Not only did television audiences migrate to paid cable television, there were also prominent internal tropisms in digital media. Both phenomena parallel what Iyengar and Hahn (2009) identified: there is growing evidence that when voters identify biases in the news channels, they seek alternative sources of information that are more consistent with their political preferences. The expansion of cable TV and the existence of numerous informational options on the Internet create a much more fragmented and competitive informational environment than that of 20 years ago, giving the reader/viewer a much wider range of sources to choose from (Ramírez-Alvarado, 2007). In the Venezuelan case, starting from the 2013 turning point, an explosion of new digital media was generated.

While changes of media ownership were occurring, with their editorial lines causing a reduction in audience, and with audiences migrating to digital media (or from one digital media to another) online tactics of disinformation from the government also changed, innovated, and adapted to the new landscape. It is then that those in power forged the new closing of digital spaces: from 2013 the broadband service provided to universities was reduced, with interruptions and website blocking practices becoming more and more frequent (Uribarrí & Díaz, 2018). The Venezuelan government pioneered the use of bots to create opinion trends on Twitter, known as *astroturfing* (Howard, 2006). Three different tactics used by the government have been identified (Puyosa, 2018): (i) use of official governmental accounts and automated accounts to reach the trending topics daily; (ii) promotion of distraction tags through the use of cyborg accounts and bot accounts, with the use of emotional, scandalous, misinformative, offensive and/or false messages; (iii) kidnapping of opposition tags to distort their speeches and interfere conversations of various communities of opponents. In the Venezuelan case, and contrary to what is suggested by Giglieto et al. (2019), disinformation seems to fundamentally come from the hand of the creators/issuers of disinformation (MacLeod, 2018), while the analysis of the propagators-intended or not- of said disinformation has been understudied (Deltell et al., 2013; Forelle et al., 2015). On the other hand, the information blockade promoted by the government fertilizes the territory for the proliferation of false news related to both the ruling party and the opposition. As radio stations, online media and websites are blocked, and print media outlets in the country are closing, the pressing need to understand what is happening grows, which explains why many Venezuelans turn to social media to stay aware of news (Ramírez-Alvarado, 2020).

Methodology

In order to carry out this investigation, 1216 telephone interviews were conducted through cell phones in Venezuela. The survey firm More Consulting carried out the field work, which took place between January 20th and 29th of 2020. The demographic of the study consists of people older than 18 years registered in the national electoral registry. The type of sampling consisted of a random selection of municipalities previously classified according to different strata (cities of large, medium, and small size, rural and urban, with various levels of poverty). In these municipalities, a selection was made of both the telephone samples and interviewees by dynamization of quotas (by region, sex, and age). The sampling error is 2.81%, with a confidence level of 95%.

The questionnaire as a whole includes questions related to interest in politics, news consumption, trust in the media, and concern about disinformation, among other issues. For this work, the answers pertaining to the following research questions are analyzed:

RQ1: *In a polarized society like that of Venezuela, are there notable differences between the ways of informing themselves among pro-government and pro-opposition supporters?*

RQ2: *What are the types of digital disinformation that Venezuelans are most concerned about?*

RQ3: *Is it possible to notice a different sensitivity to the different forms of digital or online disinformation based on the political self-definition of Venezuelans, their age, their gender or their educational level?*

Analysis of information sources

According to the figures reported by World Internet Stats (CITE), the 23.6 million Venezuelan citizens had Internet access by December 2019, which would be equivalent to a rate of penetration of 83.0% (using the governmental regulator agency Conatel as a source). Global Digital Inside (2020), however, handles the lower figure of 72% rate of penetration by January of 2020. This number does not use CONATEL as an official source, as it has been accused of altering the statistical measurement to artificially inflate the penetration numbers (Uribarri, 2018). The figure is identical to that given by the investigation's sources for the entire region (72% in January 2020).

However, this research does not use this web penetration data, because although our survey finds that 79% of the respondents have access to the Internet, with 67% stating to be users of social networks (the same proportion that Data Report claimed for the region as a whole in February of 2020), only 34% of the surveyed population identify digital sources as their main means of information. When asked about the sources of information, respondents were asked which news sources they had used the previous week, and of these news sources they were asked to identify which they considered to be the main one. The results indicate that the dominant medium among the surveyed population continues to be television as a source of news information. However, there is clear evidence of "cross-mediality" consumption, or cross-media use, within what Chadwick (2013) conceptualizes as the hybrid system. Therefore, when asking the question, emphasis was placed on the "main source of information."

The questionnaire included several questions with the goal of categorizing the ideological position of the Venezuelans surveyed. One question asked participants to self-position in terms of ideological left/right. Another question inquired about the participants' perspective on the Venezuelan regime as a democracy or a dictatorship. A third question, which is used in this analysis, asked the participants to position themselves in one of the following categories: (a) "Committed to Maduro" (Signifying support for current Venezuelan president, Maduro; this category will be coded as "Oficialista"), (b) "Chavista, but not madurista" (signifying support for Chavez but not for his successor), (c) "Committed to the MUD" (Signifying support for la Mesa de Unidad Democrática, the opposition coalition), (d) "Part of the opposition but not aligned with the MUD," or (e) "All politicians are equal."(This category will be coded as "not aligned" and will be later integrated with those who refrained from answering the question). Subsequently, in order to simplify the visibility of the data, and for the purposes of modeling, these categories were re-coded into only three: options (a) and (b) were integrated as "Chavistas," options (c) and (d) were unified as "Opositores," while option (e) was integrated with those they refrained from answering under the category of "Not aligned."

The responses to the question concerning the main source of information show important differences in the sources of information used by those who are in favor of the Maduro government and those who oppose it (Table 11.1). While the participants that support Maduro's government and/or Chavez' government, called "Chavistas" have preferences for traditional media (51.4% for TV), the participants supporting the opposition, called "Opositores," are predominantly informed by digital media (39% for RRSS). The participants so-called non-aligned, claimed TV is their main source (39.4%), although with a less significant rate than their "Chavistas" counterparts. This trend is reinforced by data on newspaper usage through the Internet or apps. Social networks are the main source of news information for 39% of "Opositores," for 22.3% of the non-aligned, and down to 14.7% for "Chavistas;" newspapers on the Internet or in apps are the main source of news information for 12.7% of the "Opositores," falling to being the main source for only 7.1% of the non-aligned, and only 3.4% for the "Chavistas."

Table 11.1 Main source of news information used the previous week, by political self-positioning (January 2020)

	Chavistas	*Opositores*	*Not Aligned*	*Abs. Freq.*
Television news bulletins or programs	51.4%	26.3%	39.4%	**470**
24 hour news television channels	13.8%	6.5%	10.0%	**121**
Radio news programs or bulletins	7.0%	7.9%	6.7%	**87**
Printed newspapers	2.8%	0.8%	2.3%	**24**
Websites/apps of newspapers	3.4%	12.7%	7.1%	**95**
Websites/apps of news magazines	0.3%	1.6%	1.7%	**16**
Social media	14.7%	39.0%	22.3%	**308**
Blogs	0.3%	0.0%	0.6%	**4**
Through conversations with family, friends, or acquaintances	4.9%	1.9%	7.5%	**62**
None of these	1.5%	2.7%	2.1%	**26**
NR/DK	0.0%	0.5%	0.2%	**3**
Frequency	**327**	**369**	**520**	**1216**

In order to better visualize the relative impact of the main news sources on distinct political segments, they were regrouped to differentiate between analog and digital sources (Table 11.2).

Types of disinformation, agents that cause it, and ways to combat it

As we have pointed out in the previous pages, the term "disinformation" includes very diverse practices in matters such as intention, content, and emitters, so it is worth wondering whether if this diversity of forms of disinformation is of equal concern to Venezuelans. When the respondents were

Table 11.2 Main source of analog/digital news information by ideological self-positioning

	Chavistas	*Opositores*	*Not aligned*	*Frequency*
Main news source is analogic	75.0%	41.5%	58.4%	702
Main new source is digital	18.7%	53.3%	31.7%	423
Through conversations with family, friends, or acquaintances	4.9%	1.9%	7.5%	62
None of these	1.5%	2.7%	2.1%	26
NR/DK	0.0%	0.5%	0.2%	3
Frequency	327	369	520	1216

asked about these modalities of "problematic information," the results indicate that for both "Chavistas" and "Opositores" categories, the most worrying factor (55.7%) is mediocre journalism, that is, data errors, simplified news, misleading or headlines that might serve as lures to obtain visits or clicks (Table 11.3). The second most worrying modality (52.3%) consists of news in which the facts are modified or rigged to favor partisan interests (in this case, the concern is greater among "Opositores" than among the pro-government faction: 56.6% vs. 52.9%). The third most recurrent answer was about concern for news that are entirely made up for commercial or political reasons, which worry 49.3% of the participants. In fourth place, 47% of those surveyed reported concern for false news or fake news by politicians or others with the intention of discrediting. In contrast, only 30% of the respondents seemed to be concerned with headlines that look like news but are actually advertisements, and only 1 in 5 respondents (19.9%) were concerned about satires or news that are totally invented to make people laugh.

As a counterpart to the previous question, respondents were also asked the following: "Which of the following disinformation agents do you find most worrying? In other words, in which of the following actors would the

Table 11.3 Type of disinformation most worrisome, ordered by ideological self-positioning

To what extent, if at all, are you concerned about the following …

	General	*Chavistas*	*Opositores*	*Not aligned*
Poor journalism (factual mistakes, dumbed down stories, misleading headlines/clickbait)	55.7%	59%	58.6%	51.7%
Stories where facts are spun or twisted to push a particular agenda	52.3%	52.9%	56.6%	48.9%
Stories that are completely made up for political or commercial reasons	49.3%	52.9%	54%	43.7%
Headlines that look like news stories but turn out to be advertisements	30.7%	34.6%	31.7%	27.5%
Stories that are completely made up to make people laugh (satire)	19.9%	22.6%	19.6%	18.4%
The use of the term fake news (e.g. by politicians, others) to discredit news media they don't like	47.4%	50.1%	54.2%	41%

Note

The results include "very concerned" + "extremely concerned" answers.

Table 11.4 Disinformation agent more worrisome, due to ideological self-positioning

Which of the following disinformation agents is most concerning to you? In other words, in which of the following actors would the use of fake news be more serious?

	General	*Chavistas*	*Opositores*	*Not aligned*
Actions from journalists or the media	30.6%	35.5%	27.6%	29.6%
Actions from politicians or political parties	29.4%	19.6%	41.7%	26.7%
Actions from foreign agents or international interference	21.4%	31.2%	12.5%	21.5%
Actions from groups of activists	5.9%	4.6%	6.0%	6.7%
Actions from ordinary citizens	5.6%	4.3%	6.0%	6.2%
NR/DK	7.2%	4.9%	6.2%	9.2%

use of fake news be more serious?" (Table 11.4). Here again the answer varies depending on the self-reported ideological spectrum: for the participants under the "Chavistas" category, journalists and the media seem to be of most concern (35.5%), closely followed by foreign agents (31.2%). For the participants under the "Opositores" category, the use of "fake news" by political actors was reported as most concerning (41.7%).

Concerns about disinformation

To explore concerns and sensitivity toward disinformation, one of the questions in the questionnaire inquired about the level of agreement with the following statement: "Regarding online news, I am concerned about what is true and what is false on the Internet" (Table 11.5). Considering the participants' answers, and following the trend, there seems to be a stark difference between the positions of the respondents depending on ideological affiliation, with 69.4% of the "Chavistas" category agreeing or strongly agreeing with the statement. While only 57.4% of "Oppositores" and 55.6% of "Not Aligned" participants agreeing with the statement.

Table 11.5 Concern about disinformation according to ideological self-positioning

Thinking about online news, I am concerned about what is real and what is fake on the internet.

	General	*Oficialistas*	*Opositores*	*Not aligned*
Strongly disagree + tend to disagree	18.7%	24.8%	10.6%	20.6%
Neither agree nor disagree	18.8%	18.0%	18.2%	19.6%
Tend to agree + strongly agree	59.5%	54.7%	69.4%	55.6%
NR/DK	3.0%	2.4%	1.9%	4.2%

Considering this data, however, it's uncertain whether or not this difference might the product of ideological polarization or just a spurious relationship, consequence of the fact that "Opositores" respondents might consume mostly digital media as a source of news information, or another unidentified demographic variable. To clear this doubt, a Poisson regression model was performed with the intention of explaining concern about disinformation as a function of various demographic variables that could be influencing the questions regarding level of concern about disinformation. Concern about disinformation was assumed as a Dependent Variable with ideological self-positioning, gender, educational level, and the main source of information as independent variables.

From the premise that ideology can have a significant impact on the level of concern about disinformation, two variables were used: ideological self-positioning and the question regarding Venezuela as having a democratic or dictatorial government ("Do you believe that we are in democracy or dictatorship?"). This question serves as an indirect way of measuring ideological approach, being less explicit than the right/left self-positioning question. With a significance value of less than 0.05, none of the variables related to polarization (ideological self-positioning or perception of democracy/dictatorship) was significant, indicating that the current model exceeds the null model. In other words, the null model indicates that these independent variables do not explain the dependent variable. Thus, ideological variables do not affect concern about disinformation. In a country that is perceived as deeply polarized, this result is undoubtedly striking.

However, other variables can influence the concern about disinformation. After analyzing the results, we propose a disinformation model that is linked to two variables: educational level and main source of information.

> **Concern about Disinformation = - 0.554 Completed Elementary school education - 0.478 Incomplete Secondary/High school education - 0.384 Completed Secondary/High school education - 0.451 Incomplete Technic/University degree- 0.211Completed University/Master's degree - 0.161 Analog.**

Concern about misinformation seemed to decrease in parallel to educational level, meaning participants with less educational level seemed less concerned with misinformation, with participants with higher educational levels being more concerned. Concern about misinformation also lessened among participants that reported the use of digital media as the main source of news information. These results allow us to infer which populations are most vulnerable to the phenomenon of disinformation: those who, being less educated and resting more on analogue sources for information, are less concerned about finding false news on the internet.

Table 11.6 Poisson regression coefficients

	Coeff	*S. E.*
Elementary School	−0.554 **	0.1460
High school not completed	−0.478 **	0.1234
High school completed	−0.384 **	0.0843
Some university (not completed)	−0.451 **	0.0944
University or Master's degree	−0.211 **	0.0765
Analogical main source	−0.161 *	0.0797

Note
*$p < 0.05$.
**$p < 0.01$.

Discussion and conclusions

Throughout this chapter we have examined how media consumption and the incidence of disinformation occur in the Latin American context, taking Venezuela as a case study. The first research question (RQ1) interrogates whether, in a society that perceives itself as highly polarized as that of Venezuela, there are notable divergences in ways of reporting news between pro-government participants and pro-opposition participants. This research confirms previous findings (Fernández & Rodríguez-Virgili, 2017, 2019) in the sense that in Venezuela there are clear differences in media consumption between government supporters and opponents: the former opt for traditional medias such as television and the latter prefer digital medias and social networks. Indeed, television channels, whose editorial management is dominated by the government, are used as a means of political information by the government supporters (51.4%); while, on the contrary, opposition supporters are predominantly informed by digital means (39%). For the self-classified as non-aligned, television is still their main source of information, but in a considerably less significant way (39.4%) than for the pro-government participants, as they tend to turn toward social networks more frequently than pro-government participants (22.3% of the unaligned and 14.7% of the government supporters). These results confirm the selective exposure theory, which states that media consumption is influenced by the predispositions of the audience, which seeks to confirm or reinforce their opinions on the content of the information (Lazarsfeld, Berelson, & Gaudet, 1948). As discussed in the theoretical framework, citizens seek information that aligns as closely as possible with their previously existing ideas on political reality (Iyengar & Hahn, 2009; Stroud, 2010; Walter et al., 2019). This return to selective exposure theory is based on two premises: the multiplication of channels to obtain information and the emergence of a journalism model distanced from objectivity, allowing for partisan exposure (Stroud, 2011). Both of these premises are prominent and fulfilled in the Venezuelan case study.

However, there seems to be no apparent differences between ideological groups regarding the types of digital disinformation that most concern them, an issue that was raised in our second research questions. The Venezuelan citizens surveyed, regardless of whether they were pro-government, pro-opposition, or non-aligned, seemed to be concerned about the misinformation caused by poor journalism, that is, data errors, simplified news, deceptive headlines or that serve as a mere lure. In the same way, they also expressed concern about misinformation caused by modified news or rigged news to favor partisan interests. In the latter case, a slight difference is observed between the pro-opposition "Opositores'" category (56.6%) and the pro-government "Chavistas" category (52.9%). Results also show that they are concerned, but to a lesser extent, about news being entirely made up for commercial or political reasons as well as fake news used by politicians or others with the intention of discrediting. Thus, as seen in the theoretical framework, the intimate relationship between the crisis of journalism and disinformation, and how partisan journalism might be affecting and eroding trust in the media is once again confirmed.

Differences are again detected between ideological groups regarding concerns about the severity of the disinformation agent. For those participants ideologically aligned with the Venezuelan government, the pro-government "Chavista" category, the use of fake news by journalists and the media seems to be of more concern, as well as the use of fake news by possible foreign agents. For the participants aligned with the Venezuelan opposition, the "Opositores" category, disinformation spread by political actors seems to be of more serious concern.

All in all, the main finding of this research lies in the variables that affect levels of concern about digital disinformation in Venezuela. In this case it is not about ideological self-positioning but fundamentally about the participants' educational level and their main sources of information. Following this argument, the authors of this work propose a simple digital disinformation model to detect sensitivity and concern about this global problem. The model consists of disinformation as a function dependent on educational level and the main source of information:

$$\text{Disinformation } f(d) = a \text{ (educational level)} + b \text{ (main source of information)}.$$

This model would allow identifying and locating population groups that might be more vulnerable to digital disinformation. Much remains to be understood about this phenomenon, which, although not new, constitutes a novel threat to liberal democracies and, in general, to institutions. Undoubtedly, it will be necessary to continue deepening the study of disinformation, as this model could be applied in different Latin American countries to verify its validity. Considering crossed-sectional analysis and comparative analysis between countries as essential to advance knowledge of this global phenomenon, this study proposes the above model as a modest but useful contribution.

Note

1. **Acknowledgment:** This chapter is part of a project entitled "Disinformation in Venezuela," financed by European funds contributed to the Venezuelan chapter of Transparency International. Authors declare that they have no conflict of interest. Authors would like to thank Dr. Jennifer Campos for her valuable statistical advice. They also thank Beatriz Nieto Fernández for her precious help in proofreading the manuscript.

References

Allcott, H., & Gentzkow, M. (2017): Social media and fake news in the 2016 Election. *Journal of Economic Perspectives*, 31(2), 211–236. doi:10.1257/jep.31.2.211

Bastos, M.T., & Mercea, D. (2019): The Brexit botnet and user-generated hyperpartisan news. *Social Science Computer Review*, 37(1), 38–54. https://doi.org/10.1177/0894439317734157

Bennett, W. L., & Livingston, S. (2018): The disinformation order: Disruptive communication and the decline of democratic institutions. *European Journal of Communication*, 33(2), 122–139. doi:10.1177/0267323118760317

Boczkowski, P. (2017): La posverdad. Las noticias falsas y el futuro del periodismo. *Revista Anfibia*. Retrieved from: http://www.revistaanfibia.com/ensayo/la-post verdad/.

Bradshaw, S., & Howard, P. (2017): Troops, Trolls and Troublemakers: A Global Inventory of Organized Social Media Manipulation. *COMPROP Working Paper Series*, Oxford University Retrieved from: https://ora.ox.ac.uk/objects/uuid:cef7e8d9-27bf-4ea5-9fd6-855209b3e1f6/download_file?safe_filename=Troops-Trolls-and-Troublemakers.pdf&file_format=application%2Fpdf&type_of_work=Report

Bradshaw, S., & Howard, P. (2019): *The Global Disinformation Order*. The Computational Propaganda Project at the Oxford Internet Institute. Retrieved from: https://comprop.oii.ox.ac.uk/wp-content/uploads/sites/93/2019/09/CyberTroop-Report19.pdf

Campbell, W. J. (2001): *Yellow Journalism: Puncturing the Myths, Defining the Legacies*. Westport: Praeger.

Cañizales, A., & Matos-Smith, M. (2015): El caso de Globovisión y la implantación del modelo mixto-autoritario en el sistema de medios. *Revista Iberoamericana*. 15(59), 127–140.

Chadwick A. (2013): *The Hybrid Media System: Politics and Power*. New York: Oxford University Press.

Chadwick, A. (2019): The New Crisis of Public Communication: Challenges and Opportunities for Future Research on Digital Media and Politics. *Online Civic Culture Center*. Retrieved from: https://www.lboro.ac.uk/research/online-civic-culture-centre/news-events/articles/o3c-2-crisis/

Deltell, L., Congosto, M. L, Claes, F., & Osteso, J. M. (2013): Identificación y análisis de los líderes de opinión en Twitter en torno a Hugo Chávez. *Revista Latina de Comunicación Social*, 68, 696–718. doi: 10.4185/RLCS-2013-997

Fernández, C. B. (2018a): Ciberpolítica 2018: Tendencias en Latinoamérica. In Wesseman, K. (ed). Nuevas campañas electorales en América Latina (pp. 147–162). Montevideo: Konrad Adenauer Stiftung.

Fernández, C.B. (2018b): Medios rojos y espectadores azules: cuando las audiencias deciden emigrar. Selectividad ideológica de las audiencias ante la estatización de la información en Venezuela. Revista Contratexto, 29, 181–198.

Fernández, C. B., & Rodríguez-Virgili, J. (2017): El consumo de información política de los públicos interesados comparado con el del electorado general. Los casos de las elecciones de Argentina, España y Venezuela de 2015. *Revista de comunicación*. 16(2), 60–87. https://doi.org/10.26441/RC16.2-2017-A3

Fernández, C. B., & Rodríguez-Virgili, J. (2019): Electors are from Facebook, political geeks are from Twitter: Political information consumption in Argentina, Spain and Venezuela. *KOME International Journal of Pure Communication Inquiry*. 7(1), 42–62. doi: 10.17646/KOME.75698.62.

Forelle, M. C., Howard, P. N., Monroy-Hernandez, A., & Savage, S. (2015): Political bots and the manipulation of public opinion in Venezuela. Retrieved from: http://papers.ssrn.com/sol3/papers.cfm?abstract_id=2635800

Freelon, D., & Wells, C. (2020): Disinformation as political communication. *Political Communication*, doi: 10.1080/10584609.2020.1723755 volume 37, issue 2, pages 145-156.

Giglietto, F., Iannelli, L., Valeriani, A., & Rossi, L. (2019): "Fake news" is the invention of a liar: How false information circulates within the hybrid news system. *Current Sociology*, 67(4), 625–642. doi:10.1177/0011392119837536

Global Digital Insights. (2020, January). Retrieved from http://www.datareportal.com/

Gronke, P., & Cook, T.E. (2007): Disdaining the media: The American public's changing attitudes toward the news. *Political Communication*, 24(3), 259–281.

High Level Expert Group on Fake News and Disinformation (HLEG). (2018): A multi-dimensional approach to disinformation: Report of the independent high level group on fake news and online disinformation. *European Commission*. Retrieved from: https://ec.europa.eu/digital-single-market/en/news/final-report-high-level-expert-group-fake-news-and-online-disinformation

Howard, P. (2006): *New Media Campaigns and the Managed Citizens*. Cambridge University Press, Cambridge, Massachusetts.

Iyengar Shanto, & Hahn, Kyu (2009): Red media, blue media: Evidence of ideological selectivity in media use. *Journal of Communication* 59(1), 19–39.

Iyengar, S., & Westwood, S. J. (2015): Fear and loathing across party lines: New evidence on group polarization. *American Journal of Political Science*, 59(3), 690–707.

Jack, C. (2017): Lexicon of lies: Terms for problematic information. *Data & Society*, 3. Retrieved from: https://datasociety.net/library/lexicon-of-lies/

John, N. A. (2016): *The Age of Sharing*. Cambridge, UK: Polity Press.

Kalogeropoulos, A., Suiter, J., & Eisenegger, M. (2019): News media trust and news consumption: Factors related to trust in news in 35 countries. *International Journal of Communication*, 13, 3.672–3.693.

Khaldarova, I., & Pantti, M. (2016): Fake news. *Journalism Practice*, 10(7), 891–901. doi:10.1080/17512786.2016.1163237

Lasswell, H. (1927): *Propaganda Technique in the World War*. New York: Peter Smith.

Lazarsfeld, P., Berelson, B., & Gaudet, H. (1948): *The People's Choice*. Nueva York: Columbia University Press.

Lee, E., & Shin, S. Y., (2014): When the medium is the message: How transportability moderates the effects of politicians' Twitter communication. *Communication Research*, 41(8), 1088–1110.

Macleod, A. (2018): *Bad News from Venezuela: Twenty Years of Fake News and Misreporting*. New York: Routledge.

Molina, M. D., Sundar, S. S., Le, T., & Lee, D. (2019): "Fake news" is not simply false information: A concept explication and taxonomy of online content. *American Behavioral Scientist*. doi:10.1177/0002764219878224

Monitoreo Ciudadano (2020): Caden-ó-metro. Contador de horas de Nicolás Maduro en Cadena Nacional de Radio y Televisión en Venezuela. Retrieved from: www.monitoreociudadano.org/cadenometro

Munger, K. (2020): All the news that's fit to click: The economics of clickbait media. *Political Communication*, 37(3), 376–397. doi:10.1080/10584609.2019.1687626

Nickerson R. S. (1998): Confirmation bias: A ubiquitous phenomenon in many guises. *Review of General Psychology*, 2(2), 175–220.

Nieborg, D. B., & Poell, T. (2018): The platformization of cultural production: Theorizing the contingent cultural commodity. *New Media & Society*, 20(11), 4275–4292.

Nielsen Report (2013): «*Medición de audiencias*». Agosto, Caracas.

Nielsen, R. K., & Ganter, S. A. (2018): Dealing with digital intermediaries: A case study of the relations between publishers and platforms. *New Media & Society*, 20(4), 1600–1617.

Oyedeji, T. A. (2007): Incredible Media or Incredulous Audience: The effects of Polarization and Partisanship on Media Credibility. *AEJMC Annual Convention Program*, Washington D.C.

Paniagua, F., Seoane, F., & Magallón-Rosa, R. (2020): Anatomía del bulo electoral: la desinformación política durante la campaña del 28-A en España. *Revista CIDOB d'Afers Internacionals*, 124, 123–145. doi: doi.org/10.24241/rcai.2020.124.1.123

Primera, M. (2014): El mapa venezolano de las redes sociales. *Yahoo Noticias*. Retrieved from: https://es-us.noticias.yahoo.com/el-mapa-venezolano-de-las-redes-sociales-234757537.html

Puyosa, I. (2018): Venezuelan Government Strategies for Information War on Twitter. *Center for Latin American and Caribbean Studies (CLACS)-Brown University*. Retrieved from: http://dx.doi.org/10.2139/ssrn.3459724

Ramírez-Alvarado, M. (2007): Escenarios de comunicación en una Venezuela polarizada: del Grupo Cisneros a la Ley Resorte. *Revista Zer*, 22, 283–300.

Ramirez-Alvarado, M. (2020): Post-Truths and Fake News in Disinformation Contexts: The Case of Venezuela. In Hernández-Santaolalla, V., & Barrientos-Bueno, M. (Eds.), *Handbook of Research on Transmedia Storytelling, Audience Engagement, and Business Strategies*. Hershey: IGI Global, 306–320.

Resende, G., Melo, P., Sousa, H., Messias, J., Vasconcelos, M., Almeida, J., & Benevenuto, F. (2019): (Mis)information dissemination in WhatsApp: Gathering, analyzing and countermeasures. *WWW'19: The World Wide Web conference*, 818–828. https://doi.org/10.1145/3308558.3313688

Salaverría, R., Buslón, N., López-Pan, F., León, B., López-Goñi, I., & Erviti, M. C. (2020): Desinformación en tiempos de pandemia: tipología de los bulos sobre la Covid-19. *El profesional de la información*, 29(3). https://doi.org/10.3145/epi.2020.may.15

Serrano-Puche, J.; Fernández, C. B; Rodríguez-Virgili, J. (2018). Political information and incidental exposure in social media: the cases of Argentina, Chile, Spain and México. *Doxa Comunicación*, 27: 19–42.

Serrano-Puche, J. (2017): Meta-analysis of digital consumption in the contemporary media ecosystem: Key factors and emotional implications. *Revista Mediterránea de Comunicación*, 8(1), 75–85. doi: 10.14198/MEDCOM2017.8.1.6.

Stroud, N. J. (2010): Polarization and partisan selective exposure. *Journal of Communication*, 60, 556–576.

Stroud, N. J. (2011): *Niche News: The Politics of News Choice: The Politics of News Choice*. Oxford: Oxford University Press.

Sunstein, C. R. (2017): *#Republic. Divided Democracy in the Age of Social Media*. New Jersey: Princeton University Press.

Tucker, J. A., Guess, A., Barberá, P., Vaccari, C., Siegel, A., Sanovich, S., Stukal, D., & Nyhan, B. (2018): *Social Media, Political Polarization, and Political Disinformation: A Review of the Scientific Literature*. Hewlett Foundation. Retrieved from: https://hewlett.org/wp-content/uploads/2018/03/Social-Media-Political-Polarization-and-Political-Disinformation-Literature-Review.pdf

Uribarri, R., & Díaz, M. (2018): Políticas públicas para el acceso a Internet en Venezuela. Inversión, infraestructura y el derecho al acceso entre los años 2000-2017. *Derechos Digitales*. Retrieved from: https://www.derechosdigitales.org/wp-content/uploads/CPI_venezuela.pdf

Valenzuela, S., Halpern, D., Katz, J. E., & Miranda, J. P. (2019): The paradox of participation versus misinformation: Social media, political engagement, and the spread of misinformation. *Digital Journalism*, 7(6), 802–823. doi/full/10.1080/21670811.2019.1623701

Van der Linden, S., Panagopoulos, C., & Roozenbeek, J. (2020): You are fake news: political bias in perceptions of fake news. *Media, Culture & Society*. https://doi.org/10.1177/0163443720906992

Walter, N., Cohen, J., Holbert, R. L., & Morag, Y. (2019): Fact-checking: A meta-analysis of what works and for whom. *Political Communication*, https://doi.org/10.1080/10584609.2019.1668894

Wardle, C. (2017): *Fake new: It's complicated*. Retrieved from: https://firstdraftnews.org/fake-news-complicated/

Wardle, C., & Derakhshan, H. (2017): *Information Disorder: Toward an Interdisciplinary Framework for Research and Policymaking*. Strasbourg: Council of Europe. Retrieved from: https://rm.coe.int/information-disorder-toward-an-interdisciplinary-framework-for-researc/168076277c

12 Social media in a post-truth age

Discursive roles of fake news about Marielle Franco

Priscila Muniz de Medeiros and Natália Martins Flores

Introduction

In the last few years, the rise of political and social tensions has brought a series of challenges to societies all around the world. In Brazil, progressive and conservative tensions turned the 2018 presidential elections into a fierce dispute. One representative moment in this turbulent time was the murder of Rio de Janeiro' City Councilwoman Marielle Franco seven months before the October elections. She and her driver were shot on the evening of March 14, 2018 while leaving a political event in downtown Rio.

Franco was born and raised in a Brazilian favela and was building a political career defending minorities, especially black and poor people from the favelas. She received the fifth-highest number of votes (46,502) in 2016 in the Rio municipal elections and integrated the left-wing Socialism and Liberty Party (PSOL). Despite being new, she was gaining a foothold in the Rio de Janeiro City Council. In February of 2018 she had a position on a commission which monitored and reported police abuse during the federal military intervention of the city to combat narco-trafficking gangs. She was actively reporting these abuses at City Council sessions as well as on social media. This is the reason why policemen involved with the Rio de Janeiro's *milícia* were the first suspects of her murder. In March 2019, two former police officers were arrested as suspects of the crime, but the investigators were still looking for the mastermind. Franco's death had worldwide repercussions. The mystery of who killed her or ordered her murdered has attracted international attention. Along with being on the front page of newspapers, many rumors have also emerged on social media accusing her of being connected to organized crime. A text published on a right-wing news website became the most shared content about her death on social media. Public figures replicated similar false content on WhatsApp, Facebook, and Twitter, which added more severity to this case. Accordingly, the media was forced to focus on the defense against these false narratives.

In this chapter we present an analysis of the discursive circulation and narrative construction of Franco's death on social media. We are interested in mapping the discursive formations (DFs) that supports "fake news" narratives in order to understand the strategy behind the online propagation of this content. We also want to understand the discursive functions of fake news, considering the new communication architectures and the hyperpolarization in Brazilian politics. We employ Discourse Analysis as a methodological procedure, focusing, especially on Foucault's (1969, 1971) and Maingueneau's (2011) perspective on DFs.

Digital public sphere and polarization in Brazil: The rise of an information schizophrenia

Fake news is a great concern among scholars, politicians, and citizens across the globe. This kind of content is constantly accused of interfering in elections by destroying the reputations of political adversaries. Despite the popularity of sharing fake news, the definition of the expression "fake news" itself does not have a consensus. Ireton and Posetti (2018) argue that the use of fake news helps to undermine the credibility of information that meets quality standards, since "news" would mean verifiable information in the public interest, and content that does not share these principles would not deserve the label, even if preceded by the term "fake." Wardle and Derakhshan (2017) also refrain from using the term fake news because they consider it "woefully inadequate to describe the complex phenomena of information pollution" (Wardle & Derakhshan, 2017, p. 5). Instead, critics prefer broader terms such as "information disorder." Wardle and Derakhshan (2017) propose a commonly known classification in which they identify three types of information disorders: misinformation, disinformation, and malinformation. For this paper, we will concentrate on the idea of "disinformation," "when false information is knowingly shared to cause harm" (Wardle & Derakhshan, 2017, p. 5).

An even broader, widely used concept is "post-truth." It became popular after being chosen in 2016 as the "Word of the Year" by the Oxford English Dictionary. It defined post-truth as "relating to or denoting circumstances in which objective facts are less influential in shaping public opinion than appeals to emotion and personal belief." McIntyre (2018) argues that even if falsehoods are not new, the idea that facts are less important than feelings in shaping our beliefs about empirical matters seems to be. "Thus, what is striking about the idea of post-truth is not just that truth is being challenged, but that it is being challenged as a mechanism for asserting political dominance" (McIntyre, 2018, Preface, para. 4). The author adds that post-truth is not a simple denial of the existence of a single objective truth, as relativists and postmodernists have stated for decades. Post-truth "is not so much a claim that truth does not exist as that facts are subordinate to our political point of view" (McIntyre, 2018, Chapter 1, para. 14). For McIntyre, it is as important to understand what post-truth is as understanding why it occurs. We will try to contribute to this questioning by analyzing Franco's case through an approach that utilizes technology shifts, political contexts, and discourse concepts.

Based on the studies supported this paper, we understand that there are at least three factors that helped create the perfect environment for the current worldwide disinformation era. The phenomenon is connected to the new communication architectures: the credibility crisis in traditional media, political polarization, and the rise of ideological bubbles created by social media's algorithms. Additionally, we identified three other factors, particular to Brazil's reality, which helped increase the effects of the 2018 disinformation crisis: the control of traditional media by only a few companies, the massive use of social media by Brazilians, and low education levels.

Journalists and scholars have been giving different reasons for the credibility crisis in traditional journalism. Some denounce bad journalistic practices as the main cause of the crisis, arguing that economic and political interests drove mainstream journalism away from the quality standards that would assure its connection to reality (Baptista, 2019). Others go further by linking the credibility crisis to the impartiality myth itself. They argue that traditional journalism built its legitimacy on a lie—the possibility of an impartial report of the facts. Now that the lie has been revealed, it melted away the once powerful journalistic legitimacy (Marcondes Filho, 2019). Even if we agree that bad journalism motivated by economic and political reasons is central to the crisis, we understand that the problem goes deeper, since the myth of impartiality can no longer thrive in a society marked by a decentralized media ecology.

In Brazil, the organization of the mass media into strong oligopolies made the fall of the impartiality myth even more dramatic. A survey published in 2018 by the NGO Reporters Without Borders placed Brazil as the country with the worst indicators for media plurality among 12 researched developing countries. Before the splintering in news sources, media concentration enabled political discourse in Brazil to be more homogeneous than in countries with more media diversity. The lack of diversity in political points of view would strengthen the idea of impartial reporting of facts.

The new media ecosystem allowed the emergence of new protagonists in the gatekeeping processes, which created a dynamic of decentralization. On the one hand, this dynamic allowed individuals and groups that used to be excluded from the mediatized public sphere to have voice and visibility. On the other hand, most of the new information emissaries are not familiarized with the professional codes of conduct, impairing the quality of the scattered contents (Amaral & Santos, 2019).

At first, the new plurality allowed Brazilians to access different points of view of the same facts. It was the "checkmate" for traditional journalism's monopolistic claim that it would be a mirror of reality. Subsequently, people started denouncing traditional media as partial, choosing what they assumed to be an "impartial" information sources aligned to their personal beliefs. Furthermore, in different countries, including Brazil, populist politicians started to accuse media vehicles of spreading fake news every time the information was not in their interests. Globally, traditional media has been constructed as the major enemy of conservative populist political discourse—along with immigrants.

The doubts about credibility in traditional journalism created a reference crisis. According to a 2019 Digital News Report from the Reuters Institute, in Brazil trust in news has fallen 11% in the last year. "Brazilians have the highest level of concern about misinformation and disinformation in our survey and high use of social media facilitated the spread of inaccurate information during the election" (Carro, 2019, para. 12).

The Reuters survey added that "Brazilians remain some of the heaviest users of social media in the world and usage of all the top social and messaging brands has gone up significantly again over the last year" (Carro, 2019). The survey also shows that WhatsApp is a primary network for discussing and sharing news in Brazil, where 53% of the population use it with this aim. This is what makes Brazil the leader in WhatsApp use for news among the researched countries. "Around half of our Brazilian (53%) and Malaysian (50%) samples use WhatsApp for news, compared with 9% in the UK, 6% in Australia, and just 4% in both the United States and Canada" (Newman, 2019, para. 11). Along with the high levels of social media usage in Brazil, there are great problems in its educational system. A 2018 survey showed that 29% of the population between the ages of 15 and 64 are functionally illiterate, which means their reading and writing skills are inadequate to clearly understand and interpret texts (Inaf Brasil, 2018). The loss of references, the wide exposure to diverse sources of information, and little ability to interpret information became an even more toxic combination after the hyperpolarization of Brazilian politics.

The polarization of the political debate can be understood as the reduction in the political diversity to only two poles in a process of discourse alignment (Ortellado & Ribeiro, 2018). A new kind of polarization, characterized by a strong emotional bias, is a global phenomenon connected to the rise of social media (Abranches, 2019). Such emotions, as a result of conflicts between groups, are more likely to be amplified among active militants (Mason, 2016). By allowing citizens to participate in the emission of media messages, the new communication environment enabled the rise of digital activists, reaching out to hyperpolarized public spheres all over the globe. Hyperpolarization in Brazilian politics had a clear starting point with the 2013 protests against the rise in transport fees in which thousands of Brazilians took to the streets. According to Ortellado and Ribeiro (2018), it was after those manifestations that the Brazilian digital public sphere started to substantially change.

Facebook then emerged as an important audience binder, working as a tool for political mobilization and enabling the emergence of new political groups (Ortellado & Ribeiro, 2018). The political goals of the 2013 protesters shifted from a clear agenda (opposing higher transport fees) to a less tangible list of claims and dissatisfactions that even united people with opposite demands. The streets became mirrors of Facebook profiles with thousands of people holding posters with his or her own particular claim. Ortellado and Ribeiro (2018) argue that the shift of agendas in the 2013 protests strengthened the polarization in Brazil. At first, civil society was united in a struggle against politicians and business representatives, for they were seen as being responsible for the rise in transport fees. Eventually, the struggle between civil society and political and economic oligarchies was replaced by the strong polarization between right and left.

By analyzing Facebook posts on political pages, Ortellado and Ribeiro (2018) showed that by 2013 the interactions were divided into four clusters, separated into two axes: right/left and politicians/civil society. Civil society pages of both right-wing and left-wing publishers did not interact with political pages, even though they shared the same ideology. By 2014, the separation between political parties and civil society disappeared since the interactions between the two kinds of pages rose. Simultaneously, interaction between left-wing and right-wing pages decreased. It was the beginning of polarization and by 2016, the polarization was consolidated, since the clusters amalgamated, creating a dualistic structure. "On the one hand, left-wing parties, identity movements and human rights formed an only cluster; on the other hand, right-wing parties, anti-corruption movements and penal populism formed the other" (Ortellado, 2018, para. 8). The author adds that the huge separation between the clusters in the Internet indicate that the interactions between them are minimal.

Researchers and other kinds of social actors have been arguing that the splintering of news sources caused by the liberation of the emission pole, which is a phenomenon where a great amount of people who used to be consumers start to use media to disseminate their own content (Lemos, 2009) along with the social media algorithms of relevance construction has led people to live in ideological bubbles (El-Bermawy, 2016; Lee, 2016; Parisier, 2011; Yeginsu, 2017). There is no scientific consensus over the existence, the importance, or the political consequences of filter-bubbles or echo chambers in what concerns the consumption of media. Efforts have been made to analyze the degree to which exposure to different opinions and social media content varies among individuals with different political positions.

While in the United States, a research showed a substantial amount of overlap in the ideological distributions of Twitter accounts followed by users on opposite ends of the political spectrum (Eady et al., 2019). In Brazil, other research showed the existence of information clusters in Twitter conversations about polemic political facts in the country (Recuero et al., 2017). The Brazilian research concluded that there are filtering processes that make the nodes of each political group give visibility only for information that coincides with their political positions. Such different results can obviously be due to methodological issues, but we cannot rule out the possibility of the influence of regional particularities.

If a group of citizens has access to information that suits only one pole of the political dispute—including fake news—its members will less likely be confronted with different versions. Even when they are confronted, emotions and passions raised by the polarization phenomenon will influence their likelihood of believing the fake news denials. This is even more serious if we consider the crisis of reference created by the credibility crisis in traditional journalism, which in Brazil increased because of its historical media concentration. In a country with terrible education levels, media literacy is not widespread, which is what makes such discernment even harder. These factors combined allowed the emergence of an "information schizophrenia" in Brazilian society.

By information schizophrenia, we mean the loss of contact of civil society with reality, which is promoted by disinformation campaigns. Educational issues make it harder for Brazilians to distinguish between good or bad information or between rumors and facts. Yet, hyperpolarization raises "confirmation bias" (Bakir & McStay, 2017), a tendency people have of validating only information that confirms their pre-existing beliefs, which is basically the essence of post-truth. If reality was consensual in the age of mass media, with variations over how people interpreted it, in the era of post-mass media such consensus is gone, and so different groups live under the dome of *entirely different realities*.

We can interpret the post-mass media era through a Foucauldian perspective as a context where the own nature of Discursive Formations comes to the first scene. The reality of social media bubbles exposed how discourse builds specific truth regimes (Foucault, 1969, 1971) to groups and societies in given historical periods and social contexts. Discursive subjects and objects, that is, who we are and what we talk about, only exist in relation to a given truth regime, to a specific *DF* that sets a pair of rules to enunciations (Foucault, 1971). This functioning can help us to explain the way distinct identities and world perspectives are formed in the political and social spectrum.

A discursive approach

The approach used to analyze the discursive construction of Franco's death is based on the fact that social media and journalism texts are related to a broader social and historical context. Accordingly, a methodological strategy can help us identify the historical background that unfolded after this discursive event. We take into account that textual marks assign a discursive identity to Franco based on social identities displayed by Brazilian discourses. Our methodological procedure then consists in collecting this textual evidence and interpreting it in the light of knowledge of social identities.

The notion of DF gives us some interesting directions to unfold the relations between linguistic material and social context. It was created by Foucault (1969, 1971) to highlight the dispersion of a discourse in a set of time and gains of a variety of forms in discourse analysis, depending on the adopted theoretical approach (Maingueneau, 2011). In Maingueneau's categorization (2011), the notion is used as a non-topic unit based on the interpretation of the analyst, differing from pre-formatted elements of topic units, which are explicitly in the text as discursive genres and linguistic marks. For Maingueneau (2011), DF is a central element to discourse analysis, as it permits the transgression of the frontiers of textual marks in a permanent relation between "inside" and "outside,"—that is, discourse and interdiscourse.

Our methodological procedure consists in analyzing the interdiscursive movements displayed by a dispersed *corpus* of texts regarding Franco's death. These *corpora* include fake news disseminated on social media about Franco in the form of texts and images. This data collection was compiled via access to the Brazilian fact-checking pages of Boatos.org, E-farsas, and Aos Fatos using the keywords "Marielle Franco" on their websites' research mechanisms. We focused on content published from March 2018 to March 2019. The search produced 36 texts (18 from Boatos.org; 5 from E-farsas; and 13 from Aos Fatos). The interpretation of this material allowed us to map their predominant DFs.

The circulation of Marielle Franco's death between social and traditional media

The false narratives about Franco rapidly emerged on social media after her murder, starting on the morning of March 15, 2018. The rumors were spread on Twitter and eventually reached WhatsApp between the evening of March 15 and the afternoon of March 16. The main narrative affirmed that the councilwoman was connected to Rio narco-trafficking groups and was engaged in their defense. Supposed photos of Franco with Marcinho VP, the leader of a criminal group, were dispersed through WhatsApp; it was announced that they had previously been married.

The rumors reached a crescendo when political actors started to share this content. The right-wing Deputy Alberto Fraga and Judge Marília Castro Neves were the main sources of these rumors through their personal Facebook pages. As public figures, they helped to legitimize the false narratives about Franco. Newspapers such as *Folha de S. Paulo* and *Veja* magazine took notice of this activity in social media from these individuals and started to produce pieces quoting the errors as well as the judicial consequences that the fake news campaign could bring to Neves and Fraga.

Right-wing websites played an important role in the dissemination of false narratives about Franco. A data-mapping from the Monitor of Political Debate on Digital Media Project (in Portuguese: *Monitor do Debate Político no Meio Digital*) traced a total of seven news items about the case that were disseminated on social media. Among them, a text published by the right-wing site *Ceticismo Político* was the most prolific, with 232,000 shares on the first day. The piece used some information published by *Folha* regarding false comments made by a judge about Franco. Instead of replicating the content of *Folha* that showed that the judge was being prosecuted because of her statements, *Ceticismo Político* inverted the discourse logic and created a new title: *"Judge breaks PSOL narrative and says that Marielle got involved with bad guys and is a 'common corpse.'"* (In Portuguese: *"Desembargadora* ***quebra narrativa do PSOL e diz que Marielle se*** *envolvia* ***com bandidos e é 'cadáver comum'"****).* The other journalistic websites adopted the same declaratory strategy, quoting and endorsing the judge's false claims, as revealed by some of the headlines: *"Judge says that Marielle 'was engaged with bandits'"* (*"Desembargadora diz que Marielle 'estava engajada com bandidos'"*) (*Veja* magazine), *"Judge of TJRJ accuses Marielle of partnering with the Red Command"* (*"Desembargadora do TJRJ acusa Marielle de parceria com Comando Vermelho"*) (GGN News), a narco-trafficking organization. Neither of them worried about revealing that this declaration was a false one (MONITOR, 2018).The political group *Movimento Brasil Livre* (MBL) also replicated the Facebook post. They emerged in the 2013 protests and since then have grown into a right-wing social movement.

One important question we will try to answer concerns the reasons why right-wing social actors felt the need to deconstruct Franco's image by spreading fake news about her. Although representative of important causes such as human rights and gender issues, at a national level, she was not one of the most popular left-wing politicians. She was new and she was not running for important political positions. Given this fact, why was it so important for right-wing groups to use social media to incisively attack her reputation? Why divide the country between those who mourned her death and those who were convinced she deserved it? Namely, why did some political groups feel the need to turn her into an evil figure using strategies that included disinformation?

In the current hyperpolarized Brazilian political scenario, we can clearly observe the dispute between two opposite DFs—the progressive and the conservative. This conflict mixes political and moral discourses. Gallego et al. (2017) state that the relationship between moral and political discourse is not new in Brazil. But they believe that, in the recent past, moral discourse used to be instrumentalized by political discourse. Presently, the opposite seems to be happening. For the authors, the former polarization between a liberal right that would defend a meritocracy based on free enterprise and a left that would defend political interventions to promote social justice was not replaced, but it started to be subordinated to a new antagonism between a punitive conservatism and a comprehensive progressivism.

In order to list the main agenda of each political field in Brazil, Gallego et al. (2017) presented questionnaires to activists from both sides. The results could give us clues about the main argumentative modules in each DF. Two other papers have helped us in this mission: Souza (2017) and her observations on human rights discourses in right-wing Facebook pages; and Alonso (2019), with her reflections over the Bolsonarist moral community. For this paper, we have focused on urban violence topics, which are central for the discursive disputes over Franco's death. It was the main topic discussed by

Franco in her statements as a participant in the police violence review committee. In 2017, Brazil's murder rate was 31.6 homicides per 100,000 inhabitants—the highest homicide rate of its history (*Atlas da Violência*, 2019). This reality transforms violence into a recurrent discussion topic for Brazilians, especially in a pre-election scenario. Thus, urban violence, along with corruption, was one of the main topics of the 2018 presidential election. The theme, however, appears connected to other social issues, such as racism.

From the three previously mentioned studies, we can verify that in statements connected to the progressivist DF, the police are more violent with black citizens than with white ones. Another important value shared by this moral community is that human rights must be universal. Also, for Brazilian progressivists, education and politics that promote social equality are the best ways to fight criminality, not penal populism. Franco's discourses and political projects were clearly connected to this DF.

In regard to what concerns the conservative DF, some of its main discourses reveal the following: criminals must be punished with more jail time, the death penalty should be applied for serious crimes, crime-committing minors should go to jail, good citizens must have access to guns, and human rights hinder the fight against crime (Gallego et al., 2017). Souza (2017) adds that right-wing discourses in Facebook groups produce a sense effect of the deconstruction of the purpose of human rights advocacy, associating its practices to the defense of bandidos. Alonso (2019) states that for the Bolsonarist moral community, human rights should be guaranteed only for the "right humans," and not for bandits. The author also draws attention to the fact that this moral community "is structured based on a belief that is shared in binary codes that divides the world in good and evil, sacred and profane, family people and indecent, good citizens and bandits, ethics and corrupted, nationalists and globalists" (p. 52).

This binary perspective plays a central role in the conditions of the possibility of the discourses about Franco. She was considered a defender of human rights. In the punitive conservatism of the DF, human rights are "bandits' rights," therefore human rights defenders would actually be "bandit defenders." This aspect of the DF simplifies criminality issues into an easy formula in which criminals play the roles of villains and police officers play the roles of heroes. Since the conservative DF states that human rights advocates defend bandits and police officers are heroes, Franco's death by the hands of criminal police officers—the hypothesis since the beginning of the case—is a narrative that would not fit. The text below is one of the first fake news messages on WhatsApp about Franco:

> **Extract 1:** *Is it true? Who was Marielle? She got pregnant at 16. She was married to Marcinho VP. She was a cannabis user. She was elected by the Comando Vermelho. She defended a rival faction in the Acari neighborhood in Rio de Janeiro. She recently dismissed six employees. But it was the police who killed her!!!* (Boatos.org, E-farsas, Aos Fatos).

The last sentence of the message is ironic, since it tries to build the idea that she was involved with drug dealers and criminal groups and such connections would have gotten her killed and not the police. The mentioning of Marcinho VP (a drug dealer and former leader of a criminal organization) and Comando Vermelho (criminal organization) are central to such a discursive strategy. According to Boatos.org, another similar message circulated adding that Franco was the daughter of the most popular drug dealer in Brazil, Fernandinho Beira-Mar, and that he financed her election campaign. A third message shared on WhatsApp followed the same discursive logic, arguing that Comando Vermelho was responsible for financing her political campaign:

> **Extract 2:** *She was elected by the Comando Vermelho. The favela funded her. Drug trafficking funded her, drug trafficking put her in there* [on City Council] (Boatos.org, E-farsas, Aos Fatos).

Inside the punitivist conservative DF, criminal police officers are an impossible paradox. Disinformation campaigns arrived in order to "equalize" the facts to a narrative that would fill in what is sayable in such DF. Fake news was used to convince people that Franco was not killed by militias, but by drug dealers, the same bandits that, as a human rights defender (or bandit defender, for the DF), she used to defend. To "prove" that she (and the left) used to defend bandits, other fake news was created, such as the message below:

> **Extract 3:** *Believe it if you want!!! Today, a bill proposed by that Marielle has been approved, and it reserves 20% of the vacancies for public jobs for minor offenders in the city of Rio de Janeiro. That's exactly what you have read. Soon it will be an advantage to be a minor offender. Crivella, you must veto that indecence!* (Boatos.org).

The existence of a bill proposed by Franco that would give privileges to crime-committing minors would strengthen the discourse that accuses human rights defenders of defending bandits. Therefore, it would help to keep intact the binary codes that sustain the punitive conservatism of the DF. The text below is another example of fake news elaborated to convince people that Franco was a bandit defender. The message asks the reader to watch a video in which Franco was supposedly defending outcasts:

> **Extract 4**: *Please take 4 minutes to watch this video and draw your conclusion about who the councilwoman saint Marielle Franco really was. Take a look at Marielle's performance, screaming in the House defending outcasts and saying that her muse is MC Carol, a funk singer with very dirty lyrics, by the way. Watch Councilor Carlos Jordy's video* (Boatos.org).

Fact-checking pages have shown that it was not Franco in the video, but another politician from her party. The video shows a black woman complaining about the police slaughter of seven black people in the Salgueiro favela. We can still hear her voice when the image is replaced by texts stating that the dead people were bandits.

In the binary schema, good citizens versus bandits is not the only Manichaean duality in the fake news discourse. As presented in Extract 1, the first information about "who was Marielle" states that she got pregnant at 16. Such disinformation is meant to create a moral judgment about her character based on a shared belief that women who have a child at a young age are indecent. The archetype of the promiscuous woman, typically associated with women from favelas who have sexual liberty and racist stereotypes about black and mulatto women being more sexual and engaged with bad men, is mobilized by these discourses to construct an image of Franco opposed to the archetype of the pure and innocent women with moral family values. In Extract 4, Franco is represented as a screaming woman who has as her muse a Brazilian funk singer that sings dirty songs. In Brazil, funk is a popular musical genre from the favelas, characterized by rap cadences over electronica-style beats and heavy bass, that is under constant attack due to the sexual content in some of its lyrics.

Maybe the biggest example of fake news with the goal of associating Franco's image to that of a promiscuous woman is a photo that started to circulate some days after her death. The photo puts this binary into a visual image. It is a woman wearing little clothes and sitting in a man's lap. The text that accompanied the picture stated: "Councilwoman Marielle and Marcinho VP. I don't need to say a word. The image speaks for itself." The elements in the picture also evoke a conservative discursive memory for which this kind of clothes and the act of sitting in a man's lap are incompatible with the morals of a woman with family values. The people in the image are neither Franco nor Marcinho VP. Fact-checking websites found the origin of the picture; it was first published in a Fotolog page that had the word "whores" in its title. The picture's subtitle mentioned a brothel in northeastern Brazil. This particular origin strengthens the suspicion that the image was not any randomly chosen picture. It was carefully selected with the aim of creating an "alternative reality" that works as an amalgam that preserves the integrity of punitivist conservative DF.

Personal ties attributed to the private life of Franco acquired a public existence and influence in some other conjunction of texts. In this sense, her background in the favela seems to justify her political action. Souza (2017) argues that conservative DF stigmatizes people from the favelas and their cultural manifestations, especially black people which are stereotyped as criminals. In our analyzed corpus we could verify some discursive marks that share such values. In Extract 2, we can read the sentence "The favela funded her" among the other sentences that mention criminal groups connected to drug trafficking. In Extract 4, a funk-singing muse is an element employed in order to blur Franco's image. Such fragments imply that the symbol of the "favela" and other symbols connected to it, such as "funk" music, have negative connotations in those discourses. In the binary codes of punitivist conservative DF, the favela and its symbols are placed on the "evil side." Extract 5 is another fake news message that circulated on WhatsApp. Most of the discursive elements discussed are present in the text (the binary between the police and criminals, comprehension of human rights as defense of criminals), but this time we see a clear racial issue in the statement:

> **Extract 5:** *Marielle' killer has been discovered!!! ((Thiago Macaco.)) He's not a police officer, he's not white, he's linked to TRAFFIC [drug trafficking]. The media doesn't talk about Marielle anymore. Why??? Where is the racist, homophobic white policeman that the left and Globo invented?? What now, Globo and rubbish PSOL, why are you silent? Why are you not at the police station defending this oppressed young man, who had no opportunity? Thiago Macaco is a victim of this society; he is just like those bums that you defend so much! I'm waiting for a statement from you bunch of junk bum defenders* (Boatos.org).

In order to maintain the discursive coherence of the punitivist conservative DF, fake news about Franco also worked in the deconstruction of the fundamental basis of the opposite DF. The existence of racist police officers is enunciated as a media construction and not a reality. The proof of this would be that Franco's murderer was not a white policeman, but a black criminal, the same kind of person that the media and Franco's party (PSOL) used to defend. The attack on traditional media is also present in this and in other analyzed messages (Globo is the main Brazilian TV channel).

As we have discussed, in the first moments, the fake news about Franco had the clear aim of equalizing the narratives about her death into something that would satisfy the moral beliefs that integrate the punitive conservative DF. In March 2019, however, two former police officers were arrested as suspects in her murder. This event started a new moment of fake news circulation, this time in a more pragmatic way and targeting not just Franco's image any longer, but other politicians in major political positions and political parties. Most of the fake news were trying to associate the suspects to the conservative president, Jair Bolsonaro, or to the main representative of the progressive Workers' Party, the former president Lula.

Conclusion

The current disinformation crisis is strongly connected to the political polarization that emerged within a new communication architecture, in which the emission of messages is decentralized. This is quite different from what used to happen in the mass media age. Such decentralization also contributed to the crisis in traditional journalism, which in the post-truth age, is translated as a reference crisis. Truth now is less about careful investigation of facts and more about the suitability of the messages to one's previous beliefs and ideology. Considering the Brazilian context, our study helped to understand the discursive roles of fake news in this scenario.

At first, disinformation campaigns against Franco after her death did not have a clear, immediate, and pragmatic function. This was because she was not a major name in Brazilian politics and more importantly, there was no need to convince people not to vote for her. Therefore, we can list at least two discursive purposes of such discourses. The first one is more obvious: in a scenario of hyperpolarized politics, after her murder, Franco became a symbol of what is perceived in contemporary Brazilian culture as leftist values and causes, such as human rights, feminism, and anti-racism. The political scenario turned her into a metonymy of the left itself. When she died, in March 2018, Franco became *the part for the whole*. To attack her image was, therefore, to attack the left itself.

Our analysis showed another important role of such discourses: they were meant to maintain the ideological coherence of the punitivist conservative DF. The fake news analyzed was not randomly chosen with the aim of blurring the councilwoman's image. Textual and visual elements were thought to "equalize" the facts to the idyllic Manichaean world discursively created by conservative Brazilians. Such coherence is important to maintain group ties, which are made of moral precepts. The confirmation bias connected to such moral precepts is also why some people were willing to believe in fake news that could be easily refuted.

References

Abranches, S. (2019). Polarização radicalizada e ruptura eleitoral. *Democracia em risco? 22 ensaios sobre o Brasil hoje*. São Paulo: Companhia das Letras.

Alonso, A. (2019). A comunidade moral bolsonarista. *Democracia em risco? 22 ensaios sobre o Brasil hoje*. São Paulo: Companhia das Letras.

Amaral, I., & Santos, S. (2019). Algoritmos e redes sociais; a propagação de fake News na era da pós-verdade. In J. Figueira & S. Santos (org) (Eds.). *Fake News e a nova ordem (des)informativa na era da pós-verdade* [Google Books version]. Retrieved from https://books.google.com.br/books/about/As_fake_news_e_a_nova_ordem_des_informat.html?id=0LewDwAAQBAJ&redir_esc=y

Atlas da violência 2019. (2019). Retrieved from: http://www.ipea.gov.br/portal/index.php?option=com_content&id=34784&Itemid=432

Bakir, V., & McStay, A. (2017). Fake news and the economy of emotions: problems, causes, solutions. *Digital Journalism*. doi:10.1080/21670811.2017.1345645 Vol.6, Issue 2, pgs.154-175

Baptista, C. (2019). Digitalização, desinformação e notícias falsas: uma perspectiva histórica. In Figueira, J.; Santos, S. (org) (Eds.), *Fake News e a nova ordem (des) informativa na era da pós-verdade* [Google Books version]. Retrieved from https://books.google.com.br/books/about/As_fake_news_e_a_nova_ordem_des_informat.html?id=0LewDwAAQBAJ&redir_esc=y

Carro, R. (2019). *Digital news report: urban Brazil.* Retrieved from http://www.digitalnewsreport.org/survey/2019/brazil-2019/

Difusão dos boatos sobre Marielle Franco. Observatório da imprensa. (2018, March 03). *Monitor do debate político no meio digital.* Retrieved from http://observatoriodaimprensa.com.br/monitor-do-debate-politico-do-meio-digital/difusao-dos-boatos-sobre-marielle-franco/

Eady, G. Nagler, J, Guess,A. Zilinksky, J, Tucker, J. (2019). How many people live in political bubbles on social media? Evidence from linked survey and Twitter data. Sage Open Special Collection Social Media and Politics, v.9, issue 1, pgs. 1 -21. doi:10.1177/2158244019832705

El-Bermawy, M. M. (2016, November 18). Your filter bubble is destroying democracy. *Wired.* Retrieved from https://www. wired.com/2016/11/filter-bubble-destroying-democracy/

Foucault, M. (1969). *L'arquéologie du savoir.* Paris: Éditions Gallimard.

Foucault, M. (1971). *L'ordre du discours.* Paris: Éditions Gallimard.

Gallego, E., Ortellado, P., & Ribeiro, M. (2017). Guerras culturais e populismo antipetista nas manifestações de apoio a Lava Jato e contra a reforma da previdência. *Debate, v. 9, n. 2,* pp. 35–45. Retrieved from http://opiniaopublica.ufmg.br/site/files/artigo/7.pdf

Inaf Brasil 2018. (2018). *Resultados preliminaries.* Retrieved from http://acaoeducativa.org.br/wp-content/uploads/2018/08/Inaf2018_Relat%C3%B3rio-Resultados-Preliminares_v08Ago2018.pdf

Ireton, C., & Posetti, J. (2018). *Journalism, Fake News & Disinformation: Handbook for Journalism Education and Training.* Paris: UNESCO.

Lee, T. B. (2016, October 26). How social media creates angry, poorly informed partisans. *Vox.* Retrieved from https://www. vox.com/policy-and-politics/2016/10/26/13413292/socialmedia-disrupting-politics

Lemos, A. (2009). Nova esfera conversacional. In D. Kunsch (Ed.), *Esfera pública, redes e jornalismo (*pp. 9–30). Rio de Janeiro: E-papers.

Maingueneau, D. (2011). Formação discursiva, unidades tópicas e não-tópicas. In R Baronas (Ed.), *Análise do Discurso: Apontamentos para uma história da noção-conceito de formação discursive (*pp. 63–91). São Carlos: Pedro & João Editores.

Marcondes Filho, C. (2019). Apresentação—Fake News: o buraco é muito mais embaixo. In J. Figueira & S. Santos (Eds.), *Fake News e a nova ordem (des)informativa na era da pós-verdade* [Google Books version]. Retrieved from https://books.google.com.br/books/about/As_fake_news_e_a_nova_ordem_des_informat.html?id=0LewDwAAQBAJ&redir_esc=y

Mason, L. (2018). *Uncivil Agreement: How Politics Became Our Identity.* Chicago: University of Chicago Press.

McIntyre, L. (2018). *Post-Truth* [Kindle version]. Retrieved from http://www.amazon.com/

Newman, N. (2019). *Executive Summary and Key Findings of the 2019 Report.* Retrieved from http://www.digitalnewsreport.org/survey/2019/overview-key-findings-2019/

Ortellado, P. (2018, June 08). Legados de junho: como o levante da sociedade civil contra o estado virou briga entre "coxinhas" e "petralhas." *Revista Época.* Retrieved from https://epoca.globo.com/politica/noticia/2018/06/legados-de-junho-como-o-levante-da-sociedade-civil-contra-o-estado-virou-briga-entre-coxinhas-e-petralhas.html

Ortellado, P., & Ribeiro, M. (2018). Polarização e desinformação online no Brasil. *Friedrich-Ebert-Stiftung, Análise, n. 44*. Retrieved from http://library.fes.de/pdf-files/bueros/brasilien/14629.pdf

Parisier, E. (2011). *The Filter Bubble*. New York: The Penguin Press.

Recuero, R., Zago, G., & Soares, F. (2017). Mídia Social e Filtros-Bolha nas Conversações Políticas no Twitter. *XXVI Encontro Anual da Compós*. São Paulo: Compós.

Souza, F. (2017). Os manos não são humanos direitos? *VIII Seminário de Estudos em Análise do Discurso*. Recife: SEAD.

Wardle, C., & Derakhshan, H. (2017). *Information Disorder: Toward an interdisciplinary framework for research and policy making* [E-book version]. Retrieved from https://edoc.coe.int/en/media/7495-information-disorder-toward-an-interdisciplinary-framework-for-research-and-policy-making.html

Yeginsu, C. (2017, December 27). When Harry met Barry: The BBC Obama interview. *The New York Times*. Retrieved from https://www.nytimes.com/2017/12/27/world/europe/obamaprince-harry-interview.html

13 Collaborative journalism versus disinformation

An approach to fact-checking projects in Mexico, Argentina, Colombia, Brazil, and Spain

Amaya Noain-Sánchez

Introduction

Viewpoint diversity and media pluralism are seen as essential conditions for a well-functioning democracy. From this premise, scholars underline the important role played by Social Network Sites (SNS) as a source of information, since it is expected to be drawn from a diverse, multi-perspective range of sources (Bruns, 2011). SNS, therefore, come to disrupt the traditional elite control of media while, at the same time, amplify the political voice of non-elites and minorities (Castells, 2011). This fact is particularly relevant in Latin America where there is a long tradition of market concentration and campaigns of disinformation, which have been a common strategy of traditional media monopolies to threaten and dismantle democracies. Nevertheless, as the proliferation of politically biased, fake news stories has become widespread on SNS, the initial optimism about its potential has given way to concern that users manipulated. Particularly, hoaxes and false information spread quickly when it comes to the SNS Facebook, Twitter and, more recently, instant messaging on WhatsApp. In the last case, disinformation is particularly worrying, since in this environment "news is spread in closed exchanges and messages are encrypted, making it impossible to know how what is being spread or how many people are seeing it" (Owen, 2018: para 01). Furthermore, "false information does not just come as text, but as images and memes" (2018: para 01). In this context, the emergence of fact-checking platforms plays an essential role not only as far as news verification is concerned, but also in the maintenance of the media pluralism whose control would mean a serious threat to our democracies. The study of this phenomena is particularly relevant in Latin American and Spain where there is concern about disinformation eroding democratic political processes, and its attached values in the context of regional elections is increasing.

Against this background, we aim at analyzing six platforms that allow us to draw the global scene of the phenomena of collaborative journalism in Latin America and Spain.

This chapter is organized as follows: (1) by reviewing existing literature, we explore different dimensions of disinformation online, discussing, therefore, the possible impact on decision-making processes; (2) by using qualitative case study and quantitative methods of content analysis, we approach the fact-checking environment and the development of collaborative journalism, focusing on cases in Mexico, Brazil, Colombia, Argentina, and Spain; (3) we provide an overview of the huge array of methods used to verify items of news, photographs and the like; (4) we evaluate essential aspects such as: transparency and accountability, communication of results, and interaction, thus analyzing the role played by collaborative platforms in tackling disinformation; (5) finally, we conclude by discussing the outcome of fact-checking platforms, throwing light on the potential steps to be taken to reduce the effects of disinformation on social media, and placing emphasis on the future of fact-checking as a technique to monitor public discourse.

The landscape of disinformation

The rise and rapid growth of SNS represents one of the fastest growing phenomena in the 21st century, evolving from leisure-oriented venues into platforms where a significant part of social interaction takes place today. These new public spheres have become spaces for the distribution and consumption of information about political and civic events, providing users with useful tools to share information and views about their governments and policies. The growth in the use of social media to find news (Newman et al., 2017) has, however, a side effect: the production, consumption and dissemination online of false, misleading and manipulated information, which has become a serious concern in many countries in recent years. Particularly, during the last United States presidential elections, the role played by SNS (mostly Facebook) gained attention, particularly because of its capacity to influence the voters and the results of the elections through the information they allowed to be distributed. Of all the issues regarding this topic, the one which draws the most attention was the so-called "fake news" phenomenon. This concept is defined as "fabricated information that mimics news media content in form but not in organizational process or intent" (Lazer et al., 2018) and may also include pieces of content related to news satire, news parody, fabrication, manipulation, advertising, and political propaganda (Tandoc et al., 2018). This term encompasses everything from false content fabricated in pursuit of advertising revenues (Subramanian, 2017), to state-backed misinformation campaigns. However, despite the terminology of "fake news" being quite popular, it is highly imprecise, vague and deals narrowly with broad phenomena. Furthermore, it has become an emotionally charged, weaponized term used to undermine and discredit journalism (Wardle & Derakshan, 2017). To tackle the inaccuracy of the terminology, the Council of Europe describes the three different dimension of the phenomena: (a) misinformation related to false information shared, but no harm is meant; (b) disinformation, that is to say, false information knowingly shared to cause harm; and (c) mal-information, when genuine information is shared in order to cause harm, for example by moving information designed to stay private into the public sphere (European Commission, 2018a: 10). Particularly, disinformation encompasses a spectrum of information types, defined as: "false, inaccurate, or misleading information designed, presented and promoted to intentionally cause public harm or for profit" (2018: 10).

The landscape of disinformation has been a wide subject of study for many (Allcott & Gentzkow, 2017; Guess et al., 2018; Graves, Nyhan & Reifler, 2018) and is linked to the widespread crisis of confidence in the media and public institutions (Nielsen & Graves, 2017), and a change in their central role as distributors and gatekeepers, by broadcasting and printing mass media in the current environment dominated by digital, mobile, and social media platforms (Bell et al., 2017; Nielsen & Ganter, 2017). Several pieces of research suggest manipulated content has made up only a very small fraction of the total information exposure of citizens (Allcott & Gentzkow, 2017). Nonetheless, in this new environment, "content flows and reaches web users in an isolated way, with no context and with a weak link to the particular medium which publishes the news," thus lacking any formal cue to interpret or detect bias (Cepeda, 2019: 12). Furthermore, as news is distributed depending on the previous users' interests collected by the platforms, there is a high risk of being inside a "filter bubble" (Pariser, 2011) which may narrow a user's point of view, leading to the "cyberbalkanization." This is the idea that the segregation of the Internet into small political groups with similar perspectives to a degree that they show a narrow-minded approach to those with contradictory views (Bozdag & van den Hoven, 2015). Within this framework of unsourced or biased information and distrust in the media, non-partisan and transparent fact-checking platforms share the goal of promoting truth in public discourse, contributing efficiently to the demand for accountability which is the key to strengthening democracy. Its importance has been highlighted by the European Commission since "a dense network of strong and independent fact-checkers is an essential requirement for a healthy digital ecosystem" (European Commission, 2018b: 9).

The rise of "fact-checking"

Fact-checking platforms are a mixture of "divergent practices, missions and organizational forms, a broadly shared concern with promoting democratic discourse and accountable government" (Graves, 2018: 14). The first organization dedicated to publicly evaluating the truth of political claims, *Spinsanity,* appeared in the United States in 2001 (Graves & Amazeen, 2019). It was an external *post hoc* fact-checking platform by three college graduates who presented their project as "a nonpartisan watchdog dedicated to unspinning misleading claims from politicians, pundits and the press" (Spinsanity, 2004). In 2003 this was followed by the non-profit website *FactCheck.org,* still active, which is run by professional journalists based at the University of Pennsylvania (Graves, 2016). Both gave rise to the launch of similar initiatives on two conventional media platforms: *The Fact checker* (Washington Post) and *PolitiFact* (St. Petersburg Times, now Tampa Bay times), spreading the model in the United States and then globally. These first initiatives can be defined as "a style of reporting dedicated to assessing the truth of political claims" (Graves et al., 2016: 1). Nonetheless, as the media landscape has changed, so has the scope of the projects: in addition to assessing political claims, it also focuses on debunking viral disinformation that circulates on social media. Fact-checking represents an emerging ecosystem, giving rise to a "transnational movement which includes journalists and non-journalists engaged in practicing and promoting an emergent form of accountability" (Graves, 2018: 14). As the diversity of the projects matches the global picture, its categorization seems complicated. The fact-checkers themselves come from a range of backgrounds, including journalism, but also political science, economics, law, public policy, and from diverse activist groups (Graves & Cherubini, 2016) introducing even more heterogeneity. Nonetheless, the authors propose a categorization which is rooted in the phenomenon's own evolution. They distinguish between (a) outlets based in traditional newsrooms and (b) independent projects based almost entirely in NGOs and/or alternative media outlets. Therefore, according to Graves & Cherubini, the so-called "Newsroom Model" incubated within media outlets benefits from the reach and resources of their media parent, with the disadvantage of remaining dependent on editorial interest and financial support. Whereas non-profit fact-checking outlets, the "ONG Model" operate independently of editorial and business constraints, though they lack the dedicated editorial resources and reliable audiences that fact-checkers based in media companies can count on (2016: 8–10). The number of each type depends on the region, but, as an overall trend, political fact-checking in North Western Europe has been led by legacy newsrooms, while the NGO Model is widespread in Eastern Europe and in Latin America (2016: 10–11). Some of these platforms, additionally, can be defined as "collaborative journalism," that is to say, a growing practice in the field of journalism that entails a cooperative arrangement, be it formal or informal, between two or more news and information organizations (Stonbely, 2017). This practice, which aims to supplement each organization's resources and maximize the impact of the content produced, must be carried out by both professional and amateur reporters.

Fact checking platforms have experienced substantial growth in recent years. The last report published by the Duke Reporters' Lab in September 2019 counted 195 active websites and organizations (Stencel & Luther, 2019). Particularly, in Latin America, a region facing problems in achieving genuine media democracy, there are 22 platforms, whereas in Spain, 4 platforms aim to tackle the problem of disinformation during elections. The majority of initiatives have emerged inspired by *Chequeado* in Argentina, which was launched in 2010 and is one of the first projects making use of a collaborative approach to cover elections and political information. These sites began their operations linked to an electoral process, with the exception of *Colombiacheck* which, at the beginning, focused on the peace process that Colombia was conducting with the FARC, the Revolutionary Armed Forces of Colombia—People's Army. Once negotiations finished, it moved its attention to the 2018 presidential and congressional elections. However, despite covering mainly topics related to national politics, they also verify messages regarding a wide variety of topics such as social issues, economics and the environment.

Methodology

Prior to our analysis, and following previous research (Vizoso & Vázquez-Herrero, 2017: 133) we have carried out a cross-sectional study of the papers and reports whose subject matter focused on three key points: (a) the phenomena of disinformation; (b) the characterization of fact-checking projects, including case studies; (c) research into SNS. and news sharing. Developed in the framework of a Systematic Literature Review (Ramírez-Montoya & García-Peñalvo, 2018) the aforementioned academic texts were collected form *Web of Science* and *Scopus* databases.

By using a methodology that combines qualitative and quantitative approaches, we selected a sample of fact-checking platforms from countries with a current population of more than 30,000 million habitants (United Nations, 2019). This phase of the study was supplemented by data from the Duke Reporter's Lab census and aims at offering a broad overview of the kind of organizations involved in fact-checking across Latin America and in Spain. This allows us to obtain a first selection of 21 platforms: 10 in Brazil, 3 in Mexico, 2 in Colombia and in Argentina and 4 in Spain. Within these, nineteen of them remained active in September 2019, while two of them, one in Brazil (*Truco*) and one in Argentina (*Macrimento*) were identified as inactive. There was no platform active in Peru at the time of the analysis, therefore it was excluded from the primary sample. Subsequently, we undertake a first characterization, collecting data from their websites and underlining features such as: year of launch, ownership, type of business and model, distinguishing between "Newsroom Model" and "ONG Model" (Table 13.1). Among these platforms, only six fulfill the requirements of the selecting criteria, which was, "collaborative journalism." The rest are defined, according to the information displayed on their web sites, as non-collaborative projects. That is the case of the privately owned, ad-supported sites *Boatos, É Isso Mesmo* and *UOL, Spondeo Media;* as well as the independent satire site *E-Farsas.* When it comes to the particular case of *Poliétika*, we decided to exclude it since it is not developed either by professionals or by amateur reporters. It is an example of so-called "citizen Journalism." Finally, *Agência Lupa, Portal EBC's Hoax, Detector de mentiras, El Objetivo* and *La Chistera* are excluded as they do not demonstrate a cooperative arrangement (formal or informal) between two or more news

Table 13.1 Fact-checking landscape in the countries analyzed

	Platform	*Country*	*Year of launch*	*Collaborative journalism*	*Ownership*	*Business/model*
1	**Agência Lupa**	Brazil	2015	No	Revista Piauí	Private/Newsroom Model
2	**Aos Fatos**	Brazil	2015	Yes	Independent	Non-profit/NGO Model
3	**Boatos**	Brazil	2015	No	Independent	Private/ ad-supported site
4	**Comprova**	Brazil	2018	Yes	Independent/ first draft	Non-profit/NGO Model
5	**Isso Mesmo**	Brazil	—	No	Globo	Private/ ad-supported site
6	**E-farsas**	Brazil	2002	No	Independent	Private/ ad-supported site
7	**Estadão Verifica**	Brazil	—	No	Grupo Estado	Private/Newsroom Model
8	**Portal EBC's**	Brazil	—	No	EBC	Private/Newsroom Model
9	**UOL Confere**	Brazil	—	No	UOL	Private/ ad-supported site
10	**Chequeado**	Argentina	2010	Yes	Independent/a project of the foundation of public voice	Non-profit/NGO Model
11	**El Sabueso**	Mexico	2015	No	Animal político	Private/Newsroom Model
12	**Spondeo Media**	Mexico	2018	No	Spondeo	Private/ ad-supported site
13	**Verificado**	Mexico	2017	Yes	Independent	Non-profit/NGO Model
14	**Derector de mentiras**	Columbia	2014	No	La Silla Vacía-Univisión	Private/Newsroom Model
15	**Colombia Check**	Columbia	2016	Yes	Independent/ Consejo de Redacción	Non-profit/NGO Model
16	**El Objetivo**	Spain	2013	No	La Sexta-Newtral	Private/Newsroom Model
17	**La Chistera**	Spain	2016	No	El Confidencial-(Titania Compañía Editorial)	Private/Newsroom Model
18	**Madito Bulo**	Spain	2014	Yes	Independent/ first draft	Non-profit/NGO Model
19	**Poliética**	Spain	2014	No	Independent/ citizens	Non-profit/NGO Model

Source: Own elaboration from data of the Duke Reporters' Lab.

Table 13.2 Transparency and accountability

			Transparency of methodology						
				Categories/scales/meters					
	Platform	Funding sources	Explanation of methodology	True	False	Intermediate	Correction politics	Staff transparency	Principles/ ethics code
1	**Aos Fatos**	Mentioned and explained	Mentioned and explained	Verdadeiro (true)	Falso (False)	Exagerado (exaggerated) Impreciso (imprecise) Contradictorio (contradictory) Insustentável (unsupportable)	Yes	Position biography	Own code
2	**Comprova**	Non-mentioned	Mentioned	Evidência comprovada (Proven Evidence) Imagem legítima (Legitimate Image) Evento legítimo (Legitimate Event) Localização verificada (Legitimate location)	Falso (False)	Enganoso (misleading), Alterado digitalmente (digitally altered), Contexto errado (wrong context), Sátira (satire)	No	Non-detailed	Own code
3	**Chequeado**	Explained and detailed	Mentioned and explained	Verdadero (true), Verdadero+ (True+)	Falso (False)	Verdadero, pero (true but), Discutible (Disputable) Apresurado (Hasty), Exagerado (exaggerated) engañoso (misleading), insostenible (untenable)	Yes	Position biography e-mail Twitter	Own code FCIN code
4	**Verificado**	Mentioned	Mentioned and explained	Verdadera (True)	Falso (False)	Engañoso (Misleading)	No	Biography	No
5	**Colombia-check**	Explained and detailed	Mentioned and explained	Verdadera (True)	Falso (False)	Verdadero pero (true but) Cuestionable (Disputable) Inchequeable (cannot be checked)	Yes	Position biography e-mail	Own code FCIN code
6	**Madito Bulo**	Explained and detailed	Mentioned and explained	Resuelto (sort out)	Bulo (False)	Inverificable (cannot be proved), En investigacion (investigating)	No	Position biography Twitter	Own code FCIN code

Source: Own elaboration with data from the platforms.

and information organizations. These sites are developed by journalists working for the same news organization.

Once the sample was selected, we undertook the case study (qualitative approach) of these six fact-checking platforms. This primary phase allows us to obtain information about transparency and accountability. Secondly, we undertook a content analysis (Krippendorff, 2004) of the six platforms. This second phase aims to analyze the way in which results are communicated. Thus, an analysis sheet was applied to the platforms selected, taking into account, among others, the parameters summarized in Tables 13.2 and 13.3.

Table 13.3 Communication of results

		Interaction	*Presentation of results*		*Complementary resources*	
	Platform	*SNSs/ messaging/ newsletter*	*Place of results of checks*	*Average of sources*	*Specific sections*	*Educative/ technological resources*
1	**Aos Fatos**	Facebook Twitter WhatsApp Instagram Newsletter	Corpus section name	4.9	Investigamos, Tempo Real, Manuais, Aos Fatos Lab, Eleições 2018, Especiais	Aos Fatos Lab
2	**Comprova**	Facebook/ Twitter/ Instagram WhatsApp	Titles text box corpus photograph	3.6	No	No
3	**Chequeado**	Facebook Twitter Instagram Newsletter	Titles corpus photograph	6.5	El Explicador, Chequeado Investigación, Hilando fino, Falso en las redes, Mitos	Chequeado educación
4	**Verificado**	Facebook Twitter Pinterest	Corpus	3.5	No	No
5	**Colombiacheck**	Facebook Twitter WhatsApp Instagram Newsletter	Text box corpus photograph	4.1	Investigaciones, Especiales, Chequeos, ZOOM, Podcast	No
6	**Madito Bulo**	Facebook Twitter WhatsApp Instagram Newsletter Telegram	Titles summary corpus photograph	6.4	Buloteca, Maldita Hemeroteca, Maldito Bulo, Maldita Ciencia, Maldito Dato, Maldita te explica	Maldita Educa, tools for journalists

Results

Transparency and accountability

Organization

None of the platforms analyzed are affiliated with any established media company and, therefore, not based on traditional newsrooms. The six fact-checking outlets operate out of traditional newsrooms, backed by NGOs linked to a foundation or as independent projects supported by crowdfunding. Four such outlets are projects of established foundations concerned broadly with strengthening democratic institutions. The majority of them follow the model of *Chequeado,* a project of the Foundation of Public Voice which was legally registered in September of 2010. Other examples with this organization are *Colombiacheck,* a project conceived and developed by Consejo de Redacción (CdR), a local news organization that promotes investigative journalism. The project was launched in June 2016 and currently counts on financial support from the Open Society Foundation. *Maldito Bulo,* part of Maldita.es, is another a non-profit association dedicated to fact-checking and sponsored by the independent organization First Draft. Finally, *Comprova* is a partnership of 24 Brazilian media organizations, coordinated by the Associação Brasileira de Jornalismo Investigativo. The platform, also supported by First Draft, benefits from financial and technical support from The Google News Initiative and Facebook Journalism Project. While these platforms combine the foundations' support with individual contributions, other outlets such as *Aos fatos, Verificado* are completely independent or housed in a purpose-built charity or NGO and supported by crowdfunding such as *Verificado,* an independent, volunteer-run project led by several journalists from northern Mexico, which relies on individual contributions.

Funding

The six platforms show a high level of transparency when it comes to organization and statement on ownership. Nonetheless, not everyone offers in-depth details on its funding sources. While *Aos fatos, Chequeado, Colombia Check* and *Maldito Bulo* present a detailed account of their funding, the same evidence has not been published in detail by *Comprova,* which only mentions their funding with a brief explanation and giving very little details. On the contrary, *Chequeado* sets one of the best practices among analyzed platforms. The detail and depth in which the platform discloses its financial information is worthy of being highlighted. As with other platforms it provides an overview of spending and the form in which it is registered. Additionally, it makes public the names of people, organizations and companies that donate, as well as its annual budget. In line with this, *Colombiacheck* and *Maldito Bulo* fully disclose information about their ownership and current funding.

Methodology

Defining a step-by-step methodology is the starting point for any fact-checking project. The majority of platforms analyzed (five) made their methodology public and explained the criteria they use to select, research, write, edit, publish, and correct their fact checks. *Chequeado, Maldito bulo, Colombiacheck* and *Aos fatos* are examples of sites with a fact-checking methodology that is sound and reliable, since it discloses clear, easy-to-reach information. Nevertheless, in spite of the fact that information about methodology is crucial, one of the sites analyzed (*Comprova*) barely outlined how it operates, and in two cases, there is no specific section on the home page (*Comprova, Verificado).*

Fact-checkers also vary in their approach to selecting claims to investigate. As an overall trend, the verification process follows the eight-steps method model of *Chequeado*: (1) "select a public claim"; (2) "outweight its relevance"; (3) Check the original source; (4) check the official source; (5) check alternative sources; (6) contextualize the information; (7) Confirm or debunk claim; and (8) rate (Chequeado, 2019).

To offer an assessment after verification, the platforms make use of a huge array of different categories, scales of truth and meters, which range from three options (*Verificado)* to nine categories (*Comprova, Chequeado),* thereby including an abundance of nuances between false or true (See Table 13.2), and sometimes, even more than one label for true statements (*Comprova, Chequeado*).

As for the corrections politics, four platforms show clear sections, allowing users to send claims through different means of contact. When this correction is related to fact-checks, *Aos Fatos* and *Chequeado* show this information on a public page that lists the updates and corrections, and *Colombiacheck* commits itself to responding to these claims in less than 48 hours. The rest of the platforms lack a public page listing all the corrections on its website.

Ethical commitment

As far as the principles that platforms commit to follow during the verification process, three of them (*Chequeado, Colombiacheck*, and *Maldito Bulo*) are signatories of the International Fact-Checking Network (IFCN, 2016) code of principles, and the same three have elaborated their own codes. Additionally, *Aos Fatos* which follows the IFCN standards, have published their own code, as well as *Comprova*- a very brief code in this case.

Among the commitments mentioned, the platforms underline: (a) nonpartisanship and fairness, providing unbiased and accountable information (to avoid bias, pieces are edited by at least two people on *Chequeado*); (b) a policy preventing staff from direct involvement in political parties and advocacy organizations- "We do not defend any ideology, nor do we carry out political activism or of any other type" (*Colombiacheck*); (c) open data, transparency and accountability (*Aos fatos)*; (d) integrity and ethical commitment (*Comprova*).

Transparency of staff

As regards the staff, we evaluate if there is a section on the site summarizing all authors and key actors behind the fact-checking project, and if it is clearly listed with their biographies with contact details included. In this respect, four platforms provide clear and easy-to-reach information about its board and staff members, including position (four), twitter account (two), e-mail (two), and biography (five).

Communication of results

Structure

The platforms deliver their outcomes in diverse presentations. Two of them placed the result in the titles, one in the summary, five in the *corpus* of the article and, four through illustrative photography. As the verification result is communicated through labels corresponding to different categories, scales and meters, platforms present it by showing distinctive printing characters or even symbols (one), which may appear inside a text box (one) or using colors depending on the result of the check (three). It is important to underline that we have not found emoji symbols or cartoon lie-detectors with facial expressions, as happens in other non-collaborative projects such as *El sabueso*.

In terms of structure, four of the platforms present a clear organization with different sections where contents are easy to reach. *Chequeado*, for example, provides an archive section, with many subsections (*El Explicador, Chequeado Investigación, Hilando fino, Mitos*) aimed at explaining some the most controversial topics checked. In line with it, *Aos fatos* displays on its website menu the option to view its stories database by label. It also randomly displays on its *Termometer* section a variety of verifications about politicians from different political parties, accompanied by a link that provides access to a fact-checking list of each one. It is also remarkable that the archive section of *Maldito Bulo,* called *La buloteca,* allows users to read through false items of news. Furthermore, the thorough way in which the platform distributes its content in specific sections deserves recognition, focusing on topics such as science (*Maldita Ciencia*) immigration (*Maldita Migración*) and gender inequality (*Maldito Feminismo*). *Colombiacheck* is also well-structured, though with fewer sections. On the contrary, the home page of *Comprova* and *Verificado* show few specific sections and their scope is not fully clear.

Format and type of content

All of the initiatives analyzed have websites and carry out their main activities on the internet by making use of a format similar to cybermedia. Their contents, the results of the checks, are presented as articles that may include headline, subtitles, lead, and the *corpus* of the article. In the *corpus*, the sources that were consulted in order to verify doubtful information are listed, including links. The average number of sources consulted goes from 3.6 per article (*Comprova*) to 6.5 (*Chequeado*). The articles are usually accompanied by videos, pictures, and graphics from social networks or other media, so that users can tell the difference between true and false content. Some platforms, as it is the case of *Colombiacheck,* include podcasts as well as a huge array of sections with supplementary reports, aimed at contextualizing the information. In particular, the articles on *Chequeado* and *Maldito Bulo* are committed to a greater comprehensiveness, reaching the category of in-depth reports. In parallel, platforms create resources that go from educational content to technological tools. In this respect, *Maldito Bulo* stands out, not only do they include specific sections that play an essential role as far as contextualization of information, *they* also provide journalists and citizens with technological tools to help them in debunking false information. As for educational aspects, it is necessary to underline the quality and variety of educational content developed by *Chequeado*—the platform also runs an educational program to stimulate critical thinking.

Interaction with readers and media ties

With the exception of *Verificado*, platforms encourage readers to send claims to fact-check by providing a dedicated section/call for action or including a form that explains to readers what can be fact-checked. This is the case of the sections: *#vamosaosfatos, nós checamos para você*, from *Aos fatos*; *Chequeo Colectivo* from *Chequeado;* or *pergunte ao Comprova* from *Comprova*, among others. Users can also contribute by suggesting topics to be fact-checked using WhatsApp (in four platforms). This service works particularly well on *Comprova* and *Colombiacheck*, where messages are answered in less than four hours. Fact-checkers can also be reached on social media platforms, such as Facebook (six), Twitter (six), or Instagram (five), and in four cases, users can opt to receive a newsletter. Finally, readers from *Maldito bulo* can submit hoaxes thanks to its browser plug-ins.

In addition to its journalistic work, fact-checkers employ a wide range of strategies to increase their media footprint. These strategies go from standard media relations to producing stories for particular news organizations. Two of the cases are remarkable: *Chequeado* presents its verifications in weekly columns in three national media platforms, and *Maldito Bulo* collaborates with various radio and TV programs.

Discussion

The results reveal that the model of the Argentine platform *Chequeado* continues to be a benchmark for other fact-checkers, and that its implementations are closely followed by *Maldito Bulo, ColombiaCheck* and to a lesser extent, *Aos Fatos*. Although there is room for improvement, these four stand out for their high standards in terms of transparency and reporting of results. Two of them (*Chequeado* and *Maldito bulo*) are also notable for the variety and quantity of content aimed at contextualizing information, as well as the educational aspect and the multitude of resources they make available to both the public and other journalists. They also carry out important research work on the introduction of technological tools. Some of these aspects can be improved in the other platforms. *Comprova* in particular should undertake improvements related primarily to transparency, whereas the initiative *Verificado* should reinforce aspects such as communication of results, and interaction with users as well as enhance their poorly developed website.

When it comes to transparency, which is a key point in increasing reader confidence in the activities of the fact-checkers, we have to underline the following aspects: firstly, not all the fact-checking projects analyzed provide detailed information on their funding. This fact is very palpable in one of the platforms (*Comprova*) and may well lead to the belief that their fact checks are unrealizable and/or potentially influenced by their unknown financiers. In the case of those fact-checking projects relate to a specific medium and, therefore, depending on the funding of the media group, this condition may be detrimental to reader trust in the platform. It may be seen as a product influenced by the editorial line and thereby not objective in its verifications. It is therefore striking that the platforms studied in this chapter, which are independent and are attached to the NGO model, do not take advantage of their independent condition, by providing details that may enhance the readers' trust in the platform.

Secondly, it is noteworthy that although we are dealing with collaborative journalism, the nature of these collaborations, as well as the roles and membership of both journalists and experts in other media are not always specified. As in the first aspect, the lack of information as far as members' names, contact details, background, and/or other affiliations is concerned may have a detrimental effect on the reliability of the platforms.

Finally, with regard to the transparency of the methodology, it is important to note that one of the aspects that creates value for these platforms is that the procedure being followed is well explained and can be verified and replicated by readers and journalists. This also means that the information will contain the documentary sources necessary for verification and the links to locate and contextualize the fake news. In this way, transparency becomes a useful tool for the public, enabling them to verify information personally.

Apart from transparency, and placing emphasis on the methodology procedures, the main obstacle comes from the abundance of categories chosen by the platforms to transmit the results of the verification to the reader. Users show a certain preference for corrections that include some kind of veracity scale, as it makes the verdict easily understandable and accessible

(Amazeen, et al., 2015). However, the fact that there are different grades in a platform's categories may lead to confusion. Binary categories such as "True" or "False" are easily understandable, as well as other categorical verdicts such as "out of context" or "cannot be proved." Nonetheless, the labels that are in between such as "true, but ...," "exaggerated" and the like, can be problematic for the reader. Sometimes the scales offer several different categories to convey the same opinion, which is also absolute, and would not therefore permit any nuances. In fact, these are often so subtle that they can be difficult to interpret. It should be kept in mind that one of the reasons why fake news spreads so quickly is that it simplifies content within a Manichean framework, allowing the easy categorization of information. It facilitates rapid understanding and encourages the reader's acceptance. However, if platforms use confusing verification categories, the reader may be lost in nuances that detract from the content of the verification itself. The fact that the reader is forced to memorize what each category means may result in the correctness and verification of the information not spreading as quickly as the fake content does. However, all this does not take into account that the different platforms do not share a homogenized grading system, which contributes to further confusion, and may lead to distrust.

As far as the code of principles is concerned, some of the platforms that were investigated have not developed their own code, or the one they publish on their website is too brief and limited. This is particularly striking when one realizes that fact-checking is based on rigorous work with high ethical standards, not on external interests. These considerations should be put in writing and strictly complied with by workers on the platform, although this does not always occur. As for the presentation of content and the communication of the results, the best structured and most cohesive websites are those that have the specific resources and useful tools for searching such content. Some platforms include online news search engines which greatly facilitate browsing between the checks. It is remarkable the enormous amount of resources that some make available to the reader and the educational work and content they do, which transcends the limits of the platform itself. Among the formats, the use of video is especially successful in published fact-checking and other content, as it has a greater communicative power, making it a more effective tool than simple text. Some platforms also create very elaborate audiovisual content and others complement their information with podcasts. As for interaction, although platforms give the readers the tools to send complaints or suggestions, not all the platforms inform the reader how it will proceed in case a reader is not satisfied with the response or correction. Finally, in terms of interaction, the use that some platforms (*Comprova, Colombiacheck, Maldito Bulo*) make of the instant messaging system WhatsApp is notable, due to the feeling of closeness it can instill in the user. The fact that verification goes beyond the limits of the website and is disseminated by similar means to those used in fake news is crucial for the correction to reach the largest number of people.

Conclusion and proposals

In this study we have taken a quick snapshot of the current fact-checking picture in several Latin American countries and Spain, taking five collaborative journalism platforms as a sample. By focusing on these fact-checkering platforms, we have highlighted the strengths and weaknesses that fact-checking must address in order to consolidate itself as a worthwhile option in fighting disinformation. For this reason and given the nature of fact-checking, we have primarily evaluated all those aspects that are directly involved: truthfulness, information objectivity and credibility, verification procedure correction and, finally, its explanation, contextualization and informative capacity. As a result, and although some of the aforementioned aspects could be improved, the study shows that the platforms that were analyzed do generally carry out their journalistic work, aimed at achieving these objectives.

However, given that there is room for improvement, we set out a number of proposals that should be kept in mind:

- Increase Transparency to increase trust. Transparency plays an essential role in legitimizing the activities undertaken by fact-checking sites. By detailing the process involved in each of the stages of the verification, platforms show how accountable they are, increasing reader trust in their work.
- Indicate the key sections that verify the platform's transparency on the home page.
- Declare its funding annually, detailing what percentage of the budget comes from each source.
- Since these are collaborative platforms, specify the nature of the collaborations, indicating the roles and membership or origin of both journalists and experts.
- As it is essential that anyone can "check the checker," sources and methodologies must be provided in enough detail that readers could replicate the fact check.
- Simplify the truth scales in a maximum of four categories: "True," "False," "Out of context," "cannot be proven," to increase understanding as well as the impact and usage of verification. The other nuances can be explained as part of the news. That way the meaning of the information will be clearer.
- Standardize the truth scales, so that they are the same for all platforms. This way the reader will be able to interpret the results regardless of the platform and country they choose.
- With regard to the code of principles, while it is true that the majority subscribe to the International Code, it would be desirable for each of them to draft their own code in a more complete manner, stressing the importance of the ethical commitments entered into by the platform.

Similarly, and given the importance these platforms are gaining in the current information landscape, the international organization could lay the foundation for these codes of ethics and principles by further developing its own code.

- Increase explanatory and contextual content, especially in video format.

The implementation of these changes could contribute to improving and standardizing this new type of old journalism that modern news reporting demands.

References

Allcott, H., & Gentzkow, M. (2017). Social Media and Fake News in the 2016 Election. *Journal of Economic Perspectives 31*(2), 211–236.

Amazeen, M. A., Thorson, E., Muddiman, A., & Graves, L. (2015). A Comparison of Correction Formats: The Effectiveness and Effects of Rating Scale versus Contextual Corrections on Misinformation. Retrieved from http://www.americanpressinstitute.org/wpcontent/uploads/2015/04/The-Effectiveness-of-Rating-Scales.pdf.

Bell, E., Owen, J. Brown, P. D.; Hauka, C., & Rashidian, N. (2017). The Platform Press: How Silicon Valley Reengineered Journalism. Tow Center, Columbia Journalism School. Retrieved from https://www.cjr.org/tow_center_reports/platform-press-how-silicon-valley-reengineered-journalism.php

Bozdag, E., & van den Hoven, J. (2015). Breaking the Filter Bubble: Democracy and Design. *Ethics and Information Technology, 17*(4), 249–265. DOI:/10.1007/s10676-015-9380-y

Bruns, A. (2011). Gatekeeping, Gatewatching, Real-time Feedback. *Brazilian Journalism Research*, *7*, 117–136.

Castells, M. (2011). *Communication Power*. Oxford: Oxford University Press.

Cepeda, J. (March 19, 2019) *Social media: Social threads or threats to human rights?* Doc. 14184 Report. Council of Europe. Retrieved from http://assembly.coe.int/nw/xml/XRef/Xref-XML2HTML-EN.asp?fileid=27472&lang=en

Chequeado (2019). Método. Retreived from https://chequeado.com/metodo/

European Commission (2018a). *A multi-dimensional approach to disinformation. Report of the independent High level Group on fake news and online disinformation.* Luxembourg: Publications Office of the European Union, 2018.

European Commission (2018b) *Tackling online disinformation: A European Approach*. Retrieved from https://eur-lex.europa.eu/legal-content/EN/TXT/PDF/?uri=CELEX:52018DC0236&from=EN

Graves, L. (2016). *Deciding What's True: The Rise of Political Fact-Checking in American Journalism*. New York: Columbia University Press.

Graves, L. (2018). Boundaries Not Drawn: Mapping the Institutional Roots of the Global Fact-checking Movement. *Journalism Studies 19*(5), 613–631.

Graves, L., & Amazeen, M. A. (2019). Fact-checking as Idea and Practice in Journalism Editor (Nussbaum, J), Location Oxford. In *Oxford Research Encyclopedia of Communication*. Oxford University Press, doi:10.1093/acrefore/9780190228613.013.808, ISBN 9780190228613

Graves, L., & Cherubini, F. (2016). The Rise of Fact-Checking Sites in Europe (Reuters Institute Digital News Report). *Reuters Institute for the Study of Journalism*. Retrieved from https://ora.ox.ac.uk/objects/uuid:d55ef650-e351-4526-b942-6c9e00129ad7

Graves, L., Nyhan, B., & Reifler, J. (2016). Why do journalist Fact-check? The role of demand- and supply-side factors. Retrieved from https://www.dartmouth.edu/~nyhan/journalist-fact-checking.pdf

Guess, A., Nyhan, B., & Reifler, J. (2018). Selective Exposure to Disinformation: Evidence from the Consumption of Fake News During the 2016 US Presidential Campaign'. Retrieved from https://www.dartmouth.edu/~nyhan/fake-news-2016.pdf

IFCN (2016). International Fact-Checking Network' code of principles. Retrieved from http://www.poynter.org/fact-checkers-code-of-principles/

Krippendorff, K. (2004). *Content Analysis: An Introduction to Its Methodology* (2nd ed.). Thousand Oaks, CA: Sage.

Lazer D. M. J. et al. (2018). The Science of Fake News. *Science*, *359*(6380), 1094–1096.

Newman, N., Fletcher, R., Kalogeropoulos, A., Levy, D., & Nielsen, R. K. (2017). *Reuters Institute Digital News Report 2017.* Oxford: Reuters Institute for the Study of Journalism.

Kleis Nielsen, R., & Ganter, S. A. (2017). Dealing with digital intermediaries: A case study of the relations between publishers and platforms. *New Media & Society, 20*(4), 1600 -1617. https://doi.org/10.1177/1461444817701318

Owen, L. H. (2018, June 1). WhatsApp is a black box for fake news. Verificado 2018 is making real progress fixing that. *Nieman Lab*. Retrieved from https://www.niemanlab.org/2018/06/whatsapp-is-a-black-box-for-fake-news-verificado-2018-is-making-real-progress-fixing-that/

Pariser, E. (2011). *The Filter Bubble: What the Internet Is Hiding from You*. New York: Penguin Press.

Ramírez-Montoya, M. S., & García-Peñalvo, F.-J. (2018). Co-creación e innovación abierta: Revisión sistemática de literatura/Co-creation and open innovation: Systematic literature review. *Comunicar*, *26*(54), 9–18. Retreived from https://www.doi.org/10.3916/C54-2018-01.

Spinsanity (2004). About Spinsanity. Retrieved from http://www.spinsanity.org/about/

Stencel, M., & Luther, J. (2019, September 16). From Toronto to New Delhi, fact-checkers find reinforcements. *Duke Reporters' Lab*. Retreived from https://reporterslab.org/from-toronto-to-new-delhi-fact-checkers-find-reinforcements/

Stonbely, S. (2017). Comparing Models of Collaborative Journalism. *Center for Cooperative Media*. Retrieved from https://collaborativejournalism.org/wp-content/uploads/2017/09/Models-for-Collaborative-Journalism-research-paper.pdf

Subramanian, S. (2017, February 15). Inside the Macedonian Fake-News Complex. *Wired*. Retrieved from https://www.wired.com/2017/02/veles-macedonia-fake-news/

Tandoc Jr. E. C., Lim Z. W., & Ling R. (2018). Defining "Fake News." *Digital Journalism*, *6*(2), 137–153, doi: 10.1080/21670811.2017.1360143

United Nations (2019). World Population Prospects: The 2019 Revision. Retrieved from https://population.un.org/wpp/

Vizoso, A., & Vázquez-Herrero, J. (2019). Fact-checking Platforms in Spanish. Features, Organisation and Method. *Communication & Society*, *32*(1), 127–142.

Wardle, C., & Derakshan H. (2017, September 27) Information Disorder: Toward an interdisciplinary framework for research and policy making. Council of Europe, Retrieved from https://rm.coe.int/information-disorder-toward-an-interdisciplinary-framework-for-researc/168076277c

14 Conclusions: Daily life, public engagement and the prospective impacts of digital media

David Ramírez Plascencia, Barbara Carvalho Gurgel and Avery Plaw

Living in hyper-mediated societies

Currently in Latin America everyday activities are been shaped by the popularization of information technology. Smartphones, tablets, and smartwatches take the digital experience far beyond the limitations of the domestic and workplace connectivity, allowing more flexible and diverse forms of sharing data and expand interpersonal communication (Vanden Abeele, 2016). Information about relevant social events socialize instantly, reaching a worldwide public in a matter of a few minutes. But there are many cases, as it has been argued through this volume, that the information and news is not as trustworthy as it should be. Thanks to the lower price of mobile devices and the diversification of Internet access, (cable, satellite, cellular, fiber optic) every day more people are able to adopt these technologies to improve their social and economic conditions: to criticize government actions on social media, to take online courses, to get a new job, or to chat with their relatives at the homeland, as it happens with those who have been compelled to journey into other countries looking for better labor opportunities or escaping from political repression, scarcity, or war (O'Malley, 2015). Latin Americans are no passive consumers of information but dynamic users who generate and share content across diverse virtual platforms. This "democratization" of technology, however, causes an overload of data where reliable and deceitful sources compete to catch public interest (Anderson & Rainie, 2017). In this context, societies require the support of free and trustworthy media which promotes free speech, public accountability, data trustworthiness, and the open debate on critical issues as racism, migration, and free market among others.

The first volume of **The politics of technology in Latin America**, centers on how governments and businesses dwell with the process of technologization in the region, in what way they include digital media to comply with their structural goals: to protect citizens and expand public services in the case of public administrations. Companies, conversely, focus on integrating technology to make their procedures, products, and wholesales more efficient. Though, as Volume I described, there are complexities about balancing private and public interests: governments should protect people's property and lives without disturbing human rights; and corporations look to innovate by adopting digital media but with the obligation of keeping consumers' private data at the same time. This second part of the project: **The Politics of Technology in Latin America (Volume 2)** studied the incorporation of digital media into people's daily activities; not just for entertainment purposes but to expand social relations and explicit their political views (Valenzuela et al., 2016), and how technology has unlocked new possibilities for traditional journalism. In Latin America, however, the process of informatization has been unequal, with important differences, not just among countries, but within them. There are contrasting adoption levels among rural and urban contexts, particularly about the quality of connectivity which limits the growth of services that require high-speed, like videos on streaming, for example (IBD, 2019). For that reason, it is imperative not only to emphasize the advances on Internet connectivity and the popularization of devices that enable the access to social media platforms, video streaming, ecommerce and, even videogames, etc., but to understand that there are still social barriers that cause an uneven access not just regarding Internet but to basic services as education, security, and health. While the number of Latin Americans able to access the Internet is increasing, the speed is slow, and the equipment is deficient. These lacks magnify as people have to dwell with natural disasters and social contingencies, as it happened in 2020 (Patrick, 2020).

By June 24 of 2020, there are about 9.22 million cases and nearly 477,000 deaths caused by the COVID-19 virus (ECDC Europe, 2020). Though, the real impact of the pandemic is far from being known since there is a significant shortage of tests and their accuracy could be affected by diverse logistic obstacles: timing, barriers to collect raw materials, and the lack of proper equipment for testing (Campbell & Hutter Epstein, 2020). In addition, many countries are having problems to correctly gather and record the information as the pandemic spreads. Many suspicious cases of COVID-19's casualties have been reported as "unknown/undetermined" deaths (Ahmed & Berehulak, 2020). Around the world, governments have taken extreme measures such as limiting people's mobility and restricting economic and public activities, allowing only those considered as essential such as agriculture, grocery stores, medical services, and police. These forced lockdowns have caused (And will cause) huge negative effects on the global economy. In April 2020, the oil price collapsed, some countries were compelled to trade their product below zero because of the low demand and the lack of storage tanks to keep the surplus (Krauss, 2020). The International Monetary Forum (IMF) has warned that the global growth will suffer a huge decline compared only to the Great Depression of the 1930 decade (Elliott, 2020). As people stayed at home during quarantines, digital media usage blasted up, Netflix's subscriptions triggered, and the Internet flows grew massively. The pandemic, however, has exposed how deep digital inequality is in the region. While a minority could remain at home enjoying video streaming, working from home, studying online, many people have been compelled to continue their job because it was considered as essential in the case of farmers, grocery employees, or healthcare workers or because of the shortage of resources to follow the public ordinances. Education in Latin America manifested this inequality as well (Hernández Arriaga, 2020). Students continued their education at home, and teachers and schools adopted digital tools which require high Internet speeds as the case of ZOOM or watching videos on YouTube. Many children and youth were not able to properly attend their classes online because of inadequate technological equipment and connectivity and the support of their parents who were working even during the quarantine. This situation stressed even more regarding students with disabilities or belonging to an indigenous community (Moreno & Ortíz, 2020).

This conclusion will discuss key topics related with the use of digital media in Latin America; particularly how the region is moving toward a mediatization of social and economic activities in a context of political polarization and disinformation, distrust toward traditional institutions, economic incertitude, and the persistent health and social problems associated with the COVID-19. Some of these issues are connected with: (i) everyday uses of digital media among citizens and the production of alternative discourses to contest social inequality, the integration of drones for civil and commercial uses, and the role of social media to surpass the consequences of the COVID-19 pandemic; (ii) Other subjects deal with the impact of technology in the Latin American political landscape: the irruption of alternative social movements and the use of social platforms in electoral campaigns. How digital technologies serve as spaces for civic engagement; (iii) and the prospective and problematics of digital journalism in Latin America, in what way fake news is causing social polarization and distrust toward democratic institutions in the region.

Digital media and daily life in Latin America

Emerging technologies, as the case of drones, are becoming familiar in other sectors aside the army or police forces (Strobel, 2019). Drones have been incorporated by civic organizations to support the search of missing victims of criminal organizations in remote rural zones in Mexico (The Guardian, 2015) or to enhance agriculture and improve media coverture of political and cultural events. This rising presence has compelled authorities to establish specific regulations about the suitable use of drones in the private sector: the expedition of licenses to incorporate drones for delivering packages or capturing multimedia material in tourist and entertainment activities, for example, the technical and psychological requirements to become a drone pilot. But there are some pending questions that are important to ponder, particularly regarding the boundaries amid the private and public use of drones, for example: the commercialization of armed drones, the legal liability when a mortal accident occurs, and even the limits of using these devices by individuals to record other people's intimacy. These discussions, however, are just starting of being subject of public interest in the region but they will become very relevant, as this incipient technology popularizes, allowing people to perform high-technical operations that could compromise not just their personal safety, but other people's rights. In addition, social media platforms, such as YouTube or Facebook, enjoys great popularity across the region. In these spaces, youth share their concerns and disagreements toward problems that affect them directly as the case of genre violence, drugs, criminality, political discontent, and the lack of labor opportunities (Palenzuela Fundora, 2018). YouTube has been particular useful to distribute music videos that praises for women's empowerment and the contest toward genre discrimination (Infobae, 2019). Feminist Rap, as it was possible to read in this volume, is a visual narrative that denounces the physical and verbal genre violence against women and the social and labor discrimination that undermines women' social development.

In this complex setting, people are searching social and spiritual relief in technology as a form to stand social seclusion. These spaces serve to communicate spiritual convictions and faith. Besides that, many religious organizations use Internet and social media to share public communications or stay in contact with their devotees (Cowan, 2017). The COVID-19 contingency has required them to readapt the religious cult to the quarantine normativity. The Catholic Church, for example, has used Facebook to lively transmit ceremonies and masses, giving the opportunity to follow the rites at home (Yurieff & O'Brien, 2020). Philanthropy has readapted to this complexing time as well. Through the Internet it is was possible to find plenty of cases in where digital media has assisted civil organizations to deliver food and amenities to deprived communities, and several charitable events have been organized using platforms like ZOOM to gather resources to combat the pandemic and to aid people in hard economic situations (Black, 2020). However, there are other testimonies published on newspapers around the world that revealed how technology was not entirely able to substitute all real physical interactions. In addition, social seclusion and lockdowns have reduced mental health and caused depression and even suicides during and after the confinements (Wan, 2020). With the future about the return to a "normality" after the confinements is uncertain, technologies will continue replacing physical interaction. Further studies are mandatory to comprehend the real impact of the self-isolation policies in people's mental health and to realize until where digital media could replace face-to-face communication (Holmes et al., 2020).

Civic engagement in the digital age

The remaining sections of this volume were dedicated to examining two key activities that have flourished in Latin America during the last decade: civic engagement and online journalism. As people were able to access the

Internet and acquire mobile devices, they could connect with each other on social platforms to exchange political views. Technology has allowed Latin Americans to organize civil mobilizations in ways that some years ago would have been unthinkable: share their discontent toward public issues in a global telecommunication media at almost free of cost and to speedily organize public gatherings, most of the time circumventing government censorship (Fuentes-Nieva & Nelli Feroci, 2017). In Latin America, social media has allowed the proliferation and diversification of alternative movements and spaces of social contestation as well. The use of technology inside these groups has outstandingly evolved, from the design of static websites up to flexible platforms and mobile applications that improve the logistic and coordination of the action; there are even technologies as the case of cryptography that support the exchange of protected information among the members, avoiding authority scrutiny.

This volume presented insightful chapters that testify the expansion and diversification of Latin American social movements' agendas in the region. Social media platforms have served, for example, as optimal conducts to exchange ideological ideas in between university students and local feminist groups in Mexico. These groups have approached information technologies to widely state their discontent toward the rise of femicides in Mexico. Encouraged by other movements massively shared on social media as #MeToo, broadly supported by actresses in Hollywood or The Chilean collective "Las Tesis." Mexican women have organized several actions to protest against genre violence, particularly in universities, in where there have been recent cases of sexual harassment and femicides inside the campuses. Due to these incidents, female students promoted an unending strike as a form to force authorities to resolve the crimes and to improve the safety conditions for women in campuses. During these actions digital media has become an important asset for the collective to share their agenda, objectives, generating social pressure that obliges universities and local authorities to take decisive paths toward the respect of women' rights (Villegas, 2020). Other cases exposed how some independent collectives struggle to bring digital media to deprived contexts. These organizations assisted marginalized communities to capacitate them with the learning of digital competencies that support their incorporation into the process of decision-making about prospective local public works and social policies (King, 2019).

Sometimes, however, beside investments in technological infrastructure and the training of public servers to improve civic involvement in governmental consults and enhanced public services, many public platforms lack innovation; they only virtualize traditional processes that replicate inefficiency and corruption (Adam & Fazekas, 2018). Deficient competences and the absence of financier instruments as credit cards limit the impact of public services online. In order to expand the civic involvement in public affairs it is important to equal the conditions to access community platforms besides the genre, ethnic, and economic condition (UN, 2017). While many experiences related with the use of digital media as a "weapon" to fight back social and political deprivation are rooted in urban contexts, there are examples in where indigenous people have approached media as a way to demand better conditions. Indigenous films have served to set novel narratives that let these communities to bring visibility toward their social fights, to express and broadcast their culture using their voice (Carlson & Dreher, 2018). The testimonies portrayed in these films provide further evidence on how these communities struggle to defend their culture, lands, and lives, but at the same time they illustrate how these materials will be significant, not just as elements for social revindication, but as digital testimonies to protect memory and culture for the forthcoming generations.

Journalism and media integrity in age of post-truth

Journalism has changed exponentially thanks to the arrival and the global spread of digital media (Grabowicz, 2014). The massification of Internet and the proliferation of mobile devices among the people allow the access to information faster and more enhanced way than in the traditional media. It is not just the possibility of reading online news using a computer, but how readers can leave feedback and retrieve data from news at the same time. Reading content has shifted from a unidirectional model in where readers only received the news into a new form of distribution in where they can interact with the media and with other users at the same time. They can compare instantly the coverage of diverse local and international sources about the same event, pondering the information, the multimedia elements, and the journalists' opinions on the topics. By now, journalists have at their disposition tools and devices that help them to improve their coverture and extent their public. Digital media allows the design of virtual platforms to reach wider publics, the reduction of production costs, and the enhancement of news with multimedia and interactive elements such as videos, audios, artworks, and animations that allow the exchange of information about platforms. But at the same time, this evolution has brought the closing of many local newspapers which were not able to adapt themselves to this new reality (Takenaga, 2019). Actually, there is a growing pauperization of the journalists' labor conditions (Reyna, 2020), and the growing problem of the fake news and deception campaigns which have a very negative impact on mass communication media credibility, one of the pillars that sustain modern democracies (Lee, 2019). Latin America has not been insusceptible to these changes, many newspapers have shifted from paper to digital platforms (Salaverría et al., 2019). This new form of broadcasting news has been supported mainly for the population of social media as YouTube or Facebook which enables the quick and massive dispersion of information among Latin Americans (Reuters Institute, 2020). This process of incorporating digital medial into the news production is still in progress, and not all media has survived the transition, since it requires that newspapers change their processes and to develop new forms of monetizing content (Picard, 2019). However, the same advantages that technology provides to journalism have caused, paradoxically, a rising distrust toward online news.

While the democratization of access to digital media has provided a unique way to create, publish, and exchange content, not all the data that circulate inside these spaces is reliable and come from reputable sources. Politicians and groups of interest have taken benefit of this overflow of information, particularly in social media, to found disinformation campaigns to attack their adversaries or to trigger political and social instability (Zovatto, 2019). They created disinformation crusades to justify the harassment and, even, murder political dissents and critical-minded journalists. In this polarized context, the construction of truth is less based on a careful examination of facts but on the construction of a narrative, mainly in social media, that creates an alternative explanation based on extremist ideology beliefs. While, actual presidents as Donald Trump in the United States and Andres Manuel Lopez Obrador based their electoral wins on an extensive use of social platforms like Twitter to gain electoral support among disenchanted voters who looked for non-conventional political candidates and political parties (Medina, 2018). Other examples displayed in this volume, provide evidences on how mobile applications could serve as well as conducts to promote electoral preferences but, at the same time, they could become close clusters that filters dissent voices and limit the public debate during the electoral campaigns. As a response to these rising problems that undermine democratic institutions, some organizations have created online spaces in where the people can consult if a news is real or not. These fact-checking projects have consolidated as crucial elements to limit the damage caused by disinformation, particularly regarding important political events as elections, or social incidents as protests or natural disasters and pandemics. These spaces have consolidated as important tools to increase truth-worthiness and to avoid incertitude, and polarization.

Final remarks

While there are many expectations about the prospective outcomes that the COVID-19 will bring for the social and economic landscape in the next months and years, there are few doubts that the information technologies are assuming a decisive role, not just controlling the outbreaks and the social distancing ordinances, but helping people and businesses to continue with their activities after the confinement, using digital media to sell food or goods using smartphones, and supporting scientific research that will eventually develop reliable tests and effective vaccines to combat the pandemic. Technology will continue playing a decisive role for activism as well; even during the pandemic there have been relevant movements on both sides of the Atlantic Ocean: #ICantBreathe and the renewal of the #BlackLivesMatter. These movements have gained important global support not just on social media, but on the streets as well. Along with pacific manifestations about the pursuit for equal rights and the ending of racism and police brutality, there have been other protests that have caused plundering and disturbs. But digital technologies have been incorporated by the authorities to prosecute activists also. Governments are using social media platforms to surveil the dissents' private lives to identify and prosecute them. There are even technologies recently used in China that are able to record and identify protesters by using AI facial recognition. As social media is becoming widespread in everyday activities and devices—not just smartphones or computers, but electro domestics, toys, and clothes,—there will be more concerns about how that information will eventually make users vulnerable of being under the frequent scrutiny of authorities.

In this context, journalism has a relevant role to play by serving as a social counterweight toward government decisions, and bringing into the spotlight relevant community problems, and open and horizontal debate which is particularly important in times of polarized societies and populist governments. Though, journalism is now passing through a big transition toward digital media from paper-based format. Publishing content online allows journalists to have a potential global scope and diverse social platforms to share and spread their content, and the use of digital media to reduce costs and make more flexible the process of news production. However, this shift has brought difficult tasks about how to protect the intellectual property rights of news, multimedia elements as photographs or videos, and to find an efficient form to monetize the access to the information. But above all, it is imperative that societies recall how important preserving free press is as a democratic guard, mainly in times of economic uncertainty, social discontent, and political disenchantment.

References

Adam, I., & Fazekas, M. (2018). Are emerging technologies helping win the fight against corruption indeveloping countries? (N.° 21; Background Paper, Número 21). Oxford.

Ahmed, A., & Berehulak, D. (2020, May 8). Hidden toll: Mexico ignores wave of Coronavirus deaths in capital. *The New York Times*. Retrieved from https://www.nytimes.com/2020/05/08/world/americas/mexico-coronavirus-count.html

Anderson, J., & Rainie, L. (2017, October 19). The future of truth and misinformation online. *Pew Research Center: Internet, Science & Tech*. Retrieved from https://www.pewresearch.org/internet/2017/10/19/the-future-of-truth-and-misinformation-online/

Black, M. (2020, April 22). Charitable events in Alberta go virtual during COVID-19 pandemic. *Global News*. Retrieved from https://globalnews.ca/news/6852699/alberta-covid-19-charitable-events-virtual/

Campbell, S., & Hutter Epstein, R. (2020, April). Why are coronavirus tests so difficult to produce? *BBC*. Retrieved from https://www.bbc.com/future/article/20200422-why-are-coronavirus-tests-so-difficult-to-produce

Carlson, B., & Dreher, T. (2018). Introduction: Indigenous innovation in social media: *Media International Australia*, *69*(01), 16–20. Retrieved from https://doi.org/10.1177/1329878X18803798

Cowan, D. E. (2017). Cyberspace and Religion in America. In *Oxford Research Encyclopedia of Religion*. Retrieved from https://doi.org/10.1093/acrefore/9780199340378.013.480

ECDC Europe. (2020, June 24). *Situation update worldwide, as of 24 June 2020*. European Centre for Disease Prevention and Control. Retrieved from https://qap.ecdc.europa.eu/public/extensions/COVID-19/COVID-19.html

Elliott, L. (2020, April 9). IMF chief flags up grim global economic forecast. *The Guardian*. Retrieved from https://www.theguardian.com/business/2020/apr/09/imf-chief-flags-up-grim-global-economic-forecast-covid-19

Fuentes-Nieva, R., & Nelli Feroci, G. (2017). The evolving role and influence and growing strength of social movements in Latin America and the Caribbean. *International Development Policy | Revue Internationale de Politique de Développement*, *9*(9), 323–338. Retrieved from https://doi.org/10.4000/poldev.2378

Grabowicz, P. (2014). The transition to digital journalism. *Berkeley Advanced Media Institute*. Retrieved from https://multimedia.journalism.berkeley.edu/tutorials/digital-transform/

Hernández Arriaga, M. (2020, June 5). Profesores y alumnos de zonas vulnerables ante la pandemia. *Nexos*. Retrieved from https://educacion.nexos.com.mx/?p=2344

Holmes, E. A. et al, (2020). Multidisciplinary research priorities for the COVID-19 pandemic: A call for action for mental health science. *The Lancet Psychiatry*, *7*(6), 547–560. Retrieved from https://doi.org/10.1016/S2215-0366(20)30168-1

IBD. (2019). *Internet pra todos: Disminuyendo la Brecha Digital en América Latina*. Banco Interamericano de Desarrollo. Retrieved from https://www.iadb.org/es/mejorandovidas/internet-para-todos-disminuyendo-la-brecha-digital-en-america-latina

Infobae. (2019, December 12). Una rapera española se alzó contra los feminicidios en México: Así fue la batalla de rap de la que habla todo el mundo. *Infobae*. https://www.infobae.com/america/mexico/2019/12/12/una-rapera-espanola-se-alzo-contra-los-feminicidios-en-mexico-asi-fue-la-batalla-de-rap-de-la-que-habla-todo-el-mundo/

King, K. (2019). Education, digital literacy and democracy: The case of Britain's proposed "exit" from the European Union (Brexit). *Asia Pacific Education Review*, *20*(2), 285–294. Retrieved from https://doi.org/10.1007/s12564-019-09594-0

Krauss, C. (2020, April 21). "I'm Just Living a Nightmare": Oil Industry Braces for Devastation. *The New York Times*. Retrieved from https://www.nytimes.com/2020/04/21/business/energy-environment/coronavirus-oil-prices-collapse.html

Lee, T. (2019). The global rise of "fake news" and the threat to democratic elections in the USA. *Public Administration and Policy*, *22*(1), 15–24. Retrieved from https://doi.org/10.1108/PAP-04-2019-0008

Medina, A. (2018, November 29). Las benditas redes sociales que le dieron "like" a AMLO. *Forbes México*. Retrieved from https://www.forbes.com.mx/las-benditas-redes-sociales-que-le-dieron-like-a-amlo/

Moreno, T., & Ortíz, A. (2020, May 31). Clases en línea no son para personas con discapacidad. *El Universal*. Retrieved from https://www.eluniversal.com.mx/nacion/clases-en-linea-no-son-para-personas-con-discapacidad

O'Malley, J. (2015, September 7). Stop acting surprised that refugees have smartphones. *The Independent*. Retrieved from http://www.independent.co.uk/voices/comment/surprised-that-syrian-refugees-have-smartphones-well-sorry-to-break-this-to-you-but-youre-an-idiot-10489719.html

Palenzuela Fundora, Y. (2018). Participación social, juventudes, y redes sociales virtuales: Rutas transitadas, rutas posibles. *Ultima Década*, *26*(48), 3–34. Retrieved from https://doi.org/10.4067/S0718-22362018000100003

Patrick, A. (2020, June 10). How the COVID-19 pandemic shed light on the digital divide. *Government Technology*. Retrieved from https://www.govtech.com/network/How-the-COVID-19-Pandemic-Shed-Light-on-the-Digital-Divide.html

Picard, R. (2019). Funding digital journalism: The challenges of consumers and the economic value of news. In B. Franklin & S. A. Eldridge II (Eds.), *The Routledge Companion to Digital Journalism Studies* (pp. 147–154). Routledge. Retrieved from https://www.routledge.com/The-Routledge-Companion-to-Digital-Journalism-Studies-1st-Edition/Franklin-Eldridge-II/p/book/9780367205027

Reuters Institute. (2020). *Digital News Report 2020* [Digital News Report]. Reuters Institute.

Reyna, V. H. (2020). "This is my exit sign": Job control deficit, role strain and turnover in Mexican journalism. *Journalism Practice*, *0*(0), 1–17. Retrieved from https://doi.org/10.1080/17512786.2020.1776141

Salaverría, R., Sádaba, C., Breiner, J. G., & Warner, J. C. (2019). A Brave New Digital Journalism in Latin America. In M. Túñez-López, V.-A. Martínez-Fernández, X. López-García, X. Rúas-Araújo, & F. Campos-Freire (Eds.), *Communication: Innovation & Quality* (pp. 229–247). Springer International Publishing. Retrieved from https://doi.org/10.1007/978-3-319-91860-0_14

Strobel, W. P. (2019, September 25). Military drones now common to nearly 100 nations, report finds. *Wall Street Journal*. Retrieved from https://www.wsj.com/articles/military-drones-now-common-to-nearly-100-nations-report-finds-11569403805

Takenaga, L. (2019, December 21). More than 1 in 5 U.S. papers has closed. This is the result. *The New York Times*. Retrieved from https://www.nytimes.com/2019/12/21/reader-center/local-news-deserts.html

The Guardian. (2015, October 21). Mexico to use drones as part of fresh search for missing students' remains. *The Guardian*. Retrieved from https://www.theguardian.com/world/2015/oct/21/mexico-drones-fresh-search-missing-students-remains

UN. (2017). *Consent, Participation of Indigenous Peoples in Decisions Affecting Them Vital to Advancing Their Rights*. United Nations. Retrieved from https://www.un.org/press/en/2017/gashc4203.doc.htm

Valenzuela, S., Somma, N. M., Scherman, A., & Arriagada, A. (2016). Social media in Latin America: Deepening or bridging gaps in protest participation? *Online Information Review*, *40*(5), 695–711. Retrieved from https://doi.org/10.1108/OIR-11-2015-0347

Vanden Abeele, M. M. (2016). Mobile lifestyles: Conceptualizing heterogeneity in mobile youth culture. *New Media & Society*, *18*(6), 908–926. Retrieved from https://doi.org/10.1177/1461444814551349

Villegas, P. (2020, March 9). In Mexico, women go on strike nationwide to protest violence. *The New York Times*. Retrieved from https://www.nytimes.com/2020/03/09/world/americas/mexico-women-strike-protest.html

Wan, W. (2020, May 4). The coronavirus pandemic is pushing America into a mental health crisis. *Washington Post*. Retrieved from https://www.washingtonpost.com/health/2020/05/04/mental-health-coronavirus/

Yurieff, K., & O'Brien, S. A. (2020, March 13). Finding God online: People turn to live-streaming religious services during coronavirus pandemic. *CNN*. Retrieved from https://www.cnn.com/2020/03/13/tech/religious-services-livestream/index.html

Zovatto, D. (2019). *Latin America: Political change in volatile and uncertain times | International IDEA*. IDEA. Retrieved from https://www.idea.int/news-media/news/latin-america-political-change-volatile-and-uncertain-times

Index

For Product Safety Concerns and Information please contact our EU representative GPSR@taylorandfrancis.com
Taylor & Francis Verlag GmbH, Kaufingerstraße 24, 80331 München, Germany

www.ingramcontent.com/pod-product-compliance
Lightning Source LLC
LaVergne TN
LVHW021125300926
849160LV00010B/863
9780367677893